Lady Landlords of
Prince Edward Island

Lady Landlords
of
Prince Edward Island

Imperial Dreams
and the Defence of Property

RUSTY BITTERMANN
AND MARGARET McCALLUM

McGill-Queen's University Press
Montreal & Kingston · London · Ithaca

© McGill-Queen's University Press 2008
ISBN 978-0-7735-3389-9 (cloth)
ISBN 978-0-7735-3424-7 (paper)

Legal deposit third quarter 2008
Bibliothèque nationale du Québec

Printed in Canada on acid-free paper that is 100% ancient forest free
(100% post-consumer recycled), processed chlorine free.

McGill-Queen's University Press acknowledges the support of the Canada
Council for the Arts for our publishing program. We also acknowledge
the financial support of the Government of Canada through the Book
Publishing Industry Development Program (BPIDP) for our publishing
activities.

A grant in aid of publication has been received from the Law Foundation
of Prince Edward Island.

Library and Archives Canada Cataloguing in Publication

Bittermann, Rusty, 1951–
  Lady landlords of Prince Edward Island / Rusty Bittermann and Margaret
McCallum.
  Includes bibliographical references and index.
  ISBN 978-0-7735-3389-9 (bnd)
  ISBN 978-0-7735-3424-7 (pbk)
  1. Women landowners – Prince Edward Island – History – 19th century.
  2. Absentee landlordism – Prince Edward Island – History – 19th century.
  3. Land tenure – Prince Edward Island – History – 19th century.
  4. Gentry – Great Britain – History – 19th century. 5. Landlord and
tenant – Prince Edward Island – History – 19th century. 6. Women
landowners – Prince Edward Island – Biography. I. McCallum, Margaret.
  II. Title.
  HD319.P75B58 2008   333.309717   C2008-900741-7

Typeset in Sabon 10.5/13
by Infoscan Collette, Quebec City

To Kris, Kim, and Emma

Contents

Illustrations and Maps

ILLUSTRATIONS

MAPS

Acknowledgments

Writers often complain that theirs is a solitary endeavour, but this book would not have been possible without the assistance of archivists and librarians in institutions on both sides of the Atlantic. We are grateful to the staff of all the repositories listed in the bibliography, everyone of whom provided us with prompt and professional assistance. Three institutions deserve special mention. As always, it was a pleasure to work at the Public Archives in Charlottetown, and we continue to be amazed that such a small staff, working in cramped quarters, can do so much. At the National Archives of Scotland, we were able to work our way through two extraordinary collections of private papers with the assistance of helpful staff and extensive computer indexes. When we learned to our consternation that the Hammersmith Archives would be closed for its annual inventory for all but one day of that research trip, the archivist made sure that all we had asked to see was waiting for us when we arrived, along with other things that she thought, quite correctly, we might find useful.

We gratefully acknowledge funding from the University of New Brunswick, the New Brunswick Law Foundation–University of New Brunswick Faculty of Law Endowment Trust, and St Thomas University that assisted with our travel and research costs at these and other archives and enabled us to use the incomparable collection of the British Library in London. The Endowment Trust also provided assistance with the costs of permissions to reproduce material for illustrations, making it possible to use the cover image of Georgiana Fane held by the Tate Gallery. We thank the following institutions and individuals for granting permission to use material for the illustrations: British Library, London; London Metropolitan Archives, London; National Archives of Scotland, Edinburgh; Public Archives and Records Office of Prince Edward Island, Charlottetown; Tate Gallery, London; D. Mallet; and Sue Pierson. Chapter 5 is a revised version of an article by Rusty Bittermann, "Lady Landlords and the Final Defence of Landlordism on Prince Edward Island: The Case of Charlotte Sulivan," published in *Histoire sociale/Social History* 38 (Nov. 2005): 203–33. It is used here with permission of and thanks to that journal.

In the research for this and other projects, we have enjoyed assistance and encouragement from many generous people. We thank them all, particularly Dean Philip Bryden of the Faculty of Law, University of New Brunswick, for his enthusiastic and timely support to both of us. We gratefully acknowledge the Law Foundation of Prince Edward Island, which provided a generous grant in aid of publication. At times, the multiple responsibilities of academia left too little time for colleagues, friends, and family. We have dedicated this book to our daughters – Kris, Kim, and Emma – not as recompense but in tribute to them as they make their own ways in the world.

Note on Names

Historians focus on change and continuity, and proper nouns pose a particular challenge in this regard. Individuals of differing times, places, or status may use various names or spellings of names to identify the same person or place, and names of people as well as places change over time. In identifying places, we generally use the modern name. Thus throughout the book we refer to the island that the Mi'kmaq called Abegweit and the French Île Saint-Jean as Prince Edward Island, even though the British gave it this name only in 1799. We also use current spelling and so drop the apostrophe from Kings and Queens Counties and write Charlottetown as one word. The conventions of scholarly writing require, quite appropriately, that we identify women as well as men by their surnames. But in places in this book, we refer to the four lady landlords who are its focus by the more familiar Anne, Jane, Georgiana, and Charlotte, the names that we began to use for them as we read their correspondence and gained insight into their lives and characters. This choice prevents confusion with relatives who share the name and provides continuity through changes in surname on marriage or when a husband inherited a title. The use of the title "Lady" also poses a problem. According to British usage, Anne, as the wife of the second Viscount Melville, and Jane, as the wife of the tenth Earl of Westmorland, were entitled to call themselves, respectively, Lady Melville and Lady Westmorland or the Countess of Westmorland. But Jane's daughter, Georgiana, was addressed or referred to in elite British society either as Lady Georgiana or Lady Georgiana Fane, as a courtesy only. Contemporaries on Prince Edward Island, however, referred to her as Lady Fane, and it is by that name that she is remembered in Island place names.

Lady Landlords of
Prince Edward Island

1.1   Broom House, c. 1911, Charlotte Sulivan's residence in Fulham. LMA, 77.0, BRO, 4026C

I

Imperial Land Policy and Women Landlords in Prince Edward Island

In July of 1867 Prince Edward Island's attorney general, Joseph Hensley, made a business call at a fine mansion overlooking the Thames, seven miles west of central London.[1] Broom House (see illus. 1.1) was the residence of Charlotte Sulivan, and Hensley's visit concerned her plans for the 66,000-acre Prince Edward Island estate Sulivan had recently inherited from her father. The estate, which had been in her family since the eighteenth century, had become increasingly valuable. Prince Edward Island contained some of the best agricultural lands in coastal British North America, and in the century since Britain had acquired the colony from France in the Seven Years War, it had prospered. When British travel writer Isabella Lucy Bird visited the colony in the mid-1850s, she noted the Island's "brilliant green" colours, the "gently undulating" landscape, and its "soft" soil, all of which made the Island "very suitable for agricultural purposes," although she noted, "I never heard of any one becoming rich through agricultural pursuits." The north shore of Prince Edward Island was, Bird wrote, "extremely pretty" – "small villages, green clearings, fine harbours, with the trees growing down to the water's edge, and shady streams." She described Charlottetown, the colony's capital, as "prettily situated on a capacious harbour" and "with the exception of Quebec ... considered the prettiest town in British North America." Bird also noted that "everywhere, even twenty miles inland, and up among the woods, ships may be seen in course of construction. These vessels are sold in England and the neighbouring colonies; but year by year, as its trade increases, the island requires a greater number for its own

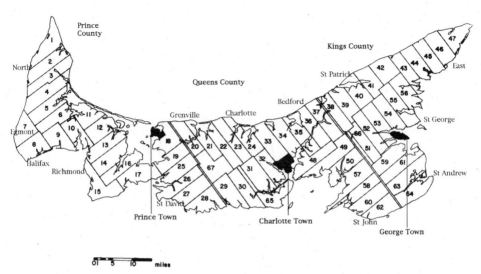

Map 1.1   Samuel Holland's plan of Prince Edward Island. Derived from a map drawn by Holland and reproduced as an insert in United Kingdom, *Acts of the Privy Council of England, Colonial Series, 5*.

use." A good land base for agriculture, timber that might easily be hauled to water for export, and a vibrant shipbuilding industry had, as Bird noted, laid the basis for prosperity and growth. By the time of Hensley's visit to Broom House, Prince Edward Island had a population of roughly 90,000.[2]

Large estates such as Charlotte Sulivan's, however, were a political problem on the Island. British imperial planners provided the foundation for such estates when they first distributed land rights in the colony in the 1760s, granting most of the Island's 1.4 million acres in 20,000-acre lots to about a hundred proprietors (see map 1.1).[3] Subsequently, concentration of property ownership became a source of grievance; indeed, it became the central political issue in the colony for most of the next century. By the late 1860s, much of the land that had once been held by proprietors had been sold as small freeholds or purchased in large blocks by the Island government. The persistence of landlordism in the colony remained a contentious issue, however. In 1867 hundreds of thousands of acres were still in the hands of proprietors, more than a third of the rural population were tenants or squatters, and resistance to the leasehold system was widespread and well entrenched.[4]

Hensley had come to Broom House in the hope of persuading Charlotte Sulivan to sell her estate to the Island government. His initiative was part of an ongoing effort to reduce landlordism on the island through voluntary sale of proprietors' holdings, so that the government might then resell these lands in small parcels to tenants and other Islanders. In the decade and a half since the government had begun buying landlords' estates, it had acquired roughly 400,000 acres of land, the largest single purchase being the 212,900-acre Cunard estate in the year prior to Hensley's call at Broom House.[5] Sulivan was not the only Island landlord Hensley visited in Britain, but she possessed the largest estate held by a landlord living outside Prince Edward Island and quite possibly the largest estate still in private hands. In 1867 the only estate of similar size was that of resident landlord Robert Bruce Stewart.

Sulivan's response would be central to Island politics during the crucial years of the late 1860s and the early 1870s, as it would help to determine whether the land question would be resolved by agreement or compulsion. Ultimately, persuasion failed, and in 1875, after the colony had become a Canadian province, the Island government enacted a Land Purchase Act that forced landlords to sell their estates to the provincial commissioner of public lands. Resistance to voluntary sale from proprietors of small estates might not have been an urgent political problem for the Island government, but continued absentee ownership of an estate the size of Charlotte Sulivan's certainly was. Embedded in this political issue of landlord-tenant relations and the possible need for expropriation to resolve it was the question of Prince Edward Island's relationship with the new federation of Canada uniting the British North American colonies of Nova Scotia, New Brunswick, and Canada (Quebec and Ontario). In the years prior to Hensley's visit, the Colonial Office had repeatedly blocked the Island legislature's attempts to resolve the land question. In the context of the 1860s, imperial officials, eager that the colony join Confederation, linked the possibility of a legislative solution to Prince Edward Island's land question with Island agreement to become part of Canada.[6] Sulivan's response to Hensley, then, was important not just to resolution of the century-long land question in the colony but as well to the political manoeuvring concerning its relationship to the new Dominion of Canada.

Women did not always have such economic and political power in Island affairs, nor had the imperial planners who established the

political structures and property relations for the Island in the eighteenth century intended to empower women by their decisions. In
the 1760s, when the Lords Commissioners for Trade and Plantations developed land policies for Britain's newly acquired island
possession in the Gulf of St Lawrence, their focus was exclusively
male. The commissioners sought to ensure the speedy settlement of
the Island and as well to reward those associated with the imperial
government's successful prosecution of the Seven Years War in
North America and elsewhere. That endeavour had been male; there
were no women among the naval and army officers who directed
the assaults on Louisbourg in 1758 and the town of Quebec in
1759, no women among the government officials who oversaw the
war effort, and no women at the forefront of the merchant community involved with the war and the subsequent occupation of
French territory. Thus those who received land on Prince Edward
Island as a spoil of war were all men.

Recipients of Island lots included officers in the military, such as
Admiral Augustus Keppel, who had commanded British naval
forces off the coast of France during the war; Vice-Admiral Charles
Saunders, who had served as commander-in-chief of the British fleet
that fought its way up the St Lawrence in 1759 and brought Major-
General James Wolfe's troops to Quebec; and Colonel Simon Fraser,
who had served with distinction during the sieges of Louisbourg
and Quebec.[7] Other recipients were government officials such as
Philip Stephens, secretary to the Lords of the Admiralty; John
Pownall, secretary to the Lords of Trade; and James Murray and
Guy Carleton, governor and lieutenant-governor of Quebec respectively; as well as merchants such as James and William Hunter, John
Williams, and Joshua Mauger.[8] The commissioners' plan for the
Island required that it be surveyed and divided into large lots (see
map 1.1). The Crown surveyor, Samuel Holland, who also received
a lot on the Island, drew up a plan with sixty-seven lots, called
townships, grouped into three counties with county seats, called
royalties, for each. On 23 July 1767, lots were allocated by a lottery
to those to whom the commissioners had decided to give land.[9]

The distribution scheme for Island land tended to reward groups
of men working together to shape imperial policy and to benefit
from British military success. Admiral Keppel and Vice-Admiral
Saunders, for instance, had initially presented a group petition for
a grant of the entire Island, and Colonel Simon Fraser had joined

with other officers of the 78th Regiment to request 146,000 acres.[10] Subsequently, those receiving lands on Prince Edward Island worked together to convince the imperial government to establish the Island as a colony separate from Nova Scotia in 1769.[11] Male power and male networking determined the acquisition and control of real property on the Island when it first became part of the British Empire. In time, however, women came to enjoy the benefits of imperial expansion in British North America. And as they did so, they came to play a significant role in the evolving land question on Prince Edward Island.

The first woman to join the male club of Island landlords was Susanna Torriano. In the fall of 1774 the Island's governor, Walter Patterson, granted Torriano a 450-acre island near the colonial capital of Charlottetown.[12] The grant of Governor's Island, as it was known, did not put Torriano in the same league as those who received 20,000-acre lots, but it made her the only woman to receive an original grant, other than the small town lots and pasture lots granted within the colony's three royalties of Charlottetown, Princetown, and Georgetown. Torriano, who was listed as a "spinster" on the grant of Governor's Island, had arrived on Prince Edward Island as part of Walter Patterson's household four years earlier and was reputedly his mistress.[13]

Unlike Susanna Torriano, most of the women who became Island landlords acquired their properties by inheritance. Some, such as Flora Townshend, did so when they became widows. Townshend, the daughter of Chief Justice Peter Stewart, was born into one of the most prominent Island families. Her husband, William Townshend, was collector of customs on Prince Edward Island, as well as owner of Lot 43 in the eastern part of the Island.[14] Following her husband's death in 1816, Flora Townshend acquired a life estate in the township.[15] Her management decisions provoked vigorous tenant resistance in the 1830s, generating major confrontations between law officers and tenants on her estate and heightening political tensions in the colony.[16] Other female proprietors, such as Maria Fanning, inherited Island estates from their fathers. Fanning acquired lands on Lots 50, 65, and 67, as well as royalty properties, in 1818 after the death of her father, Edmund Fanning, who had been lieutenant-governor of the colony in the late eighteenth and early nineteenth century. Her sisters, Louisa and Margaret, inherited Island estates as well and brought these into their marriages. Maria Fanning remained unmarried and actively managed her properties in town as well as in the countryside for more than half a century, refusing all government offers to purchase her estate.[17] In 1875 she was one of the proprietors who were forced to sell most of their land to the Island government. The group included at least thirty-three other females who were sole or co-owners of Island estates, including those who were co-owners with their husbands. Women, excluding those who shared ownership with a husband or male relative, owned more than one-quarter of the fifty-seven estates purchased by the government in the years between 1875 and 1880 (see appendix).

This book explores the life stories of four of the women who owned estates on Prince Edward Island: Anne and Jane Saunders, Georgiana Fane, and Charlotte Sulivan. The decisions these women made about their estates and, ultimately, the significance their decisions held for the history of the land question on Prince Edward Island were shaped by the broader patterns of their lives and the importance of their Island estates within these patterns. Anne and Jane Saunders inherited lands from two of the original grantees, their father, Dr Richard Huck Saunders, and their great-uncle, Admiral Charles Saunders. Anne married Robert Dundas, who became the second Viscount Melville, and Jane married the tenth Earl of Westmorland. Having survived her husband, Lady Westmorland left her property to her daughter, Georgiana Fane. Charlotte Sulivan inherited her four lots from her father, Laurence Sulivan, a third-generation Island landlord.

All four of these women were non-resident landlords living in Britain, but three of them – Jane, Georgiana, and Charlotte – travelled to Prince Edward Island to visit their estates. Anne lived primarily at Melville Castle, near Edinburgh, but also resided in London and elsewhere in Britain for part of most years. Jane lived at Apethorpe, the Westmorland estate in Northamptonshire, but after she and Lord Westmorland separated in 1811, she spent much of her life travelling, primarily in Europe. As an adult, Georgiana Fane divided her time between her estate in Somerset and a residence in the Mayfair district of London, while Charlotte Sulivan lived in Fulham, on the outskirts of London. Collectively, these women's stories span most of the history of British imperial involvement with landlordism on Prince Edward Island.

Anne and Jane Saunders were minors when they inherited estates on Prince Edward Island, following the death of their mother in

1780 and their father in 1785. Although less than twenty years had passed since the grand lottery in which their father and their great-uncle acquired the lands the sisters inherited, fundamental problems had emerged which raised questions concerning the value of their titles. All of the proprietors were required to pay annual quit rents to the Crown. As well, they were obliged to settle their lands with foreign Protestants, people drawn from Europe or other parts of North America, at a rate of one person for every 200 acres, settling one-third of their land at this rate within four years and all of it within ten years.[18] Proprietors who failed to pay their quit rents were vulnerable to distraint action; Island authorities might seize and auction their chattels and as much of the land itself as was necessary to pay any arrears. Proprietors who failed to settle their estates were liable to having their land escheated – to having the Crown reclaim the grants – as the Privy Council had determined that, if proprietors failed to meet the four-year deadline for initiating settlement, the "whole" of the grant "would be forfeited to His Majesty his heirs and Successors." The deeds that the colonial administrators issued to the proprietors contained this condition.[19]

Both the quit rent obligations and the settlement conditions became problems for proprietors. Quit rents assumed new significance when proprietors successfully petitioned to have the Island established as a colony separate from Nova Scotia in 1769 and agreed that the costs of government would be borne by their quit rents. In time, this arrangement provided an incentive for government office-holders to vigorously enforce quit rent payment as their salaries were dependent upon these receipts. The risk facing proprietors who were in arrears with quit rent payments became clear in the early 1780s, as Island officials sold a number of estates at auction to recover back rents. Some of these transactions were subsequently rescinded by authorities in London because of irregularities in procedures, but proprietors remained liable for quit rent payments and faced possible distraint proceedings in the future.

The quit rent challenge was intimately related to a general proprietorial failure to fulfill the settlement terms of their grants. Had proprietors moved quickly to recruit the immigrants they were required to bring to the Island, rents and land sales might have generated the revenues necessary to pay annual quit rents. However, none of the grantees in fact fulfilled the settlement requirements, and most could only meet quit rent obligations out of other income or capital. Even after a modest influx of immigrants in the wake of the American Revolution, the total population of the Island was probably less than 4,000. The general proprietorial failure to meet the settlement terms of the grants meant that titles to all their lots were in jeopardy, as all were vulnerable to escheat action.

In the early 1790s, within five years of Anne and Jane Saunders inheriting their father's and their great-uncle's estates, demands for a sweeping escheat of landlords' grants emerged as a popularly sustained political issue in the colony. From the perspective of settlers, there were many sources for their growing dissatisfaction with the land system that had been established on the Island. One was grounded in a comparison of their circumstances with those of settlers elsewhere. In Prince Edward Island most of the land had been assigned to proprietors in 1767, and settlers could acquire lands for farming in the 1790s and earlier only by renting or buying from landlords who would sell or by squatting on land and making farm improvements for which they would have no title. In the adjacent Maritime colonies, grants of large estates subject to conditions like those in Prince Edward Island were escheated when proprietors failed to fulfill their settlement terms. Some escheats in the mainland colonies were prompted by the American Revolution, as government officials prepared to receive Loyalist refugees seeking a new life in the remaining portions of British North America. Subsequent to these escheat actions there was an abundance of Crown land elsewhere in the Maritimes, and settlers might obtain grants of small holdings directly from the Crown for the costs of the transaction fees. No such escheats occurred on Prince Edward Island in the years before or immediately after the revolution, despite proprietors' failure to fulfill the settlement terms of their grants. In the 1790s, at protest meetings and in the Island assembly, settlers and their supporters articulated their objections to this anomaly.[20]

Opposition to the proprietorial system was grounded as well in the difficulties Island settlers faced in making a living. The first British settlers on the Island had had the advantage of the improvements made by the Acadians who preceded them, but the extent of these improvements was limited. In the mid-1750s, before the Island's French population was temporarily enlarged by the arrival of Acadian refugees fleeing the effects of war elsewhere, the Acadian population was probably around 3,000.[21] In the decade and more between the Acadian expulsion of 1758 and the beginning of a significant influx of British settlers, cleared fields had begun to revert to forest.[22] Even where new settlers were able to make use of Acadian fields, they often found that the soils had been exhausted by continuous grain cropping.[23]

British settlers, like the Acadians before them, were able to use the Island's extensive coastal marshlands for hay, but farming ultimately required that they clear forested land. This was both difficult and time-consuming. Joseph Robinson, a Loyalist refugee from the Carolinas and a leader of the demand for the escheat of proprietorial land in the 1790s, suggested that even after hardwood forests, which tended to cover the best soils, had been cut and the wood burned, it took another eight to ten years before the stumps would rot sufficiently to be pulled "and in all that time scarcely any ploughing can be performed."[24] Others with an interest in extolling the agricultural potential of the Island highlighted the speed with which new settlers could learn to wield an axe and fell forests, and they noted the possibilities for manœuvring one-handed ploughs among charred stumps, but the truth was that farm-making for most settlers was an arduous, lifelong task.[25]

And then there was the climate. According to Joseph Robinson, "In the common course of the season snow falls in the month of October." By spring, "[a]fter many falls of snow, and several reductions by thaws at the close of winter, it is to be found in the woods four feet deep and upwards." It was not until about the first of May that people could begin to plough their lands. In Robinson's experience, farmers had only ten days to complete their ploughing, harrowing, and planting for wheat or oats to have time to ripen. In the winter, he said, some days were "so exceedingly cold and stormy, that it would be highly improper for persons to quit their respective habitations, although business might require their personal attendance at some distance – and during all this time of six or seven months, all that is in your power to do, is consume the various provisions stored for winter, attend your livestock, and procure fuel in order to keep yourselves from a state of congelation."[26] The climate was, as Robinson noted, colder than the Carolinas and more difficult for farming than the British Isles, where most Island immigrants had originated.

In the event, there was no general escheat in the late eighteenth century, and most proprietors weathered the quit rent collection challenge. The settlement and quit rent issues did, however, prompt imperial officials to give renewed attention to Island land policies, including the development of procedures for enforcing quit rent collection and for ensuring that settlement conditions were met. Proprietors who wished to keep their estates thus had to take the obligations in their grants seriously, and doing so required that they actively manage their properties. Some chose to sell their estates rather than face the liabilities of quit rent arrears and the risk of escheat action. In consequence, roughly one-third of Island estates changed hands at the turn of the century.[27]

In the case of the Saunders sisters and their husbands, these developments appear to have marked the beginning of recognition that they possessed an Island inheritance that required their attention. Like other non-resident landlords, they faced the challenges of managing their estates from afar and acquiring accurate information concerning Island affairs. They benefited, however, from a general upturn in the economic development of Prince Edward Island in the early nineteenth century. British timber tariffs helped to foster a growing timber trade, and in time, agricultural development and the emergence of a significant shipbuilding industry provided the basis for sustained population growth. Thousands of immigrants arrived from the British Isles in the first decades of the century. In 1807 the population was around 9,000; by 1827 it had grown to 23,000; by mid-century it would be more than 60,000.[28]

Changes on the Island in the early nineteenth century were intimately linked with developments in Britain. Economic growth in the imperial centre generated demand for colonial imports and fostered increased maritime connections with Prince Edward Island; as well, it undermined older ways of life and helped to generate the flow of migrants arriving on the Island. Concurrently, residents of Britain and its North American colonies made new claims concerning popular rights and social justice. In Britain the momentum for change found its way into the struggle for Catholic Emancipation, political campaigns against slavery, and the mobilization that ushered in the first Reform Bill, as well as into the challenges posed by Chartism and tenant agitation. In Prince Edward Island some of these impulses emerged in struggles to end landlordism.

The early 1830s marked the beginning of a sustained popular challenge to large-scale landholding on the Island and a movement to redistribute proprietors' estates as small freeholds. Anne's eldest son, Henry Dundas, and Jane's son Henry Fane both visited the

Island during the 1830s, and Henry Dundas reported on the threat that popular mobilization within the colony posed to the interests of proprietors. By the end of the decade, leaders of this challenge, which came to be known as the Escheat movement, controlled the Island House of Assembly. Although Escheators were unable to force an end to landlordism, they created a political and cultural legacy that made the proprietorial system increasingly untenable.[29] Jane travelled to the Island to view her estate during the years in which Escheators held the majority of seats in the House of Assembly, and she offered her analysis of the Island land question to policy-makers at the Colonial Office. Georgiana Fane and Charlotte Sulivan actively defended landlords from the many challenges to their interests that emerged in the years after the Escheat movement.

The imperial decision to grant responsible government to the Island in 1851 shaped the nature of the challenges that landlords faced, as it gave politicians associated with the Reform Party hope that they might use their increased power to chip away at landlordism. When in power, Reformers introduced measures that limited the advantages of holding Island estates and passed legislation authorizing government purchase of proprietors' estates, should they wish to sell. Between 1854 and 1866 the Island government bought land from several proprietors, ranging from an estate of less than 4,000 acres to the massive Cunard estate, spread across twenty-one lots and comprising about one-fifth of the Island.[30] None of those selling their estates to the government in this period were women, though the government did assess the 2,000-acre estate of spinster Mary Margaret McDonald in response to her interest in the possibility of selling.[31] Thus female landlords became proportionately more numerous than they otherwise would have been as a result of two decades of government and tenant buyouts of male proprietors.

In the decades after responsible government, proprietors found themselves in an increasingly embattled position as public opinion on the Island hardened against the leasehold system and as the legislature initiated laws that undermined the viability of landlordism in the colony. These measures included taxes levied on proprietors' lands and rent rolls, arrangements to limit landlords' control of the fishery reserves along the shore contained in the original Crown grants, and laws to protect tenants' interests in their farms. Landlords' best hope of success in resisting these initiatives lay in appeals to imperial authorities to withhold approval of objection-able colonial legislation. When Georgiana Fane assumed control of the Island property that she inherited from her mother in 1857, she became a persistent proponent of proprietors' rights. As well as campaigning against legislation that they considered inimical to their interests, the proprietors pressured imperial and colonial officials to enforce legal processes for collecting rents and evicting defaulting tenants, if necessary through the use of military force.

British authorities found themselves responding simultaneously to challenges to landed interests at home and abroad, as landlord-tenant relations in Ireland and Prince Edward Island became increasingly intractable problems requiring a political solution. Georgiana Fane arrived on the Island to inspect her estate in 1860, as an imperially appointed land commission was winding up hearings in Charlottetown concerning the land question. The commissioners failed to devise a final resolution of the conflict, and a Tenant League, modelled on a similar organization in Ireland, subsequently sought through rent resistance to force landlords to sell their estates to their tenants. The league was eventually suppressed in 1865 by the use of troops.[32]

Joseph Hensley's visit to Broom House in 1867 followed in the wake of military intervention to reinforce landlords' rights on the Island. Charlotte Sulivan told Hensley that she would not make a decision concerning her estate without first visiting and assessing the situation on Prince Edward Island herself. She did so in the fall of 1867 and subsequently decided not to sell her land to the Island government. Georgiana Fane also rejected the government's offer. In the years that followed, both women assumed central roles in what would prove to be the final struggle to protect landlord interests on Prince Edward Island, writing to the Colonial Office as individuals and as participants in collective efforts to block legislation to which they objected. Both refused to sell their estates when the Island government again sought to purchase them in the 1870s.

When, in 1875, the Island government succeeded in obtaining royal assent for legislation compelling landlords to sell their estates to the commissioner of public lands, Charlotte Sulivan was among several landlords who fought the consequences before the Island Supreme Court. Georgiana Fane, who had been fighting the legislation when she died, was represented in the judicial challenge by her heir, Ponsonby Fane. The landlords won a stunning, albeit brief, victory when the Island courts invalidated the sale orders made under the legislation. When the Island government appealed the court's ruling to the newly formed Supreme Court of Canada, Charlotte Sulivan alone defended landlord interests there – and lost. The Supreme Court decision upholding the Island's compulsory sale legislation and the proceedings taken under it marked the end of an era. Henceforth, large-scale landownership would be illegal, as subsequent legislation limited the total number of acres that any individual, resident or alien, could own.[33]

The Supreme Court decision also marked the closure of some opportunities for women to exercise political and economic power. Although the imperial decisions that incorporated Prince Edward Island within the British Empire had not anticipated that women would own large estates and assume the powers of a proprietor, over time they had done so. Indeed, they had become significant players in estate management and in the politics of the land question on the Island. This role came to an end with Charlotte Sulivan's defeat in the Supreme Court of Canada.

2

Anne Saunders, Lady Melville: Managing at Home and Abroad

No women received Crown grants on Prince Edward Island in the initial distribution of Island land, but property came into women's hands through their connections with male landowners, especially in circumstances in which there was no male heir. Anne Saunders and her younger sister, Jane, acquired substantial estates on Prince Edward Island because their great-uncle had no children and their mother, his heir, produced no sons. While they were unmarried minors, the property was managed for Anne and Jane by the men whom their great-uncle and their father had chosen as their trustees. During the more than four decades of Anne's marriage, she and her husband cooperated in managing their domestic and public life, including her Island estate. The Island property was less significant for Anne than for Jane, for Jane's daughter, Georgiana Fane, or for Charlotte Sulivan, in part because of Anne's decision to marry, as well as her choice of partner, and in part because the Island estate was, at least initially, a relatively obscure asset in Anne's inheritance. Regardless of the relative unimportance of the estate in her life, what she did with it was of considerable import on the Island. The history of Anne Saunders's and her family's experience with her Island property reveals much about the challenges of absentee proprietorship for proprietors and for those trying to make a living on the Island.

Anne and Jane Saunders were the only children of Dr Richard Huck and Jane Kinsey, the niece of Sir Charles Saunders. As Saunders's heir, Kinsey took the name of Saunders, and so did Huck when they married in 1777.[1] Sir Charles Saunders had been rewarded for his service in North America during the Seven Years War with land on

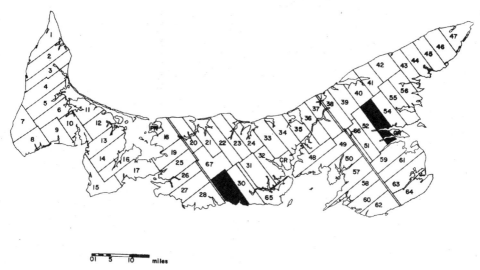

Map 2.1 The Saunders sisters' lots, Prince Edward Island.
Derived from a map drawn by Samuel Holland and reproduced as
an insert in United Kingdom, *Acts of the Privy Council of England,
Colonial Series, 5.*

Prince Edward Island.[2] He received Lot 29, a 20,000-acre tract along
the south coast of Queens County, fronting on the Northumberland
Strait, about thirteen miles west of Charlottetown (see map 2.1).
The Crown surveyor, Samuel Holland, commented favourably on
the lands and woods when he laid out the lot, noting that it was
nearly as fine as the adjacent Lot 28, which he thought would be
"very good" for agriculture. He indicated that Lot 29 included
100 acres of cleared land and four houses and barns.[3] These improvements were the product of Acadian farmers who had been deported
from the Island by the British following French military defeats in
the Gulf of St Lawrence during the Seven Years War.[4]

Dr Richard Huck Saunders was also rewarded for his military
service with land in Prince Edward Island; from him, Anne and Jane
inherited part of Lot 53 in Kings County to the east of Charlottetown.
Huck's father had been a country gentleman who died shortly after
his son's birth. Forced to earn a living, Huck apprenticed as an
apothecary and surgeon, and was appointed a surgeon with the
British army midway through the War of the Austrian Succession
(1740–48). He served at Culloden in 1746, during the final battle

of the Jacobite Rebellion; that defeat helped to impel some of the migration of Highlanders to Prince Edward Island later in the eighteenth century. After the war, Huck obtained the degree of doctor of medicine from Marischal College in Aberdeen, and he again served with the army, with a promotion to the rank of physician.[5] The Crown granted him the right to a one-third share of Lot 53 in the original distribution of Island land in 1767; he subsequently acquired another one-third from another grantee. Lot 53 is crossed by the estuaries of the Cardigan and Brudenell rivers and fronts on the estuary of the Montague River, which empties into Cardigan Bay. Samuel Holland described the soil and woods on the lot as "very good" and noted that it was well situated across the water from the Kings County royalty of Georgetown.[6]

War had been good to both Dr Huck and Admiral Saunders. During the War of the Austrian Succession, Saunders made between £30,000 and £40,000 in prize money. He subsequently married the daughter of a London banker and entered Parliament, first for Plymouth and later for Yorkshire, and continued to hold high office with the Admiralty during the Seven Years War and beyond. By the time of his death in 1775, his estate, which included lands in Norfolk and Suffolk, was worth more than £200,000. In his will, made in 1773, Saunders left most of his property to Jane Kinsey for her lifetime and then to her heirs – to her eldest son, if she had one, and if not, to her daughters in equal shares.[7]

Jane Kinsey Saunders died in 1780, shortly after the birth of her second daughter. Anne and Jane thus became the heirs to Charles Saunders's lands and fortune. Dr Huck Saunders, who had been in his late fifties when he married, arranged for nurses and governesses to care for his daughters. The family lived for some of these years at the Grove in Hampstead, a select residential district and summer retreat for some of London's wealthier professional and mercantile men, including several doctors with fashionable London practices.[8] Huck Saunders wrote frequently to Anne, thanking her for the little notes that she sent to him, offering her advice on deportment and health, and reminding her of her duty to him and, as the elder of the two sisters, of her responsibilities to Jane. In March 1783 he wrote:

> I received your letter, my dear Child, and am well pleased with both you and it – with you, because you are good; with it, because it was well-written, and shows that you are a clever

girl ... I love you dearly, for being so good and for doing so readily what you are desired. And everybody will love you if you continue to be good, which I think I can promise you will, because you know that your goodness will make my happiness ... Besides, your being good will have another happy effect. You will set a good example to your sister, and if she proves a good girl, you will have some merit in it, because she learns to be good by imitating you.[9]

A letter in October 1783 emphasized the same connection between character, reputation, and happiness:

there is nothing you will dread so much as being wicked. Wicked people are always wretched. Nobody likes them. Good people are believed by everybody, and they are happy in their own minds ... If you disobey your Papa, your Governess, your Masters, if you be not loving to your sister and good-natured to the servants, you will be looked upon as a wrong-headed, worthless girl, whom nobody will care for. You can see what pains your Papa takes to make you an accomplished girl ... You should endeavour to be a good scholar, gentle, mild, good-tempered, and affectionate to requite him for his goodness to you and to make him happy, too.[10]

Dr Huck Saunders died in 1785, leaving an estate valued at about £15,000, to be divided equally between Anne and Jane.[11] Knowing that the wealth his daughters had inherited through their mother would attract marriage proposals from the sons of the landed elite, despite the girls' lack of a title, he had done his best to ensure that they received the upbringing and education necessary for the society he expected them to join. He instructed their trustees and guardians to maintain his daughters in his house or in some other country house in an airy situation, where they were to have a private education under the care of some woman whose life fitted her to introduce them into the world when they reached a proper age. Their annual income from their inheritance was more than £3,000; so there were ample funds to carry out Dr Huck Saunders's instructions. For around £1,000 per year, the trustees rented a small house in Clapham, in Surrey, and hired a governess and staff, including a footman, coachman, cook, and several maids and menservants.

That sum also covered the household expenses, the cost of books, clothes, pocket money, and sundries, and the salaries of masters who taught the sisters music, dancing, French, and drawing. When Anne was eighteen and Jane sixteen, the trustees determined that they were ready for their introduction to fashionable society. They moved into a house rented for them in London, with a Miss Hollis to undertake their care and superintendence. Mrs Berry, their governess, a widow, left them when she married again. Even with the higher rent for the London house and the new expenses associated with these changes in their lives, their annual expenditures were still less than half their income.[12]

The trustees had to seek approval for all these arrangements from the Court of Chancery. By the end of the eighteenth century the Court of Chancery, also called the court of equity, had become the Byzantine and sometimes corrupt bureaucracy satirized by Charles Dickens in his novel *Bleak House*.[13] Nonetheless, it enjoyed a monopoly over legal proceedings involving property held in trust; thus from time to time the trustees for the Saunders sisters had to account for their use of the trust property in the Court of Chancery, and the chancellor had to approve any changes in the use of the funds. The trustees' management of Anne and Jane's property on Prince Edward Island was not exemplary. They did not ensure that the lots were settled with the requisite number of foreign Protestants, as specified in the Crown grants, and it is not clear whether they paid any of the annual quit rents required of Island proprietors. By 1779, just before Jane Kinsey Saunders died, there should have been a hundred settlers on Lot 29 and sixty-seven on Dr Huck Saunders's share of Lot 53. There were not, and the trustees did not take steps to remedy this failure; this neglect put the sisters' titles at risk.[14] In the late 1790s the Island House of Assembly claimed that there was not a single settler on either Lot 29 or Lot 53. The assembly identified another twenty-one lots that were entirely lacking in settlers and twelve more that had, on average, but three families per lot.[15]

Had the assembly had its way, the Saunders sisters and other delinquent proprietors would have lost their Island estates. From a settler perspective, the proprietary land system that British imperial planners had constructed on the Island added to their material problems both by imposing the burden of rents and by retarding developments that might have eased the difficulties new settlers faced. Population growth on the Island in the eighteenth century was below that required by the terms of the original grants and much below what the assembly thought possible, given the colony's resources. If the proprietors had complied with the terms of their grants, there should have been more than 6,500 settlers on the Island by the late 1770s and even more by the 1790s through natural increase and further immigration. According to the assembly, the colony was capable of supporting a population of half a million.[16] Instead, the Island's population in the late 1790s was around 5,000.[17]

The disruption caused by the American Revolution was partly responsible for the lack of settlers, but there were other causes, too. These included immigrant resistance to settling in a colony controlled by landlords, given the options for acquiring land directly from the Crown in adjacent colonies. As well, because some proprietors did not always have agents on the Island with the authority to issue leases, even immigrants who were willing to sign leases could not always do so, and thus risked taking up land without security of tenure. The slowness of population growth meant fewer hands to engage in the collective tasks of developing roads, fewer households to sustain schools and churches, and less reason for merchants, who were central to providing supplies and credit for settlers, to set up business on the Island.

Although the imperial government did not order the escheat of proprietary grants on Prince Edward Island at the turn of the century, it instituted more rigorous collection of quit rents and imposed a new schedule of collection that linked the level of quit rent liability with proprietors' performance in settling their lots.[18] Renewed demands for the payment of quit rents, coupled with the continuing threat of escheat actions at a later date, prompted some holders of Island lots to pay more attention to their estates and to ongoing political developments on the Island. Other proprietors chose to sell their Island estates.[19] In Anne Saunders's case, these developments were probably central to her realization that she had inherited a potentially valuable estate on Prince Edward Island, but only if it were actively managed. The change in her status from unmarried minor to married woman set the stage for Lots 29 and 53 to receive more attention.

Sometime in the mid-1790s, while Anne was living in London, she met Robert Dundas, the only son of Henry Dundas, the most

2.1   Robert Dundas, second Viscount Melville.
Engraving from mezzotint by Charles Turner,
1827, after Sir Thomas Lawrence, 1826. NAS,
GD 51/15/70/5

powerful politician in Scotland (see illus. 2.1). Since 1774 Henry
Dundas had represented various ridings in the House of Commons
and held several high offices in the government at Westminster,
including lord advocate, keeper of the signet, and treasurer of the
navy. In 1802 he was granted a peerage as Viscount Melville, a title
that Robert would inherit. Henry was also a director of the Bank
of Scotland and of the East India Company. Henry Dundas educated
Robert for the same kind of life, sending him to the Royal High
School in Edinburgh and then, accompanied by a tutor, to tour the
continent, where he studied dancing, fencing, architecture, and
German and enrolled briefly in the university in Göttingen. On his
return from Europe, Robert attended the universities of Edinburgh
and Cambridge and trained as a lawyer, becoming a member of

Lincoln's Inn in London, although he did not practise law. He served briefly in the British army and was elected to Parliament in 1794, when he was twenty-three.[20]

When Anne and Robert met, he had neither a title nor the prospect of one, but something about him pleased the young heiress, and Anne assented to Robert's request for permission to correspond with her. He wrote almost at once from Wellingborough, near Northampton, where he was stationed with his regiment, admitting with charming candour that he wrote "more for the sake of availing myself of your permission to write to you, than to convey any very interesting intelligence ... Imprisoned in a dirty, uncomfortable village, I look forward with considerable impatience to a change of quarters; and though I should, for reasons which I leave you to guess, prefer returning to London, yet next to that, I am not sorry that I am so soon to visit Scotland."[21] The relationship flourished, and Anne and Robert were married at the end of August 1796.[22]

Because Anne was still a Chancery ward, she could not marry without the approval of the lord chancellor, who was required to pass judgment on Robert's social standing and on the appropriateness of the intended application of Anne's fortune, as set out in the couple's marriage contract. Among the landed elite, marriages were usually preceded by a marriage contract, called a settlement, to ensure that the wife's property would be available for her and her children and to enable the husband to deal with his property free of the dower right of the widow, which was a life interest in one-third of her deceased husband's land. Marriage contracts also provided the wife with a maintenance allowance during widowhood, called a jointure, in lieu of dower and with pin money for personal expenses during the husband's lifetime – such things as new clothes, amusements, gifts to charities, family, friends, or servants, and other little indulgences over and above the necessities that her husband was obliged to provide.[23]

The English doctrine of marital unity subsumed the wife's legal personality into that of her husband, depriving the wife of the legal capacity to own property and precluding contracts between spouses. Thus the parties to the marriage settlement included trustees for Anne, who would, if necessary, bring legal action on her behalf in order to enforce the contract. Various connections from both families whose property rights were affected by the marriage were parties as well. Robert expected to inherit his father's lands in Scotland, but his father, only in his fifties, was likely to live a good many years yet, as was Robert's stepmother, Lady Jane Hope, aged thirty, whom Henry had married in 1793. She would have to be provided for out of whatever Robert inherited from his father. Good relations within the extended family depended on responsible use of family resources. As Henry said in writing to Anne with his blessings on her engagement to Robert, she was "the person on whom the future happiness of my life must so materially depend."[24] The final settlement approved by the lord chancellor provided Anne with £400 pounds per year pin money during her husband's lifetime and, if she survived him, with a jointure of £1,000 per year. As was usual in marriage contracts, her jointure was greater than the sum allotted for pin money, as she would have to maintain her own establishment once Robert's heir took possession of the family estate. As well, while Anne's sister, Jane, remained an unmarried minor, Robert Dundas was to have £1,000 per year from Jane's share of the sisters' inheritance to cover expenses he assumed on her behalf.[25]

All these arrangements, of course, were predicated on Anne's position as co-heiress to the Saunders estate. Admiral Saunders had hoped for a male heir; in his will he left his property to his niece's daughters and their children only if Jane Kinsey's marriage to Dr Huck produced no male heir, and then only if the daughters' husbands took the name of Saunders.[26] Robert referred Saunders's will to solicitors for an opinion on what he should do; they advised him that he and Anne should use the name Saunders. The couple did so for the first few years of their marriage, but by 1800 they were using the name Dundas, with no apparent repercussions.[27] Curiously, the Prince Edward Island lands owned by Charles Saunders and by Dr Huck Saunders are not listed in the inventories of the Saunders sisters' property prepared at the time of Anne's marriage, nor are they mentioned explicitly in other documents pertaining to the marriage settlement.[28] About half the wealth that Anne and Jane inherited from Charles Saunders was in the form of real property in Norfolk and Suffolk, in the east of England, held as entailed estates. In effect, the estates could not be sold out of the Saunders family line. Anne's husband would own the property only for his lifetime, and on his death, it would go to his male heir and, if there were none, to another family member. By the marriage contract, however, all the parties agreed that when Anne was twenty-one, she and Robert would join in "suffering a recovery" of these lands in order to "bar the entail." This meant being the defendant in a collusive lawsuit in order to obtain a judgment freeing the title from the conditions of inheritance that restricted its sale.[29] The lawsuit completed, the lands were sold in 1802 for more than £115,000. Anne and Robert were entitled to half this amount, after payment of lawyers' bills, the trustees' costs, and the cost of annuities given to various relatives under the terms of Charles Saunders's will. The other half went to the tenth Earl of Westmorland, who in 1800 had married Anne's sister, Jane. Robert Dundas invested his share in land and mortgages on land in Scotland, having obtained, at a cost of £419, a private act of Parliament permitting him to spend the money in Scotland rather than in England.[30]

Following her marriage, Anne assumed responsibility for managing Melville Castle, an extravagant mansion that Henry Dundas had built on the old Melville estate at Dalkeith, southeast of Edinburgh. Henry had acquired the 600-acre estate through his first marriage in 1765 to Elizabeth Rannie. A fifteen-year-old orphan, Elizabeth was co-heiress with her sister to her father's vast fortune made in the East India trade. Elizabeth left Henry in 1778, and he divorced her for adultery; in consequence, she forfeited the property she had brought to the marriage. During the following decade Henry began work on a new residence on the site of the old manor house on the Melville estate, in a meadow overlooking the North Esk River. Designed by fellow Scot James Playfair, Melville Castle was a three-storey rectangular building, roughly sixty by fifty-two feet, with crenellated round towers at each corner and lower wings built at each side; it looked, as one critic said, like a "toy fort"[31] (see illus. 2.2). As part of the marriage settlement between Anne and Robert, Henry Dundas agreed to transfer title to Melville Castle to Robert for life and, on his death, to his male heir or, if there were none, to his female children. In return, Anne, through her trustees, agreed to give Henry £12,000 in the form of bank annuities paying three per cent per year. Early in their marriage, with Anne still in London while Robert was with his regiment, their letters mix playful remonstrances over the other's failings as a correspondent with details of the ongoing repair, renovation, and refurbishing of Melville Castle. Robert left Anne to decide "patterns of curtains, papering, chairs, sofas or other important articles for fear of chusing something unfashionable & being therefore scolded, which I might reasonably

2.2   Melville Castle, home of Anne and Robert Dundas at Dalkeith, near Edinburgh. From W. Angus, *Seats of the Nobility and Gentry in Great Britain and Wales* (Islington: W. Angus, 1787, 1815)

expect for such an offence." Now a small hotel, Melville Castle looks from the outside much as it did in Anne's day, but without the extensive gardens that she helped to create.[32]

Raising a young family soon became the focus of much of Anne's energy, though crises in her sister's unhappy life and that of her sister's family demanded her attention as well. The three oldest children, Henry, Richard, and Robert, were born in 1801, 1802, and 1803 respectively. Jane, the first daughter, was born in 1805, Charles in 1806, and Anne in 1808. When the children were quite young, Anne remained at Melville Castle while Robert went to London to attend to his duties as a member of Parliament and, as of 1807, those associated with his presidency of the Board of Control for India. When the children were older, they and Anne accompanied Robert on his seasonal migrations between Melville Castle and London. After the death of his father in 1811, Robert entered the House of Lords as the second Viscount Melville. The following year, having declined the offer of the governorship of India, he became first lord of the Admiralty, a post he held, with one brief interruption, until 1830. Robert was offered the India governorship again in 1822 and again declined. As Anne's sons matured, they entered the professions open to the landed elite: Henry and Richard became officers in the British military, Robert a government official, and Charles a rector in Lincoln County. Her two daughters remained at home unmarried.[33]

In London, Anne and Robert were very much part of the social elite, both through his political connections and their relationship, through her sister, Jane, with Lord Westmorland and his family. They were also close friends with poet, novelist, and lawyer Walter Scott, who was a frequent visitor in London and at Melville Castle. Scott was the same age as Robert; they had been students together in Edinburgh and had both trained there as lawyers, although neither enjoyed the profession. Writing to Scott from London in January 1813, Anne reported on the challenges of trying to read his latest work while also attending to household responsibilities. These included dealing with servants and trades people, letter-writing, dining out, and providing formal education for her daughters and sons, the latter of whom she described as "most riotous school-boys." She prepared and corrected their lessons in music, languages, art, and history; she also incurred a headache by taking them to a "noisy pantomime" in Covent Garden. Anne compared her life to that of the biblical character Job, concluding that "Job's patience was not fairly put to the trial, since we have no record of his having undertaken the instruction of children, most especially in the art of through bass to which the intellects of my little girl seem more impervious than to any other piece of knowledge I have undertaken as yet to inculcate. Whether the teacher or the pupil is most at fault in this instance, I shall not pretend to determine."[34]

When King George IV decided in 1822 to visit his subjects in Scotland, Scott – Sir Walter since 1818 – orchestrated the visit, with a great deal of assistance on details large and small from Robert and Anne. Those involved in arranging for the visit met at Melville Castle to plan, and Robert Peel, then secretary of state for the Home Department, and his wife, Julia, stayed at Melville Castle before and during the first part of the king's visit. As one of the Crown's ministers from Scotland, Lord Melville signed the proclamation specifying the protocol for the king's journey from Leith, where the royal yacht docked, into Edinburgh, his arrival at Holyrood, and his other public appearances in the city. Robert's presence was required at all these events. Anne and her daughters were presented to the king, along with 450 other women, at a drawing-room for the ladies; they also attended the Peers' Ball. The king did not stay in Edinburgh but at Dalkeith House, home of the fifth Duke of Buccleuch, adjacent to the Melville estate. The Edinburgh Gas Company installed three hundred gas lamps, at a cost of ten shillings each, along the seven miles from Holyrood to the gates erected on the Duke of Buccleuch's estate in honour of the king's visit. A new road was built to connect these gates to the Melville estate, and the Midlothian Yeomanry provided an escort for the king when he took this road to Melville Castle to enjoy a cold collation before attending a performance of Scott's *Rob Roy* at the Theatre Royal in Edinburgh.[35]

In addition to educating her children and playing her role as the spouse of a leading Scots politician, Anne organized the annual household moves from Melville Castle to the south of Britain and back again. Once Robert, at eighteen, began his civil service career in London, he assisted with the details of his father and mother's migrations between Edinburgh and London. Writing to her son in November 1821, Anne discussed her impending overland journey to London. With stops on the way, including at Apethorpe, the Northamptonshire estate of her brother-in-law, the Earl of Westmorland, Anne anticipated she would arrive in London two weeks after leaving Melville Castle.[36] As the industrial revolution transformed transportation within Britain, the family sometimes travelled between north and south by steamer and later planned to travel by rail.[37] The Dundas peregrinations involved not just the family and their possessions but servants too. Writing to her son Robert in February 1834 in advance of an impending visit to London, Anne noted the inconvenience of the trip and the need to bring two handmaids, the butler, the footman, and "a little cookmaid." She hoped that Robert's housekeeper "might possibly find some person who could be decently recommended for honesty and sobriety, who could enable your own servants to keep the house, kitchen etc. in a proper state of cleanliness." As for the laundry, she would put it out.[38] In the spring of 1838 Anne intended bringing seven servants, "if we could put them up."[39] She grew tired of being constantly on the move, not just to London but elsewhere in the British Isles, as she attended to Melville family and political business, including visits with other families who owned Prince Edward Island estates, such as Sir James Montgomery at Stobo Castle in Peeblesshire and the family of Lord Selkirk at their estate in Galloway.[40]

Anne's gardens and orchards at Melville Castle were a source of pleasure when she could be there. A letter to her son Robert in the late fall of 1837 described the "gay flowers" that remained blooming on the castle grounds.[41] By the late eighteenth century, the kitchen gardens of Scotland were the envy of England and even of Europe, producing melons, cucumbers, and cherries year round and with greenhouses for grapes, pineapples, artichokes, and asparagus.[42] Anne's garden was one of these. Her plums and apricots did not always ripen, and some years there was "scarcely a peach on any outdoors tree," but the indoor trees in the orangery kept the table supplied with fruit.[43] Anne ordered plants for her garden from London, including geranium cuttings, which she asked her son Robert to deliver when he came up to Edinburgh. Geraniums, originally an African plant, had been cultivated in England since the fourteenth century.[44] Anne's son Richard, who was an officer in the navy and posted to East Asia during the first Opium War, also supplied her with flower roots, bulbs, and cuttings, shipping Asian stock to her via Sierra Leone and Robert's London address.[45] One of her daughters reported on the happy state of the roses that Anne had acquired near Ashbourne but was less enthusiastic about her father's pasturing of sheep on the lawns near the house. Intended as a "substitute for mowing (a labour he wished to curtail), [the sheep were] a signal failure as far as the beauty of the poor lawn is concerned."[46] Anne's sons sent her other gifts too, as their careers took them to various parts of the British Empire. Henry, who served with the British forces in North America and helped to suppress the 1837–38 Rebellions in the Canadas (Ontario and Quebec), sent her Native-made chair seats from Halifax.[47]

The Dundas family finances were managed jointly by Anne and Robert. Early in their relationship, Robert advised Anne on such matters as the division of inheritance goods with Jane, the payment of taxes, and the risks of paying tradesmen's bills by post.[48] As Anne acquired more experience with household management, she advised Robert on the steps she thought necessary to run Melville Castle's finances and the Melville estate. Writing to him in London early in 1802, she suggested that no more than £1,500 per year had passed through her hands for household expenses, a sum that compared very favourably with the trustees' expenditures for maintaining the Saunders sisters before their marriages. Anne thought, however, that savings would be possible if they acquired a better housekeeper/manager. She also believed that effectively collecting rents from their Scottish estates required one of them to be in Scotland. Having to work extensively through land agents was a common problem for prominent Scottish landowners who, because of their official positions, had to spend considerable time in London.[49]

Finances became increasingly problematic for Anne and Robert across the years of their marriage. The costs of travelling back and forth between Edinburgh and London and maintaining appearances bore heavily on the household budget, and Robert needed his salary as a cabinet minister. When he resigned from the cabinet in 1827, Walter Scott observed that he was sorry to see "this upright states-man and honourable gentlemen deprived of his power and his offi-cial income which the number of his family must render a matter of importance."[50] Out of cabinet for good in 1830, Robert found, as he explained to his son Robert, that it was "quite necessary to reduce my establishment [at Melville Castle] both within and without door, and one of my reductions will be my groom and saddle horse." Would son Robert be interested in hiring the groom for himself in London?[51] In 1838 Robert's sister Anne wrote to him in London to report, "Mama has made out to her own satisfaction after duly going over all her books and accounts that in spite of all our wanderings, house rent at Walton and Ramsgate etc., there has been less spent this year than usual as far as what goes thro her hands is concerned, which is great satisfaction to me as one may urge going to England *sometimes* to see you" with a clear conscience.[52]

Keeping her son Charles out of financial disaster was a constant worry for Anne. Charles was the only one of her children to marry and produce grandchildren. His limited income as a clergyman was insufficient for the apparently unlimited expenses of his growing household. Writing to her son Robert in 1838 from Charles's home, Anne warned of an impending visit Charles intended to make to London with his family. She advised Robert to store the drawing-room furnishings, as Charles's "children destroy furniture, [and] their maids have no idea of teaching the children to take care of anything, not even so far as to prevent babies from destroying the older children's playthings."[53] Anne wrote to Robert of his brother's financial circumstances in 1840, noting that although she had already given Charles "several sums" from her own savings, he was overdrawn on the £100 allowance that her husband gave her for Charles's use. She asked Robert if he could advance her £50, to be repaid when his father gave Anne the next two quarterly instalments for Charles. Later in the year she wrote to say that she had "contrived to have £200 ... in the Bank of Scotland" for Charles.[54]

In large part, Robert and Anne inherited their financial difficulties from Robert's father. Lord Melville owed about £65,000 at his death, which, as Robert said, left him in an uncomfortable position for the rest of his life. Annual interest on the debts alone was £3,500, and as well, Robert had to pay his father's widow an annual income of £2,000 until she remarried in 1814. To raise funds, Robert and Anne sold the last of the Saunders estate properties in England, and in 1823 they sold Dunira, the twenty-acre estate in Perthshire that became his father's principal residence after Robert's marriage. Together, these sales brought in about £125,000.[55] The Prince Edward Island estates initially diminished, rather than augmented, the family's income. There were quit rent bills to pay, both past and present, and settlement obligations to meet in order to protect the estate from being escheated. Perhaps Anne and Robert were deterred from selling their Island lands, unlike other Island proprietors in the years around 1800, by the complexities and costs they had encountered in selling the lands that Anne had inherited in Norfolk and Suffolk. As well, they may have been influenced by the decisions of other Scots with whom they were connected. Sir James Montgomery, lord advocate for Scotland in the 1760s and 1770s, had assembled an 80,000-acre estate on the Island shortly after the first distribution of lots in 1767, and though his experiences with developing the estate had not been happy, his family was not among those who sold their lands at the turn of the century. Yet another of their Scottish acquaintances, the fifth Earl of Selkirk, was the principal purchaser of Island estates in this period, ultimately assembling an estate of 140,000 acres scattered across nine lots. Selkirk's purchases included the one-third of Lot 53 that the Saunders sisters had not inherited.[56]

Whatever lay behind the decision to retain their Island property, Anne and Robert soon found themselves paying for the privilege. In 1804 and 1808 Robert contributed the not inconsiderable sum of £160 toward the Dundases' share of the £40 per annum quit rents that he believed were due on Lots 29 and 53. As well, he joined with Anne's brother-in-law, Lord Westmorland, co-owner of Lots 29 and 53, to retain an Island land agent and advanced funds to assist new settlers and develop the lots.[57] Anne and Robert's approach to managing their Island estate was consistent with familiar practices in Scotland and with how James Montgomery had begun to develop his lots on Prince Edward Island thirty years earlier, although they proceeded on a more modest scale and with significant differences in detail. As with the Melville estate at Dalkeith, which was carefully mapped and surveyed, the Dundases sought to bring their much larger and wilder Island estate under rational management (see map 2.2). Like Montgomery, they believed that the landlord's role included investing in the estate, and thus they authorized their agent to arrange for the construction of a mill as well as houses for tenants, to develop tree plantations, and to take whatever other steps the agent believed were necessary for the "improvement, cultivation and management" of the estate. As well, like Montgomery, they authorized their agent to give long leases.[58]

On Lot 53, management of the Dundas estate was soon affected by the ambitious development plans of their friend in Scotland and co-owner on the Island, Lord Selkirk. In 1803 Selkirk orchestrated the migration of hundreds of emigrants from the northwest Highlands of Scotland to Prince Edward Island. He chose to settle the most prosperous of these emigrants, who for the most part were from Skye and the adjacent mainland, on Townships 57 and 58 in the Orwell Bay and Point Prim region of southwestern Queens County. The poorest of the emigrants originated in Uist, in the Outer Hebrides, and Selkirk was anxious to keep them separate from the others. He ultimately settled the Uist emigrants on Lot 53. The lot had not been partitioned at the time of Selkirk's arrival on the Island, and he had not initially intended to make it available to the emigrants who travelled with him in 1803. The emigrants from Uist, however, resisted other possible places for settlement and pressed for a locale that would give them good access to the sea, as fishing had been central to their livelihood in the Hebrides. The lot, as Selkirk noted, fronted "on a fine harbour & near good fishing grounds" and thus "would be well adapted to them." The Uist settlers who first explored Lot 53 in search of a place for their settlement were favourably impressed with it. They discovered a good settlement site where a creek entered Three Rivers Harbour. There were burnt lands nearby that they could plant immediately, and the creek and bay offered large lobsters and an abundance of oysters. Island law permitted Selkirk to partition the lot unilaterally, and he did so, reluctantly, in the belief that it was necessary in order

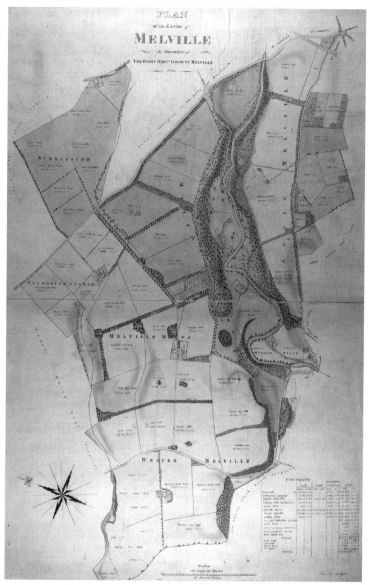

Map 2.2   Plan of the Melville estate, Dalkeith, 1831. NAS, RHP 10599

to meet the desires of the Uist settlers, taking for himself the middle third. In consequence, as of 1803, the Dundas and Westmorland portions of the lot were, by default, those that these settlers found less attractive.[59]

Selkirk spent two months on the Island in 1803, establishing settlers on his newly purchased estate, and his diary from that period records many things that landlords needed to know. He assessed the physical features of his lots, their agricultural potential, the nature of existing land-tenure arrangements, the structure of government on the Island, existing legislation, the character of the leading members of Island society, the sentiments of settlers, the state of the roads, the main patterns of the Island economy, and the cost of developing his estate, including building grist and saw-mills. Even in the short time he was on the Island, Selkirk modified his plans in response to what he learned about local conditions. Once he left the Island, he became reliant on land agents, but in dealing with the resulting problems, he and his heirs at least had the benefit of Selkirk's having begun the management of his estate with direct knowledge of the Island.[60]

Proprietors adopted various strategies for dealing with the challenges of managing Island properties. Some took up residence on the Island, while others relied on children or relatives to super-vise their affairs. Neither of these were viable options for Anne and Robert, given their position in British society, their family connec-tions, and the age of their children. Their oldest son, Henry, was two when Selkirk partitioned Lot 53, and no one from the family visited the estate until the 1830s, when both Henry Dundas and his first cousin, Henry Fane, travelled to Prince Edward Island while they were in North America with the British army.[61] Thus, like many other Island proprietors, Anne and Robert had to rely on land agents to manage their estate. And like many others, their relations with these agents were not good. Anne had noted that effective management of the Dundases' Scottish lands required that one of them be in Scotland. Their experiences with their estate in Prince Edward Island substantiated the wisdom of that observation.

When Robert Dundas and Lord Westmorland appointed a land agent for Lots 29 and 53 in 1805, they chose John Stewart, a fellow Scot born in Kintyre. Then in his late forties and temporarily resid-ing in London, Stewart was the son of the Island's chief justice, Peter Stewart, whose family had been on the Island for thirty years at the time of the appointment. A proprietor himself, having purchased part of Lot 37 in 1789, John Stewart was a central figure in Island politics and had been speaker of the House of Assembly in the late 1790s when popular protest forced the assembly to consider an escheat of proprietorial lands. He played a central role in transforming political pressure for escheat, which would have served the interests of Island tenants, into pressure for a new quit rent structure and collection procedure. The latter policy served the interests of office-holders on the Island, whose back salaries would be paid from the rents collected. As well, it served the interests of the receiver general of quit rents, who, as of 1790, was John Stewart. In the early years of the nineteenth century, Stewart travelled to London repeatedly to lobby the Colonial Office on the need for quit rent reform and to collect quit rents from proprietors resident there. In 1806 he bolstered his credentials as an invaluable source of Island intelligence by publishing *An Account of Prince Edward Island in the Gulph of St. Lawrence, North America, Containing Its Geography, a Description of Its Different Divisions, Soil, Climate, Seasons, Natural Productions, Cultivation, Discovery, Conquest, Progress and Present State of Settlement, Government, Constitution, Laws and Religion.* One can understand why Robert Dundas and other non-resident proprietors might have thought Stewart an appropriate man to act as their Island agent.[62]

Robert and Anne's choice of land agent actually put their Island affairs in the hands of Stewart's brother, Charles, as John moved to Newfoundland to take up the post of paymaster general of British forces. Charles Stewart, like his brother John, was active in Island politics; as well, he was a practising attorney. Lord Selkirk met Charles Stewart while he was on the Island in 1803 and formed a favourable impression of him. He subsequently made him one of his Island agents, as did other proprietors.[63] When John Stewart asked Charles to assume his duties as agent for Robert Dundas and Lord Westmorland, he advised him that the proprietors wanted him to construct a sawmill on Lot 29 and to establish settlers there without delay. John had received an advance of £200 pounds from the proprietors for the first task, but the plans did not unfold smoothly. He, it seems, used the £200 advance to assist in building a magnificent house for himself in St John's, Newfoundland. According to Charles's wife, Mary DesBrisay Stewart, John then shipped merchandise to Charles from St John's to make up the

£200, but the shipment proved of little resale value. The Charles Stewart family supposedly absorbed this loss, but Charles soon incurred other expenses in developing the estate, for which he claimed reimbursement from Robert Dundas and Lord Westmorland. After Charles's death, Mary submitted an account for £525 for his fee for acting as agent for five years and three months, plus more than £1,425 for supplying tenants with cows and timber, having Lot 29 surveyed, a road made, and a mill built, and outfitting a ship to take timber to Charlottetown. To set off against these expenses, the account showed about £100 in rents collected and about £1,100 in proceeds from timber sales. As had happened when Charles Stewart had submitted his accounts to a London merchant for whom Stewart had procured timber on the Island, the Melvilles and the Westmorlands found it necessary to object to the amount Stewart claimed and to dispute his authority to incur debts in their name.[64]

Anne and Robert, now Lord and Lady Melville following the death of Robert's father in 1811, learned some of what had transpired under Charles Stewart's agency through the reports from new agents appointed after Stewart's death. The first of these, William Johnston, was, like the Stewarts, a Scot. Trained as a lawyer in Edinburgh, he worked there before emigrating to Prince Edward Island in 1812. Johnston was well acquainted with the Melville family and had previously been employed by Robert's father. No doubt they believed that he could provide them with accurate information concerning events on the Island and could be trusted with management of their affairs. Johnston also obtained a series of public appointments, which, after Charles Stewart's death in January 1813, included replacing him as the colony's attorney general. Melville and Westmorland appointed William Johnston their agent in July 1813. For a variety of reasons, including poor health, he failed to provide the Melvilles, or his other proprietor principals, with regular accounts of his management of their estates.[65]

James Bardin Palmer was the Melvilles' next agent, and he too reported on problems that previous agents had created. Palmer was born in Dublin, where he practised law before moving to London. That city was not kind to him, and in 1802 he emigrated to Prince Edward Island, where he had employment as a land agent for a Dublin connection. Palmer was admitted to the Island bar shortly after his arrival and quickly became embroiled in Island feuds and politics that pitted him against both Charles Stewart and Walter

Johnston. Melville and Westmorland engaged Palmer and John Nicholas LePage, an Island merchant, as co-agents in August 1817, while Palmer was on a trip to Britain. He made such trips frequently, and the following year Ewen Cameron was appointed to exercise Palmer's authority as land agent when the latter was absent from the Island.[66]

Palmer reported late in the fall of 1817 on what had been happening on the estate since the turn of the century. As of the second decade of the nineteenth century, there were two or three tenants on the Melville third of Lot 53 and a single leased property on the Westmorland third. The leaseholder, a widow, owed rent arrears, and despite steps she had taken to pay, Johnston had forced her out of her home with legal proceedings that Palmer described as "equally cruel and unnecessary." Further, Palmer reported, the "land has been almost entirely divested of timber." There was better news about Lot 29, which was as yet unpartitioned between the Melvilles and the Westmorlands. Despite the bad road from Charlottetown to Lot 29, there were "22 or 23 old tenants, none of whom pay less than £5 annually and some pay more." As well, five new tenants from Yorkshire had settled on the estate "near the head of Westmorland River [and] have taken the usual long leases beginning at a penny per acre and increasing to a shilling." They would, Palmer thought, be good examples as farmers. Alas, according to Palmer, Johnston had advanced great sums in provisions to attract the Yorkshire settlers; one, who had been given an advance of £25, had already fled. As well, Johnston had vigorously enforced rent payments "by measures calculated to terrify new settlers – that of seizing their property, attended with most unexampled expense and apprehension."[67]

Palmer also condemned Johnston's handling of the sawmill built on Lot 29 during Charles Stewart's management of the estate. Johnston had granted a lease for the mill for a ten-year term at £50 per annum, with the right to cut pine on the unsettled portions of the lot *for milling*. He discovered that the miller was cutting and shipping pine as logs, sued him in Chancery, and lost. According to Palmer, the lease that Johnston had drawn up was "most improvident and injurious to the estate." Palmer anticipated that the commercial timber on Lot 29 would be exhausted in twenty years, at which point the mill would be worth little. He also enclosed a bill from Charles Stewart's widow, Mary, claiming almost £800 sterling

in fees and debts from her husband's time as land agent. He
promised that he would inquire into the merits of the claim, which
he considered dubious.[68]

William Johnston first learned of the loss of his agency for the
Melville and Westmorland estates from Palmer, who brought news
of the change when he returned to the colony from Britain in late
1817.[69] When Palmer demanded that Johnston provide an account
of his management of the estates and turn over the deeds, documents, and maps related to his agency, Johnston balked at rapid
compliance. He later acknowledged that "some degree of irritation
is commonly felt on these occasions."[70] Palmer brought Johnston's
failure to produce the estates' papers to the attention of the Island's
lieutenant-governor, Charles Douglass Smith, and informed Smith
of the previous mismanagement of the Melville and Westmorland
properties. He charged that the estates had been yielding at least
£120 sterling annually and that Johnston had failed to account for
these monies and remit them to his employers. For his part, Palmer
claimed that, as the new agent, he had "not received six pence from
their Lordships' estates, but on the contrary I have advanced a considerable sum in money independent of my personal trouble and
attendance on a late intricate survey and investigation of Lot 29."
As things stood, he lacked the information necessary to enforce the
payment of current rents and arrears and the revenue to pay the
estates' quit rents.[71]

Lieutenant-Governor Smith invited Johnston to respond and
brought the issue to the Island's Executive Council, as it bore on
Johnston's professional conduct and thus his suitability for his position as attorney general. Johnston's response, which the council
described as "not considered as unsatisfactory," blamed the problems on the previous agent.[72] Johnston said that he had taken over
badly managed estates and had just begun to turn things around
when the agency was taken from him. In 1813 the estates were still
"nearly wilderness," inhabited by eighteen families who were "the
poorest people in the Colony"; only by "commencing distress" was
he able to get any "trifling payment." In the four years of his agency,
Johnston had collected "between £50 and £60 and that in small
sums and inconvenient ... payments which I submitted to in order
to accommodate so poor and indigent a tenantry." Annual receipts
"really and truly did not exceed £17 – there were no arrears at the
time worth naming for most of the Tenants had paid their rent in

advance by cutting Lumber for Mr. Stewart." Johnston claimed credit for securing twelve "new Tenants of the very best description of settlers," including six from Yorkshire, and said that he had "purposely fixed them in a situation where there was an abundance of vacant land to accommodate their friends who might migrate hither and I consider it as a basis for the finest settlement in the colony." He acknowledged that there was a clause in his agency that restricted him from spending "more money than the estate yielded" and said that he had "acted in strict conformity to it." Yet Johnston, like Palmer, claimed to have advanced money to estates that were not yielding any income: "In the last year alone I made advances to the estate in Cash to the amount of £100." He agreed with Palmer that the bill submitted by Mary Stewart was excessive and "widely different from what Mr. Stewart would himself have charged." He claimed that he had been able to negotiate a reduction in the bill to £300.[73]

Whatever the truth behind the accusations and counter-accusations exchanged by Palmer and Johnston, the dispute reveals the obstacles to the Melvilles' being able to profit from new opportunities on the Island. In the early nineteenth century a buoyant timber trade, sustained by imperial tariffs, began to transform the Island economy as well as its landscape. Charles Stewart had responded to the growing demand for wood by mobilizing tenants on Lot 29 to fell and square timber and haul it to the shore for shipment to Britain. So too had the holder of the sawmill lease on Lot 29. Obviously, others had responded in similar ways on Lot 53, as Palmer noted that the timber had been stripped from the lot. Timber boats returning to the Island from Britain provided inexpensive passage for immigrants, some of whom Stewart and Johnston had hoped to establish on the estates. By 1815 the Island's population was roughly 15,000, still modest given the Island resources, and population growth was not spread evenly across the Island.[74] Island roads remained poor, not just along the Northumberland coast of Queens County, as Palmer had reported, but almost everywhere. With the exception of the road connection between Charlottetown and St Peters on the north coast, no roads were suitable for wheeled passage prior to the 1820s.[75]

Securing tenants was no guarantee that profits would follow. Although the Island's population grew significantly in the first quarter of the nineteenth century, the land-to-settler ratios were still such that it was a lease buyer's market. The Melvilles offered long leases with graduated rents, as did a number of other proprietors at this time. And like some other proprietors, they also offered incentives to attract tenants. Charles Stewart had been instructed to do so, and Johnston continued the practice, providing settlers on Lot 29 with necessities, some of which he obtained from older settlers for credit toward future rent payments. Because of limited specie, much of the Island economy was grounded in exchanges in kind, as well as promissory notes. Charles Stewart had accepted the payment of rent in labour, and Johnston, in farm produce. Rent books from Lot 29 show payment in labour in the 1840s and 1850s, as well as in oats, wheat, barley, potatoes, pork, beef, butter and cheese, cloth, timber, boards, fence rails, and cash.[76] Although some proprietors and agents resisted the practice of accepting rents in kind, insistence on cash could pose a hardship for tenants, as Johnston noted in his critique of Palmer. Both Palmer and Johnston agreed that regular rent payment was not the norm, and each criticized the other for resorting to harsh measures, such as seizing personal property, in order to collect arrears.

The Melvilles may have worried about finding a trustworthy and competent agent for their property in Scotland, but their difficulties in doing so on the Island were exacerbated by delays in receiving information, accurate or otherwise. Palmer and Johnston both suggested that the other was not forthright in his accounting, and both claimed that, despite the problems with the estates as they found them, Lots 29 and 53 had the potential to sustain flourishing settlements. One wonders how many times the Melvilles and the Westmorlands had heard the same message. Clearly, their estate cost the Melvilles money. If the nominal rent roll in 1813 was less than £40, as Johnston reported, even if tenants paid their rent in full, the sum would not cover the quit rents. And yet, according to Johnston, the proprietors had approved £1,000 in expenditures during the three years of Charles Stewart's agency, and they owed Stewart's widow another £300.[77] Both Johnston and Palmer claimed that they too had put more into the estates in effort and money than they had received from the proprietors. No wonder Anne later referred to her Prince Edward Island properties as "that miserable estate."[78]

In June 1826 the Melvilles gave the agency back to their first agent, John Stewart, who had returned to the Island from Newfoundland earlier in the decade.[79] The dynamic between Stewart and Palmer at the moment of transfer was not dissimilar to that between Palmer and Johnston earlier. Stewart requested the accounts and copies of leases, and Palmer refused, in part, it would seem, because only the Melvilles had dismissed him and Palmer thought that he and LePage retained Lord Westmorland's trust. In Stewart's view, Westmorland would have to cut his ties to Palmer before Stewart could effectively act as agent on the two lots, for Palmer was "in the most desperate circumstances and having nothing to lose, he cares not what he does." Stewart proceeded as best he could, despite the impediments Palmer put in his way, to assess developments on Lots 29 and 53. In letters dated February and April 1827, he noted that there were problems with boundary lines and that the geographical division between the Melville and Westmorland portions of the lots had not been adequately laid out. Stewart reported that tenants on Lot 29 had paid rents of more than £475 to Palmer between May 1821 and November 1826, but Palmer, despite his claims, had spent none of it on estate improvements. According to Stewart, Palmer had used some of the money – up to £150 – on the farm where his family lived, on the Westmorland side of the lot. Stewart believed the estates had generated £1,000 during Palmer's agency, but the proprietors would get none of it. He also alleged that Palmer had recently sold 300 tons of pine timber on the Melville part of Lot 29 and intended to keep the proceeds to cover his expenses while he had been agent. As well, Palmer had let the lot's sawmill on a 999-year lease at £10 per annum, with rights to cut timber across the whole of the unleased parts of the lot, for no additional payment to the proprietors. Stewart described it as "one of the most extravagant transactions I ever heard of." He had received a claim from Johnston too, alleging that Palmer had accepted payments from tenants that were in fact owed to Johnston.[80]

There was trouble from another source too. John Stewart's sister-in-law, Mary, the widow of Charles Stewart, was still pursuing her decade-old claim against the proprietors. According to Mary Stewart, her husband had established twenty-five families on Lot 29, transforming it from a "perfect wilderness" at great sacrifice to himself and his family, both in money spent and time taken from attending to his own affairs. John Stewart apologized for his sister-in-law's claim, which he said was unfounded, as Charles had been instructed not to spend more on the estates than they produced and not to contract any debts on behalf of the proprietors. The London lawyers who handled Prince Edward Island matters for the Melvilles agreed with this analysis, but the Island courts did not. In 1829 Mary Stewart obtained judgment for about £300, having sued for £1,000. John Stewart, who was present at the proceedings, changed his position and agreed that Mary was entitled to the smaller sum. With interest and costs, Lords Westmorland and Melville each paid £185; their lawyers sent a release for Mary Stewart's signature by way of Henry Fane, Anne's nephew and Jane's son.[81]

Three decades of attempting to develop the estate the Saunders sisters had inherited had produced one financial disaster after another. In the fall of 1833 Westmorland reported to Melville that "your agent Mr. Stuart [sic] seems to be considered as totally lost in mind – incapable of business and your estate totally neglected." As well, Westmorland reported that Palmer, who was still Westmorland's agent, owed him £100, which was "totally lost" because George Seymour, non-resident proprietor of Lot 13, had obtained a judgment in the Court of Chancery against Palmer "for more than he was worth." Palmer indeed was lost when Westmorland wrote, having died earlier in the year. Westmorland was correct about John Stewart too; he died the following June. Westmorland chose to appoint the Island's attorney general, Robert Hodgson, as his new agent, saying that "he writes reasonably well which [is] all I suppose can be expected from Prince Edward Island."[82]

In the 1830s both Henry Fane and Anne's eldest son, Henry Dundas, visited the Island. Not surprisingly, their reports highlighted extensive problems with the management of the estates. As Anne summarized Henry's first report in 1834, Prince Edward Island was a fine place and their land good and capable of making a return "if properly managed, which I suspect it has never been and is questionable if it ever will be."[83] Henry had not been impressed with their tenants, writing that "the present set are a lazy, indolent one, very much like the Irish who as long as they can grow enough to subsist on themselves care nothing about improving the land or paying their rent."[84] Later that year Anne told an acquaintance that Henry had been able to visit "that miserable Estate in Prince Edward Island, where he seems to have established that we have been very comfortably cheated by the Agent who is happily dead."[85] She likely meant John Stewart, who had died four months earlier, but the Melvilles had been the victims of other agents who also deserved her uncharacteristically harsh verdict.

Lord Melville had commissioned Henry to retain a new land agent, advising him that of all his tasks, the one of the "greatest difficulty and the most important" was to "select a respectable & *honest* agent, supposing that such a person can be found in the Island."[86] Melville was not happy with his London lawyers either, as they had been unable to provide him with adequate information before Henry sailed for Halifax. He complained to his son Robert that the "gentlemen in Gray's Inn have left me completely in the dark as to the state of our affairs in that quarter."[87]

Henry Dundas's attention, however, was soon drawn to the growing political challenges facing Island proprietors in the second quarter of the nineteenth century. The anti-proprietorial agitation of the 1790s had resulted in major changes in land ownership, involving the transfer of title from one group of landlords to another, and had led to modifications in landlords' quit rent obligations. But the fundamentals remained the same. Landlords continued to be required to settle their lots and pay quit rents, and the leasehold system still dominated developments on the Island. Not surprisingly, the new activism revived the demand for an escheat, a demand that had been deflected at the turn of the century into more aggressive quit rent collection.

Several of the Melville land agents played a role in the continued vitality of the escheat threat, which from the tenants' point of view was the escheat hope. In 1806 Palmer had helped to found a political organization that came to be known as the Society of Loyal Electors. Although land reform and escheat were unlikely to have been among Palmer's goals, in time the society advocated these. The imperial and local governments suppressed the society after 1813, and Palmer increasingly cast himself as a defender of proprietors' interests. During its brief existence, though, the society helped to maintain the hope of sweeping land reform and broadened the traditions of political organizing that might be used to secure it.[88] William Johnston had played a more indirect role in sustaining the hope of an escheat in the first quarter of the nineteenth century. As the Island's attorney general during the administration of Lieutenant-Governor Charles Douglass Smith, he provided the legal advice on process that allowed Smith to escheat two townships in 1818. Smith initiated the escheat proceedings and took actions to enforce quit rent collection in order to strengthen his government by enhancing the resources available to it; overall, he sought to buttress the position of the Island proprietors and to suppress unrest. But the escheat proceedings reinforced popular belief that land reform was justified and feasible.[89]

The escheat proceedings, coupled with renewed demands for quit rent payment, generated opposition to Smith among resident and non-resident proprietors. In the early 1820s John Stewart helped to orchestrate opposition to him, and he subsequently carried Island petitions for Smith's recall to the Colonial Office in London. The lieutenant-governor's land policies and the Island protest movement against him prompted the Colonial Office to, yet again, establish new rules concerning the payment of quit rents. The colonial secretary also modified the settlement terms of the original grants, allowing proprietors until 1826 to secure sufficient settlers on their estates and removing the requirement that these be foreign Protestants. On the Island, Smith's recall and replacement by a new governor in 1824 was perceived as a response to demands articulated in the colony, thus strengthening the belief in the efficacy of local political mobilization.[90]

In the decade that followed, political activity on the Island increasingly focused on land issues. The assembly passed legislation that sought to pass on some of the costs of infrastructure development to proprietors and explored ways to induce proprietors who were not developing their properties to do so. Other voices both inside and outside the assembly began to call for initiatives to escheat proprietors' holdings. Support for an escheat strengthened over the 1830s, with the Escheat movement coming to dominate the popular house in the last years of the decade. In 1831 Lord Melville heard from his brother-in-law, Lord Westmorland, concerning recent Island roads legislation, which taxed landlords for road construction and gave decision-making power concerning the construction of these roads to Islanders. These provisions were bad in themselves; worse, the new Whig government that had taken office at Westminster in 1830 had not consulted the landed proprietors before approving the Island legislation. As Westmorland phrased it, the present government "without giving us any notice or any hearing confirmed the law – it is of a piece with their whole conduct but I suppose we slaves must submit in these despotic times."[91]

Yet more alarming was the possibility of losing the Island holdings altogether. In January 1832 the Island legislature struck a committee to inquire into "whether any and what lots or townships of land on this Island are liable to escheat." It also petitioned the imperial government to establish a court of escheat and passed legislation to facilitate its operation. The Melvilles appear to have learned of this development through Lord Westmorland and he from Palmer, who was still Westmorland's agent. Palmer, of course, had once played a role in fostering the development of the popular land politics that now, in the spring of 1832, he described to Westmorland in horrified terms. Palmer warned of "the dangerous state of the landed interests here" and the threats posed by Island legislation, including the escheat bill. He noted, correctly, that publication of the assembly's escheat debates and its legislation in the Island's newspapers was fanning popular resistance to landlords and agents: "Hundreds of tenants have already refused to pay their rents and several persons have gone into the woods and marked out land for themselves." Palmer located the historical origins of these developments in the 1820s: "old Stewart [was] the fomenter of the whole mischief" because, it would seem, of his role in toppling the Smith administration and helping to construct an activist House of Assembly drawing from the "lower and sometimes ... the lowest order of Inhabitants."[92] Had Palmer written a few months later, he might have reported an escheat meeting on Lot 29.[93] Westmorland believed that this lot had sufficient settlers to be safe from an escheat in 1832, but he was not sure about Lot 53.[94]

Although landed interests on the Island and in Britain succeeded in blocking imperial approval of the assembly's escheat initiative of 1832, popular agitation for an escheat did not diminish. Indeed, in 1834 it helped to elect a new assembly that provided even more support for land reform than the previous one. Henry Dundas reported on the continuing escheat agitation in the spring of 1836, observing that there was "a party in the Island who got up a meeting a short time ago" to petition the assembly for an escheat of lots where the settlement terms had not been met. He noted that the imperial government had already repeatedly said no to the idea of an escheat, but "with such a government as the present it is necessary that the proprietors at home should be prepared to defend their interests." What they needed was an imperial initiative that would "put the question firmly to rest." This they did not get. Dundas also acknowledged that "there is no doubt that the township here has not been settled fully to the terms of the grants."[95] In November he wrote again to complain of the initiatives of the House of Assembly and to characterize it as composed of "men who cannot even write their names," a complaint that became more common two years later, when an Escheat majority dominated the assembly.[96]

On returning to his military duties after his trip to Prince Edward Island, Henry Dundas participated in suppressing a rebellion in Lower Canada (Quebec) that was informed by many of the ideas and impulses that he had complained of on the Island. In the context of Lower Canada, Dundas was able to act out his growing anger with the democratic stirrings of the 1830s. Writing on Christmas Day 1837, he described capturing a village "which was burnt next morning when we left it – not a single house, not even the Church, exempted. This place has been a nest of rebels for the last seven years."[97]

Political changes in these years were affecting the Melvilles at home too. In a letter Anne wrote in 1826 to the Melvilles' naval friend Thomas Cochrane, recently appointed Newfoundland's first resident governor, she commented on the new political order that Britain's foreign policy – and navy – was to usher in: "I for my share have seen war for so huge a portion of my life I was in the hopes not to have occasion to see any more of its glories or its pains. I see, however, that the South Americans are beginning to reap the ordinary delights of political independence by declaring war with each other, a consummation that was to be expected, I think."[98] The following year she told Cochrane: "You give me such an agreeable picture of your Newfoundland climate that seeing we are tolerably northern in our national destination, I think when all the distresses our croaking Politicians predict come upon us, I shall have some hopes of being able to make a comfortable emigration to Prince Edward Island, where a portion of land belongs to me, which Lord Melville has not yet received any profits from, but which when our British glory shall be tarnished with our alleged evil policies may give us perhaps a very comfortable asylum and primitive occupation ... I have a mortal aversion to travelling about and when I move should like it to be where I cannot be *turned out* or *recalled*, but at my own pleasure."[99] In a later letter Lady Melville acknowledged the playfulness with which she dealt with some of her concerns, noting that she had access only to serious newspapers, as "Lord Melville never allows me to see the mischievous ones because he thinks I am too mischievously inclined myself."[100]

In the month before Anne wrote of Prince Edward Island as a possible refuge, the government leader, Lord Liverpool, had suffered a stroke which ended his career and marked the beginning of the end of a quarter-century of Tory rule. It also marked the beginning of the end of Robert's position in government; he was in and out of cabinet over the next three years until he ultimately lost his position as first lord of the Admiralty with the election in 1830. Anne wrote to Cochrane from Melville Castle in the fall of 1831 to say that Robert's health had benefited from being relieved of office; she also noted that he was on his way to London to debate the Reform Bill in the House of Lords.[101] Passage of the bill in 1832 brought more change in the Melvilles' lives as it reduced the political power that had been wielded in Scotland by two generations of the Dundas family. The winds of political reform that swept Robert from office and deepened the Melvilles' financial difficulties in the 1830s were the same ones that fanned demands for land reform in Prince Edward Island and sustained tenant hopes that proprietorial estates might be escheated and redistributed to actual settlers.

In 1838, in the wake of the rebellions in the Canadas that Henry Dundas had helped to suppress, the imperial government sent Lord Durham to investigate the causes of the crisis; he came as the new governor-in-chief of British North America. Interestingly, given Durham's political reputation as a reformer occupying the space between Whig and Radical positions, Anne supported his appointment.[102] Durham investigated conditions in the Maritime colonies as well as in the Canadas and considered land policies as well as governance. An official delegation travelled from Prince Edward Island to Quebec City to testify concerning land and politics in the colony. Headed by the Island's lieutenant-governor, Sir Charles FitzRoy, the delegation included the Melvilles' latest land agent, Robert Hodgson, who was also the Island's attorney general, and other government officials, most of whom had been or were land agents. Escheat advocates sent an unofficial delegation so that the Durham commission might hear a tenant perspective on land policy. John Le Lacheur, the chosen representative, was funded by a collection to buy him a new suit and pay his passage and expenses.[103] All the delegates, official and unofficial, criticized various aspects of the proprietorial system, blaming it for the Island's retarded development.

Durham's final report and its supporting documentation were not good news for Island landlords, as the report highlighted land speculation as a fundamental problem in British North America. While recommending against escheat policies in general, it suggested that escheat might be appropriate in the case of Prince Edward Island.[104] Reading of the resumption of hostilities in Lower Canada in the fall of 1838, after Durham's departure, Anne noted that local officials did not think of the "country as restored to quietude ... I fear I may never see it so, for once raised into discontent men's minds do not so easily settle again."[105] The same might have been said of Prince Edward Island, where a party calling for a general escheat of proprietorial lands had just assumed control of the House of Assembly. As described in the following chapter, Anne's sister, Jane, visited Prince Edward Island during the years when the Escheat majority dominated the assembly, and she lived in Charlottetown for nearly a year. Despite the inauspicious timing of her visit, she made the most of it, playing the role of lady bountiful. As well, she acquired personal knowledge of the circumstances and personalities in the colony. When Jane returned to Britain from her trip, she visited the Melvilles at Melville Castle for the first time in decades. She brought with her the news of her travels, including those that had taken her to Prince Edward Island.

Through her family connections, the personal universe of Anne, Lady Melville, had come to span much of the world, including Prince Edward Island. Her husband spent more than half his life administering the naval might that underwrote Britain's expanding imperial power. Her son Henry fought to preserve the British Empire in North America, both from internal unrest and from invasion across the border with the United States. Richard made his career with the navy, seeing service in the Mediterranean, the North Atlantic, the East Indies, and Oceania, as well as in coastal China during the first Opium War. Lady Melville, however, was not an uncritical supporter of the new imperial world that Britain's politicians, traders, and military men, her family included, were creating. She was troubled by Britain's aggression against China in the first Opium War, as was Richard, and she wondered what it all portended. Writing to her son Robert in 1841, she said: "I cannot help thinking there are abundant grounds to fear that a day of retribution awaits the overweening ambition this country displays for commanding the whole world. The strange anomaly of being at war everywhere under a pretence of general Peace is a position we never were in before and one does not know what to make of the designs and intentions under which the present Rulers are conducting it."[106]

Later that year Anne, in a letter to her son Robert filled with practical advice, concluded with news about her health: "I am not altogether well, tho' I cannot say from what cause ... but the truth is I am getting old."[107] Despite her health problems, she participated in the annual family migration from Edinburgh to London, with its usual stops to visit relatives and friends. She became increasingly ill during the passage southwards and was advised by a doctor that if she wanted to return to Melville Castle, she needed to do so immediately. Never an eager traveller, she chose to return to the comfort and familiarity of her home, where she died on 10 September 1841; she was sixty-three.[108] When her husband, Robert, died ten years later, the Island estate became the property of their eldest son, Henry Dundas, the third Lord Melville. The property remained in the hands of a male proprietor until the Island government, over Henry's protests, acquired the estate under compulsory sale legislation in 1875. In correspondence with the Colonial Office, he drew on the knowledge of Prince Edward Island gained on his trips there, as did the other lady landlords profiled here. Anne, an adept manager with a supportive husband, never visited the Island, despite her playful comment about perhaps seeking an asylum there.

3

Jane Saunders, Lady Westmorland: Perpetual Motion

Jane Saunders, the younger daughter of Dr Richard Huck Saunders, was equal heir with her sister, Anne, to the large fortune and extensive properties of their great-uncle, Sir Admiral Charles Saunders, and the much smaller estate of their father. Although Jane and Anne grew up in similar circumstances, with a shared inheritance that included ownership of property on Prince Edward Island, their Island estates figured quite differently in the sisters' lives. Jane, unlike Anne, visited the Island and toured her estate there, participating actively in the social and political life of the Island. The difference was due in part to the sisters' dissimilar personalities and in part to their divergent experiences of married life.

Prior to Anne's marriage in 1796, she and Jane lived together in a furnished house in London, pursuant to the instructions their father had appended to his will for the two heiresses. The Court of Chancery approved the continuation of this arrangement for Jane alone, with a reduction of only £100 in the sum of £1,600 per year for expenses, given that the cost of renting the house and carriage, together with the companion's salary, remained as before.[1] Jane likely made the most of being a young heiress in London, no longer under the supervision of her older sister, whose criticisms she resented. Her marriage on 24 March 1800 to John Fane, tenth Earl of Westmorland, secured her a social position much superior to Anne's, who was merely Mrs Dundas, with no prospect when she married that her husband would inherit a title.

Lord Westmorland was a prominent Tory politician and office-holder.[2] He was a widower when he married Jane and, at forty-one, more than twice her age. His first wife, Sarah Anne Child, had died in 1793. Sarah had also been an heiress, the only daughter of banker Robert Child. Westmorland did not gain much financially by that match, having permanently alienated his father-in-law by marrying Sarah without his consent, when she was seventeen. Theirs was a "Gretna Green" marriage, named for the first town across the border in Scotland. Under Scots law, couples could contract a legally binding marriage simply by declaring that they took each other as husband and wife.[3] Robert Child pursued the couple in his carriage in an attempt to stop the marriage but gave up the chase, according to some accounts, after Westmorland shot the horse out from under Child's servant, who was riding ahead of his post-chaise.[4] Child never forgave Westmorland; he gave his daughter an annual allowance of £2,000, which increased to £6,000 on his death, but his will provided that Sarah's children would inherit his property only if there were no other heirs, and even then, the son who was heir apparent to the Westmorland title would inherit only if there were no other children of the marriage.[5]

This past, as well as Lord Westmorland's personality, did not incline Anne and Robert Dundas to view his courtship of Jane with favour. They would probably have preferred that she marry someone a little closer to her in age and rank, with the calmness and caution that would provide her with the steadying influence they thought she needed. Instead, as the circumstances of Westmorland's first marriage suggest, he was wilful, imperious, and apt to act impetuously without due regard for the consequences. Robert Dundas considered that Westmorland's temper would not make him easy to live with, and he predicted, sagely enough, that the marriage "will be a union ... from which no good can be assured."[6] There was gossip that money was the motive behind the match. Of course, it was common enough for a man with a title to marry an heiress from a good but not noble family in order to acquire the wherewithal to pay off debts and maintain appearances.[7] Although Westmorland had inherited a substantial estate, it seemed that he lived beyond his means. Undoubtedly, he was not indifferent to the charms of an intelligent and lively young woman who avowed that she loved him passionately, but Jane's fortune must have attracted him too.

As she was still a minor under the protection of her guardians and trustees, Lord Westmorland had to seek the approval of the Court of Chancery for their marriage. The court noted the possibility of a long period of widowhood for Jane Saunders, given the age gap between her and her intended, or even a second marriage, and it considered whether the marriage settlement would provide long-term financial security for her and any children she might have. It was not the task of the Court of Chancery to consider whether her marriage would meet her emotional needs. From the court's perspective, marriages were alliances among heirs to property who would produce more heirs. Marriage contracts provided women with some rights in the property that they brought to the marriage and some protection for themselves and their children in the context of a legal and social regime that in general enhanced men's economic and social power at the expense of women's. Even without such a contract, in a mutually affectionate and respectful relationship such as that of Anne and Robert Dundas, a husband might consult his wife on decisions about property, regardless of any legal inequality resulting from his wife's lack of legal capacity. That did not happen in Jane's marriage. Her marriage settlement provided for her share of the Saunders property to be settled on trustees, who held the property for the benefit of Lord Westmorland during his life and, on his death, for the benefit of their children, subject to payment of Jane's jointure of £4,000 per year, in lieu of dower. During Westmorland's lifetime, Jane would have pin money of £800 per year, twice what her sister Anne had under her marriage contract. According to the terms of Sir Charles Saunders's will, Jane's enjoyment of the Saunders estate was conditional on her husband taking the name Saunders, but that condition was ignored from the outset, with no consequences. Her Prince Edward Island estate was not mentioned explicitly in the marriage settlement, although Westmorland assumed the legal right of the husband to manage the estate and to collect and spend the income, without any obligation to make an accounting to his wife.[8]

By marrying Jane Saunders, Lord Westmorland acquired control over a considerable fortune, and she become a countess, presiding at social events at Apethorpe Hall, the Westmorland manor house in Apethorpe, "a picturesque ... village of stone-built and stone-tiled houses set ... amid the rich, low-lying meads" of Northamptonshire (see illus. 3.1 and 3.2). Originally built at the end of the fifteenth century, the manor house and surrounding estate came into the Fane family early in the seventeenth century. The main part of the manor house was built around an open courtyard. The ground floor was very grand, with small and large drawing-rooms, a library, a dining

3.1 Apethorpe, the Westmorland manor in Northamptonshire. From J.P. Neale, *Views of the Seats of Noblemen and Gentlemen in England, Wales and Scotland*, 2nd series, vol. 3 (London: Sherwood, Gilbert and Piper, 1826)

3.2 Front entrance to Apethorpe. From Tipping, *English Homes*, Period III, vol. 2: 1

room, and a spacious windowed gallery about a hundred feet in length that was used as the music room. An adjoining smaller rectangle with its own courtyard held the kitchen, servants' quarters, dairy, bakehouse, brewhouse, and wash house, with a conservatory, built about 1718, closing off the end.[9]

As Lady Westmorland, Jane became the stepmother to her husband's children by his first wife, Sarah Child. The eldest, John Fane, heir to the Westmorland title and known as Lord Burghersh, was studying at Harrow. In 1811, after a military career, he would marry Priscilla Anne Wellesley-Pole, daughter of the Earl of Mornington and niece of the Duke of Wellington. Lord Westmorland also had three daughters from his first marriage, and Jane claimed credit for helping them make good matches.[10] By 1805 all had married members of the aristocracy. Sarah married George Villiers, later the Earl of Jersey, and became one of the arbiters of London fashion and an active promoter of first the Whig and subsequently the Tory cause in politics. Like her stepmother, she was prone to self-dramatization. Sarah inherited the enormous fortune of her maternal grandfather, Robert Child. When she married Lord Jersey, she agreed to give £20,000 each to her father and her three siblings, yet she still had an estimated annual income of £60,000 per year from her inheritance. Westmorland's second daughter, Augusta, married Lord Boringdon, later the first Earl of Morley. She left Boringdon to live with Arthur Paget, whom she married two days after her husband divorced her in 1809. Maria, the youngest, married Viscount Duncannon, later the Earl of Bessborough.[11] Jane's children, too, were born in these busy years: Georgiana in 1801, Charles Saunders in 1802, Henry Sutton in 1804, Montagu Villiers in 1805, and Evelina, who died in January 1809.[12]

The predictable difficulties of a marriage between two people of such different ages, status, and experience were compounded for Lord and Lady Westmorland by their particular temperaments, which were likely to expose each other's weaknesses rather than provide complementary strengths. From Lady Westmorland's perspective, shared by her stepdaughter, Lady Jersey, Lord Westmorland did not treat his wife with sufficient respect, never giving her the authority and status that she deserved in the Westmorland household, countermanding her instructions to the servants, and putting the butler, rather than his wife, in charge of the dinner table. Lady Jersey said that Lord Westmorland's lack of respect for his wife was a joke among the servants. Lady Westmorland complained that her husband treated her as a rival rather than as a partner, that he resented her intimacy with his daughters, and that he besmirched her character both within the family and in the eyes of the world.[13]

Anne Dundas came to despise her brother-in-law, but she was critical of her sister too, concluding that Jane was unlikely to do what was necessary to maintain peace in the Westmorland household. In Anne's opinion, which Robert shared, Jane was unwilling to subordinate her will to another's, even her husband's, being too passionate, headstrong, stubborn, and rebellious. Before Jane's marriage, her public displays of emotion, which attracted attention and gossip, had been a trial to her more sedate and reserved sister.[14] Anne's father-in-law noted the "peculiar vivacity and eccentricity of Lady Westmorland's character from her infancy" and "the characteristic self-sufficiency and occasional violence of [her] disposition."[15] Other contemporary comments ranged from admiration for her liveliness to impatience with her restlessness. Caroline, Princess of Wales, called her "perpetual motion"; Lady Charlotte Bury, lady-in-waiting to Princess Caroline, said that Lady Westmorland "talks well on any subject, and is certainly a most amusing person ... [She] has a great charm about her, but never rests herself, and never lets anyone else rest in her presence." Sir William Hotham described her as "very quick, very good-humoured, and very eccentric. She has too much bustle about her to enjoy anything in society that is not *bruyante*."[16]

Lady Westmorland was unhappy in her marriage for many years, but she and Lord Westmorland separated only after her despair had driven her to desperate measures that nearly led to the loss of whatever freedom and independence she enjoyed.[17] In 1810, shortly after the death of her daughter Evelina, she ended a friendship with a young man when he wanted more intimacy than was appropriate. Lord Westmorland did not offer sympathy and support to his wife in the aftermath of the messy parting. Rather, he wounded and insulted her with insinuations and accusations that the friendship had gone beyond the bounds of propriety. Stormy scenes culminated in mid-July 1810 with Jane stabbing herself in the side with a knife that she had recently purchased.[18] Her husband engaged several doctors to consider her case, including three of the specialists who had attended King George III in his recurring bouts of what doctors today diagnose as porphyria, but which at the time was described as insanity. The doctors agreed that Lady Westmorland was mad and should be kept isolated and quiet for her own good. She spent the next five weeks in her room, under the constant supervision of two keepers; she was spared some of Dr Willis's harsher methods with the king, such as the use of straitjackets and a custom-made confining chair.[19]

In August, when his wife was well enough to travel, Lord Westmorland had her moved to a private asylum in Fulham, a fashionable London suburb, accompanied by a maid and the two keepers. While she was there, her eldest son, Charles, died, without her being able to see him.[20] Early in November, Jane left the asylum. In a letter to her brother-in-law, Robert Dundas, she declared that "whether it be legal or not to escape to the house of a friend when you are *sane* and confined as a lunatic I will not decide. I should think it is."[21] Throughout the lengthy family discussions of her mental state, she refused to admit that she was recovered because that would imply that she had been ill.[22] Instead, she protested, coherently and with humour, that she had never been mad. Earlier she wrote to Robert that the doctors and Lord Westmorland seemed to agree that "my *disease* is *supposing* myself to live unhappily with Lord W., whereas I am in reality enjoying the utmost felicity in my union with him."[23]

Jane's stepdaughter, Lady Jersey, championed her stepmother's cause and provided her with a place to stay when she left the asylum.[24] Anne and Robert, too, rallied to support her. Though not approving of her conduct – indeed, in Robert's opinion, "whatever may be said as to her sanity, she certainly is now, as she always has been, devoid of every sound principle or proper feeling" – both Robert and Anne opposed any steps to have Jane confined in an institution.[25] They were concerned about the consequences for their children of a suggestion of madness in the family, but they had also concluded that Lord Westmorland was acting to secure his own advantage and not out of any concern for what was best for his wife.[26] Having made some inquiries of her own, Anne decided that her sister's violence against herself was not due to any mental disorder but was a consequence of Westmorland's oppression. She had heard from more than one source that Westmorland had tried before to have his wife declared mad. Anne confirmed the story by questioning the doctor who eight years earlier had attended Jane at the birth of Charles. Had Westmorland been able to have her confined as a lunatic, he could have removed her from his house without his appearing to have done anything blameworthy and without losing the fortune she had brought to him. Without others to vouch for her sanity and to hold her husband accountable, Lady Westmorland might have suffered the fate of other women who, having been declared mad by a husband who wanted to be rid of them, spent the rest of their lives in an institution for the mentally ill.[27] During the lengthy and difficult process of securing Lord Westmorland's agreement to reasonable terms on which he and his wife would live apart, Anne came to believe that, whatever her sister's faults, Lord Westmorland was "the greatest brute alive."[28]

Robert Dundas and Lord Lonsdale, who was married to Lord Westmorland's sister and was one of the trustees of the Westmorland properties, acted as intermediaries in the negotiations between Lord and Lady Westmorland. Westmorland wanted his wife to live quietly, preferably out of London, but certainly removed from her former place in society. Robert and Anne agreed that this arrangement would be best, in order to avoid "all the gossiping tittle tattle" that would not die down if she stayed in London.[29] Jane, however, rejected the imposition of any constraints on her behaviour that would give credence to the idea that she had been mad or that would diminish her status and position in society. In a letter intended for Lord Westmorland, she stated that she would "regulate my future conduct by those habits of condition and reserve" to be expected from a woman suffering under the public manifestation of her husband's displeasure, but "at the same time ... act with the dignity of a person who is conscious of having in no respect merited so severe a misfortune." She stated that she would always "respect Lord Westmorland as the father of my children and as the man whom I loved so far above all others as to make him the guardian of my honour and happiness, and to feel it my greatest pride to bear his name. I shall endeavour to consult his wishes in the regulation of my future actions as far as I can do consistently with justice to myself." A husband who had openly withdrawn his protection from her, however, was not entitled to "preserve the right of control over her conduct."[30] Yet Jane claimed, in justice to herself and to the Westmorland name, the means to establish herself in the style appropriate to the wife of Lord Westmorland, in a house of her own in London and not in a public hotel or as a guest of others. As she wrote to Robert Dundas, if she were to be deprived of her place as a wife and mother, surely she was entitled to keep her friends.[31]

Legal handbooks of the time contained precedents for separation agreements; both the common-law courts and the courts of equity had developed a body of case law on what terms were enforceable in which circumstances.[32] By mid-1812 the Westmorlands had signed such a separation agreement, to the great relief of Anne and Robert if not necessarily to the satisfaction of the estranged couple. The negotiations, according to Robert Dundas, were "unnecessarily protracted by the thousand little objections which were stated on both sides."[33] Anne worried about her sister's propensity for rash behaviour and feared that, because of "the arrogance of her Disposition," Jane would resist a reasonable settlement if she felt that she was being compelled to "act as she should," rather than doing so of her own choice.[34] Under the final terms, Lord Westmorland retained custody of the couple's three surviving children, Georgiana, Henry, and Montagu. He agreed to give his wife plate, linen, and similar articles necessary for her to establish her own residence, to pay her outstanding bills, and to provide, through a trustee, £3,500 pounds per year for her separate maintenance. This was the equivalent of her jointure, minus both the estimated income taxes on the jointure and the annuities for the Saunders and Kinsey connections, which Lord Westmorland continued to pay.[35]

By negotiating a private settlement, the Westmorlands avoided the embarrassment of public legal proceedings, much to the relief of Anne Dundas, who did not like the thought of her sister's doings being talked of everywhere. England's ecclesiastical courts could grant a divorce *a mensa et thoro* – an order permitting the wife to live separate from her husband and relieving her of her conjugal obligations, while compelling her husband to continue to support her. Divorce *a mensa et thoro* did not give either spouse the freedom to marry someone else. That required divorce *a vinculo matrimonii*, which in England, until passage of the Matrimonial Causes Act of 1857, was available only by private act of Parliament, at great expense and with great notoriety. Lady Westmorland's stepdaughter Augusta was able to marry again because her husband chose to pursue a divorce in Parliament on the grounds of her adultery; her freedom came at the expense of her reputation. Parliament had heard and granted its first divorce petition from a woman in 1801; only three other women obtained a parliamentary divorce.[36] Lady Jersey believed that her stepmother should institute a divorce proceeding in the ecclesiastical courts for a divorce *a mensa et thoro* on the grounds of cruelty or adultery, in order to compel Lord Westmorland to give her better terms. Lady Westmorland too thought that a judicial proceeding would exonerate her of any wrongdoing. Robert Dundas, though, would not support that step as long as Lord Westmorland agreed to reasonable terms.[37]

With her separate maintenance assured, Jane began a peripatetic phase of her life, moving from one fashionable city to another. While in London still awaiting the separation settlement, she socialized with the artistic set. Poet and sexual predator Lord Byron was a guest at functions she hosted and attended, and she was one of the women who took him to task for driving novelist Lady Caroline Lamb to stab herself.[38] Jane went often to Brighton on the English Channel, an hour by coach from London. The seaside town had become a fashionable retreat for the London elite when it caught the fancy of the Prince of Wales (later George IV). In addition to the brilliant social gatherings at the Royal Pavilion, the Prince of Wales's Brighton residence, the elite enjoyed indoor and outdoor bathing in sea water and medicated steam baths and massages, called shampoos, offered at various "Turkish" baths. From 1825 on, Brighton also provided a course of waters at the German spa, an establishment presenting its clientele with a choice of water chemically treated to mimic that available at the exclusive mineral-water spas of the continent.[39] Jane also spent time in Cheltenham, a spa town in the western Cotswolds, midway between Gloucester and Tewkesbury. While she was there to take the waters in late 1811, Robert Dundas, by then second Viscount Melville, sought her advice regarding the separation negotiations with Lord Westmorland. Jane replied that he would have to wait for an answer, as she could not risk spoiling the beneficial effects of the treatment by thinking of distressing things.[40]

Lady Westmorland spent much of her time in Europe, living in Paris, Geneva, London, Milan, Florence, and Rome. In the latter two cities, in particular, she could live well on her income, and despite her ambiguous status as a woman on her own, who was neither a spinster nor a widow, she could play a leading role in the social circles of those who found life on the continent more congenial than in England.[41] Charles Greville, the infamous diarist, described society in Florence in 1830 as a mix of Italians, English, and other foreigners "in nearly equal proportions ... Nothing can be worse than it is, for there is no foundation of natives, and the rest are generally the refuse of Europe, peoples who came here for want of money or want of character. Everybody is received without reference to their conduct, past or present, with the exception, perhaps, of Englishwomen who have been divorced, whose case is too notorious to allow the English Minister's wife to present them at Court."[42] The Countess of Blessington, a member of this dubious society, noted that when the English travelled abroad, they carried with them the habits and customs of home, giving balls, soirees, and tableaux "*à la mode de Londres* ... with all its luxurious habits and dissipations."[43]

Jane, however, was not willing to overlook all evidence of scandalous dissipation in the foreign community. In the years 1826–28, while she was living in Rome, she attempted to ostracize the Count d'Orsay, a French citizen who was married to Lady Blessington's young stepdaughter. Jane would not admit either of them to her society, viewing Lady Blessington as a vulgar social climber and the marriage as a contrivance to keep d'Orsay in the household for Lady Blessington's benefit. When Jane tried to impose her views on the English community in Rome, d'Orsay objected in terms that greatly offended her and brought home the vulnerability of her position. According to Henry Fox, Lord Holland's son, Jane blamed d'Orsay's effrontery on, among others, Lord Westmorland, declaring: "Had he a grain of feeling, a spark of honor ... what remorse would he now feel to see to what insults he has exposed the woman that bears his name."[44] Jane, who had developed strong Catholic sympathies while in Rome, asked the pope, through an intermediary, to banish d'Orsay. Her daughter, Georgiana Fane, hearing of the affair in England, worried about the effect on her mother of feeling herself misunderstood by everyone and asked her influential acquaintances, including the Duke of Wellington, to write to Jane assuring her that they thought she had acted correctly. Georgiana warned them, however, not to let Jane know that no one in Paris was discussing the d'Orsay matter, as not being the subject of conversation at all would distress Jane almost as much as having her behaviour misconstrued.[45]

Fox, who was in his mid-twenties, was in Europe to avoid restrictions and responsibilities at home. He spent a great deal of time in Lady Westmorland's company, and initially he took her part in the quarrel with d'Orsay and Lady Blessington. Athough he criticized Lady Westmorland for her interference in others' business, he was inclined to agree that d'Orsay and Lady Blessington were behaving abominably. Ultimately, as Lady Westmorland became more overwrought and exhibited more evidence of mental instability, he concluded that she "is by far the most unreasonable person to deal with I ever saw, and renders it a most hopeless and thankless office to attempt in any way to assist her. I pity her less than I should any other woman in a similar situation, for ... she now feels great pleasure ... in having an opportunity of quarrelling with more than two-thirds of society, and in abusing everybody else, and in extolling her own *angelic conduct*, as she calls it, to the few victims she can obtain as an audience."[46] Fox finally cut off all contact with Lady Westmorland, returning her letters and fleeing from St Peter's Square in Rome when he spotted her "richly liveried" coachman there.[47]

A decade after this drama, Lady Blessington described Fox, who was their guest, as "a most agreeable companion, lively, playful, and abounding in anecdote," and providing amusement with his good-natured imitations of the peculiarities of others.[48] Fox was certainly a perceptive observer of character. Early in his friendship with Lady Westmorland, he noted in his journal that

> her wonderful talents and brilliant conversation make it impossible for me not to have pleasure in her society, notwithstanding the very extraordinary absurdities of her conduct. She is perhaps not mad, but no body ever approached so near it with so much reason. She has fine and generous impulses, which are almost always either perverted or entirely overwhelmed by the exuberant vanity, violent temper, suspicious distrust, or ungovernable annoyance, that obscure the better feelings of her heart. It is the same with her head. Sometimes she has very just views of people's characters and actions, but when ... she is the least blinded by one of her vague suspicions, she instantly forgets all her former observations, and only sees them as her enemies or her friends' enemy, or her enemy's friend: for she divides the world into two classes – her friends and her enemies, which supply in her vocabulary the words, good and bad. Her way of life is most extraordinary and eccentric. She entirely forgets hours and time, nor has she any mercy on the time of others. The

inconsistencies in her character are endless; and one might draw it up in perpetual antithesis. She has the greatest kindness and is capable of the greatest sacrifice for those she at the time is interested about: yet she has no feeling or permanent affection for any one, not even her children. She has the nicest observation and sees the minutest trait of character, yet she mistakes most of the people she knows and imputes false notions to them.[49]

In 1837 Jane returned to England, hoping to be reconciled with her husband, then almost blind and cared for by Georgiana. Declining to seek help from Anne or Anne's children, she arranged through acquaintances to rent a house in London. Indeed, by then she was estranged from most of her relatives, who learned of her comings and goings from others. She had even quarrelled with her stepdaughter and former champion, Lady Jersey.[50] In the following year, with no change in her relations with Lord Westmorland, she decided to tour North America and while there, to visit the estates that she had inherited from her great-uncle and her father. Her son Henry had already been to Prince Edward Island and reported back on what he had discovered. So too had her nephew Henry Dundas. Jane no doubt wanted to see the estates for herself, especially as she could anticipate that, with her husband's health failing, she might soon, as a widow, regain the legal capacity to own and manage property. As well, she felt that she was being rebuffed by her son when she sought more information about the estates and intimated that she wished to assume a more active role in managing them.[51]

Jane arrived in New York late in 1838.[52] Her relatives, concerned that she might not appreciate the difficulties of travelling in an undeveloped colony, were no doubt relieved that she did not start immediately for Prince Edward Island.[53] At that time of year, ice in the Northumberland Strait made travel to and from the Island difficult, dangerous, and at times impossible. After several months of travel in the United States, Jane arrived in Charlottetown in mid-October 1839, accompanied by her secretary and companion, Miss Chamberlain, a servant, a page, and several greyhounds. The party had travelled from Pictou, Nova Scotia, in the *Cape Breton*, which by the 1830s made regular runs between the Island and the mainland, a trip of four to five hours in good weather. George Seymour, a non-resident landlord who had inherited an Island lot from his father, visited the Island in 1840 and thought that the *Cape Breton* was "a particularly dirty" steam vessel.[54] Charlottetown, though, had its charms. A traveller in 1821 described it as "a beautiful town ... with its streets all regularly laid out. There is a large square in the middle of the town, where the Court-house, the High Church, and Market House stand, with plenty of open ground for drilling the militia, executions, etc. The houses are all of wood, and those that are well done up and painted, look very elegant, though neither warm nor durable." At the time of Jane's visit the population was around 3,000 (see illus. 3.3).[55]

Visitors with the status of Lady Westmorland or George Seymour, who was soon to be one of the lords of the Admiralty, enjoyed the hospitality of the Island's lieutenant-governor, Sir Charles FitzRoy. FitzRoy had been born into and married within Britain's aristocracy; his grandfather was the Duke of Grafton; his first wife, Mary Lennox, was the daughter of the Duke of Richmond. The FitzRoys arrived on the Island in the summer of 1837 and took up residence in Government House, completed in 1834 on a point of land at the edge of town (see illus. 3.4). Seymour said that he had never seen a better-placed dwelling; he especially appreciated its cleanliness and quiet. As he was ill during most of his visit, the latter virtue perhaps appealed more to him than to Jane.[56] Lady FitzRoy had been alarmed at the idea of playing hostess to Lady Westmorland, as her reputation for eccentricity had preceded her. She decided, however, that while her guest was "rather odd," she was entertaining, knowing everybody and with many amusing incidents to relate. Indeed, Lady FitzRoy found her generally so agreeable that she became reconciled to the task of finding, very late in the season, a suitable furnished house for Lady Westmorland and her entourage. Lady FitzRoy was impressed, too, that Jane intended to help the tenantry to establish schools and churches.[57]

With Lady FitzRoy's assistance, Jane obtained a year's lease of a house at 269 Queen Street in Charlottetown, and she lived there until August 1840 (see illus. 3.5). Shortly after her arrival, Lady FitzRoy gave "a splendid party" for her. Mrs Sidney Dealey, one of the guests, had met Lady Westmorland on the steamship from Pictou and described how she had talked "incessantly" to all and sundry who would listen, including her "favourite greyhound, which wears a silk cloak and velvet cap padded, her Ladyship says, to keep its dear little ears warm." Lady Westmorland queried

3.3 Lower Queen Street, Charlottetown, c. 1840. Photo by M. Mallet of painting by Fanny Bayfield. PARO, Acc. 2320/58-7

3.4 Government House, Charlottetown, c. 1860. Photo by Henry J. Cundall. PARO, Acc. 3466/HF 74.27.3.26

3.5 269 Queen Street, Charlottetown, where Lady Westmorland spent the winter of 1839–40, as it looked on a sunny day in 2007. Photo by authors.

Mrs Dealey on why people emigrated to the Island, and Mrs Dealey found herself quite forgetting that she was talking "to an eccentric Countess – or a Nurse of pet grey hounds – I at least think her a sensible and pleasing woman." She described Lady Westmorland as "lavishly dressed," a "determined Whig," and of the view that Americans were "the most orderly and enterprising people in the world."[58]

Early in November 1839 Jane spent two weeks on Lot 29, her estate to the west of Charlottetown in Queens County, accompanied by H.D. Morpeth, who was the latest in a series of land agents employed by her sister and brother-in-law to manage their share of the lots the Saunders sisters had inherited (see map 3.1).[59] Crapaud, the principal settlement on Lot 29, was on a good harbour, but Jane probably travelled overland. The Island government had improved the road network in the 1820s and 1830s, when Lord Westmorland had joined with other proprietors in vigorously protesting a tax on proprietors' lands to fund the work.[60] According to Lady FitzRoy,

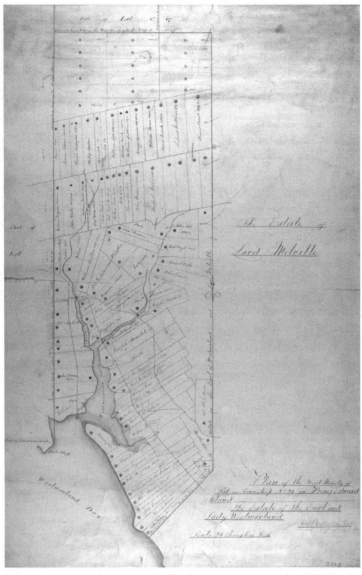

Map 3.1   Plan of the west half of Lot 29, Prince Edward Island.
NAS, RHP 2109

though, the roads were still bad; she was looking forward to the winter, when she could travel by sleigh.[61]

Crapaud took its name from the Acadian name for the nearby river, Rivière aux Crapauds, meaning river of toads.[62] Walter Johnstone described it in 1821 as a "new" settlement, "where small vessels load with timber."[63] He might have added, as the Melvilles had learned, that more often than not, the timber came from the lot without suitable payment to the lot's proprietors. The Crapaud community had begun construction of a church on land given to it in August 1839 by Lord Melville, acting through his agent, Morpeth.[64] A petition presented to Lady Westmorland, signed by twenty-four people, referred to "the general failure of our crops" and humbly requested her ladyship's assistance in completing the building, which would aid in the improvement of their morals and their continuing as "good subjects, good tenants, and good members of society." The petitioners also mentioned their difficulties in raising enough money to hire a teacher of moderate qualifications or to obtain proper school books for their children. Petitioners representing twenty-eight families from the back settlement of Crapaud, four or five miles from the main settlement, also asked Lady Westmorland for her assistance in erecting a chapel, citing their desire that the seventy-eight children of the community attend Sunday school.

Jane responded graciously to the Crapaud petitioners, thanking them for their expression of "sentiments so much in conformity with my own, on what I consider the two most important points conducive to moral happiness – piety towards God, and allegiance to the Sovereign." She said that, by her family circumstances, she was "peculiarly connected with the glorious events in times past by which these noble Provinces of North America were annexed to the British Crown," presumably a reference to the military service of her great-uncle, Sir Charles Saunders, and her father, Dr Richard Huck Saunders. She then expressed her wish, "by every little means in my power, to promote your welfare and give encouragement to industry and exertion." Jane promised to provide £100 for the completion of the chapel and £200 more for the instruction of the children, to be spent as she would determine after consultation with Lady FitzRoy, whose zeal and judgment in these matters she commended. She made a similar donation to the outlying settlers.[65]

Jane's generosity embroiled her, unwittingly, in an ongoing controversy in the community. When the Reverend Matthew Smith delivered an address of thanks to Lady Westmorland, signed by fifty-six people, they identified themselves as "the inhabitants of the Back Settlement of Crapaud and adherents to the Wesleyan Association throughout the settlement at large."[66] Publication of the address produced a flurry of letters to the Charlottetown papers. Thomas H. Davies, who described himself as "a Wesleyan missionary," wrote to refute any idea that the £100 given to the back settlement was for the benefit of one denomination only, knowing "on good information, that it is the intention of the said noble and benevolent lady" that the money be used for a free chapel, for any denomination's use, including that of the Wesleyan Methodists of the principal settlement, should they ever want to hold services in the "backwoods." Another letter questioned whether the back settlement held fifty-six persons of any denomination. Other letters followed, raising questions about who could preach in the chapel in the principal settlement too.[67] Despite the controversy, the partially constructed church was finished in 1840 and another begun, with Jane assisting with further donations. She would have been particularly gratified by the acknowledgment of her contribution by the Diocesan Church Society, which described her as "a very bright example" to other proprietors, "who by their wealth and high standing in society, may have it in their power to render such essential services to the Church and thereby to their tenantry."[68]

Jane's responses to the needs of her tenants fit closely with foundational ideas of the Escheat movement, which was challenging landlords' interests on the Island at the time when she arrived. According to the leader of this movement, William Cooper, the role of landlords was to "support and cherish" their tenants and to use their possessions to provide "employment and bread to the industrious" – the reciprocal obligation that went with the rights proprietors gained from owning a landed estate. Cooper maintained that tenants challenged proprietors' claims to the land in the 1830s in part because proprietors had simply become rent collectors and had forgotten their social obligations. This characterization of landlord behaviour certainly did not match Jane's generosity while on the Island. But her choices, and her wealth, were not the norm among Island landlords. Making her contributions directly to the tenants on Lots 29 and 53 enhanced her image and ensured that her intentions were not subverted by land agents with their own agendas.

Jane fell short of Cooper's vision of the model landlord, though, when she was confronted with the question of rents.[69]

The two petitions presented by the settlers at Crapaud, as well as requesting support for secular and moral instruction, asked for remission of rent arrears and rent reductions. The petitioners recounted how, through "persevering industry," they had been able to pay rents as long as they could do so in produce and labour. Recent crop failures, however, had put many tenants in arrears, and they asked for her ladyship's "kind recommendation in the proper quarter for a small reduction of our rents" and for permission to pay the rents in Island currency, rather than in sterling. Lady Westmorland invoked her legal disability as a married woman to sidestep this request: "With respect to everything which regards the rents, by the laws of Great Britain, I am, as a married woman, not empowered to act. If it should be the Almighty will to afflict me with what I shall consider the heaviest calamity – to be the survivor of my husband – I should then acknowledge whatever power devolves upon me to be placed in my hands by God ... and make it my study to endeavour to promote, as far as possible, in consistency with my other duties, the welfare of the persons who have been located by the authority of my husband, the Earl of Westmorland, upon those lands which I inherited."[70] Jane's careful qualification of what she might do, had she the legal capacity to do anything, shows that this speech was not mere cant; had she believed that she could alter rents and forgive arrears, she might have acted generously in this sphere too.

In July 1840 Jane spent four days visiting her estate on Lot 53, to the east of Charlottetown in Kings County, again accompanied by Morpeth.[71] She also visited Georgetown, the royalty town for the county, built on a point of land between the Brudenell and Cardigan rivers, south and east of Lot 53. In the mid-1830s there were no more than half a dozen houses in Georgetown, and a traveller complained that he could find nothing for breakfast but four eggs, procured at the cost of four dozen in Charlottetown.[72] It seems the town had grown by the time that Jane visited. According to the 1841 census, there were 556 people living in Georgetown and the surrounding royalty, with three churches and one school. The last must have been inadequately housed, since Jane contributed £2 to the erection of a schoolhouse. She was more generous in her support of the town's churches, giving £20 towards completion of work begun on an Episcopal church and £10 for the Catholic church, which served more than half the population. She donated another £10 for a Catholic church at St Margarets, on the north side of the Island, or elsewhere in the jurisdiction of the Reverend John Macdonald, himself a landlord; the latter £10 would benefit a community beyond the boundaries of the Westmorland estate on Lot 53.[73]

Jane also supported charity work in Charlottetown, donating £6 to the Ladies Benevolent Society, a project of Lady FitzRoy's, which was sustained by private donations and a grant from the House of Assembly. The society managed the Island's poorhouse and assisted those deserving of charity through weekly allowances and by providing funds to assist widows and orphans to leave the Island. The society also purchased supplies for poor women to make needlework items for sale. Jane's contributions were at the same level as those of George Seymour and the steamship magnate and Halifax merchant Samuel Cunard, who was at that time buying thousands of acres on the Island and assembling what was to be its largest estate.[74] Besides playing the lady bountiful, Jane tried to learn as much as she could about landlord-tenant relations and the conditions of the tenantry on the Island. She later sent the imperial government a report of what she learned, which her sister, Anne, not prone to praising Jane, said she had heard described as "one of the cleverest ever written by a woman."[75]

Jane's inquiries led to what Morpeth described as a "misunderstanding" between her and Sir Charles FitzRoy.[76] Landlord-tenant relations were a problem for the lieutenant-governor, one he had been grappling with almost from the day he arrived. The rent resistance and anti-landlord political activism that Jane's nephew Henry Dundas had described when he was on the Island in the mid-1830s had grown during FitzRoy's governorship. There were major confrontations between law officers and tenants in Kings County a few months after FitzRoy arrived in the colony, as angry tenants blocked the sheriff and his deputies from executing court orders at farms there and mutilated their horses. Later that fall, tenant mobilization led to the biggest mass rally to that date in the Island's history, as rural protestors in their thousands gathered at Sentiner's Tavern, on the outskirts of Georgetown, to denounce landlordism and the state policies that supported it. Although some brought arms to the rally, the popular mobilization on Prince Edward Island did not lead to a full-scale rebellion as it did in the Canadas later that winter. Henry Dundas and many of the other troops in the Maritimes were transferred to Lower Canada (Quebec) in the autumn of 1837 to deal with rising tensions there, while FitzRoy was left to spend his first winter on the Island grappling with a tenant revolt in a colony that lacked significant troops and would be isolated by ice until spring.[77]

When FitzRoy first arrived in Prince Edward Island, he was drawn to the justice of some of the positions informing tenant activism. Most particularly, he could see why the tenants who were making fields out of forests believed that they had property rights, grounded in their labour, in the farms that they were creating. As well, he was not convinced that tenants had surrendered those rights simply because they had taken leases with terms they could not meet. Distraint actions to seize tenants' livestock and goods or evictions that claimed their farms might be legally possible, but FitzRoy was not persuaded these measures were just. Figuring out how to handle the situation became the central problem of his administration. Ultimately, he divided Island landlords, both resident and non-resident, into two groups. In his reports to the Colonial Office, he described profit-focused landlords who were bringing state power into disrepute by using the courts and Island law officers to enforce unjust claims on a tenantry that had legitimate grievances, in contrast with landlords who granted tenants long leases with liberal terms, invested in the development of their estates, and provided support for schools and churches. Not surprisingly, given his class background, FitzRoy placed specific landlords from the landed elite, such as the Westmorlands and the Melvilles, in the latter group – not without some justification, at least with respect to the intentions of some of the non-resident landlords. What their agents actually did on the Island was another matter. Having made these distinctions, FitzRoy then attempted to drive a wedge between the good and bad landlords, in the belief that rapacious landlords were using the more benevolent as a cover in their lobbying campaigns for more vigorous state suppression of tenant activism. He also sought to persuade tenant leaders of the merits of working with liberal landlords and appealing to them for better terms, rather than attempting to end landlordism entirely by escheat actions or other means. By the late 1830s, however, landlord-tenant relations were too polarized for this to be a viable possibility. Landlords from both groups were demanding that the Island government defend their property rights, including the right to collect rents, and much of the rural population had come to believe that fundamental changes in the Island's land system were both necessary and possible. A year and a half after FitzRoy began trying to manage the land question in the colony, and a year before Jane arrived on the Island, an Escheat majority assumed control of the House of Assembly.[78]

Following the sweeping victory of the Escheat party in the general election in late 1838, tenant activists were in a position to use their control of the house to press their demands. Lord Durham's recommendations for ameliorating the causes of grievance in British North America had highlighted the need for land reform and for political changes that would ensure that the popular voices articulated in houses of assembly had more power in the conduct of colonial affairs. His report should have boded well for the Escheat majority in the House of Assembly, but by then FitzRoy, the self-described "liberal Whig," had become the movement's vehement opponent. In the ensuing legislative session, he did everything in his power to block Escheat's acquisition of greater political power and its plans for land reform. This included misleading the Colonial Office concerning the extent of popular support for Escheat. Even after Escheat's election victory, FitzRoy persisted in arguing that the Colonial Office should not respond to the party's demands as the Escheat assemblymen did not accurately represent popular opinion on the Island. Nor was he willing to implement any of the reforms recommended by Lord Durham after his mission to the British North American colonies, such as appointing members of the Escheat majority in the assembly to the Island's Executive Council. When Lady Westmorland arrived on Prince Edward Island, the political position FitzRoy had assumed in the colony had drawn him into making highly misleading claims in his dispatches to the colonial secretary. One can well imagine why he was uneasy about Lady Westmorland's independent investigation of the economic and political situation on the Island.[79]

Jane came to believe that FitzRoy wanted to prevent her from speaking to or associating with anyone who criticized his actions. This was probably true. Morpeth reported in a letter to Henry Dundas that, although Jane's "misunderstanding" with FitzRoy may have "lessened the pleasure" of her stay in Charlottetown, she had been able to gain "a great deal of valuable information, which she never would have been allowed to obtain, had she remained on the same friendly terms" with FitzRoy as when she first arrived. That Morpeth served as her guide when she visited her estates could not have brought FitzRoy any comfort, since Morpeth held the government responsible for many of the Island's problems and objected strongly to FitzRoy's interference in landlord-tenant relations. From Morpeth's perspective, these were a private contractual matter and FitzRoy's willingness to suggest otherwise simply fanned tenant protest. Morpeth would not likely have had much sympathy for the lieutenant-governor's analysis of the unrest in terms of bad and good landlords. He served as agent for the "good" Melvilles and Westmorlands, but his resort to legal action to enforce the claims of non-resident landlord Thomas Sorell had precipitated the riots in Kings County in the fall of 1837.[80]

When Jane left the Island in mid-August 1840, the *Royal Gazette* offered a flattering summary of her visit: "During her Ladyship's sojourn here she has endeared herself to a large portion of the inhabitants. The urbanity of her manner, her active benevolence, and the kind disposition manifested by her, have left an impression which will not be easily effaced."[81] The sentiments echoed those of an address offered to Lady Westmorland on her departure by residents of Charlottetown and vicinity and signed as well by others who had not previously had an opportunity to express "their esteem and respect" for her. This address mentioned her liberality in promoting the religious interests of the community and her "extensive, but unostentatious, charities to our destitute poor."[82] Another tribute noted that she had bestowed small pensions on "several deserving objects of charity."[83] Jane at first demurred over accepting a public address, protesting that she did not seek "public distinction" but, rather, that it was her "constant endeavour to avoid notoriety"; she was also wary lest the address be turned into "an indication of political or party spirit or feeling," perhaps a discreet reference to her differences with FitzRoy.[84]

From Prince Edward Island, Jane travelled to Quebec, Montreal, and Niagara Falls; she then returned to England on the *Britannia*, sailing from Halifax on 3 October 1840.[85] The *Britannia* was the first of Cunard's North American mail steamers, which could make the crossing in less than two weeks. In the opinion of Jane's sister, Anne, it was good that Jane had left Prince Edward Island when she did, for had she stayed, relations with the FitzRoys would inevitably have deteriorated and perhaps led to an open break.[86] Jane's decision to return to England when she did was prompted in part by a letter from Lord Westmorland, telling her that he was in poor health and asking her to gather the family around him.[87] The Melvilles feared that Lord Westmorland only wanted to escape from paying Jane's £3,500 annual allowance for her separate maintenance. Others warned her of the same possibility, and on her return to England, she continued to live apart from her husband.[88] She visited her sister at Melville Castle for the first time since the separation crisis, when Jane had felt that she did not have Anne's full sympathy and Anne, for her part, had felt that Jane would not take her advice on how to live in her new circumstances. Their reconciliation, though very welcome to Anne, was far from complete. She found Jane as difficult as ever and just as apt to attack her, although with less violence than formerly. In Anne's view, Jane was obsessed with making both her sister and Lord Westmorland recognize what she saw as their "atrocities" to her.[89]

Lord Westmorland died on 15 December 1841 at Brighton. He had been blind for some time prior to his death, but had continued to enjoy the privilege granted him by Queen Victoria to take his daily exercise on horseback in the Royal Pavilion. His daughter Georgiana was with him at the time of his death and made all the arrangements for the funeral, held at Apethorpe.[90] Jane was in Brighton as well, staying at the Bedford Hotel, an "elegant and extensive establishment" close to the Esplanades and the most fashionable parts of town. From her hotel she let it be known that she meant to be "a disconsolate widow ... determined never to be happy again."[91]

Lord Westmorland's will was unsatisfactory to everyone but his unmarried daughter, Georgiana. Lady Westmorland would receive £4,000 per year under her marriage settlement; in addition, Lord Westmorland gave her most of his carriage horses and the use and enjoyment for her lifetime of a quantity of plate and linen of her choosing, as well as her jewels, personal ornaments, and paraphernalia – her apparel and personal items of ornament suitable to her rank and degree. Georgiana was to have the linen, plate, and other things on Lady Westmorland's death. Westmorland's oldest son, Lord Burghersh, as the next Lord Westmorland, was entitled to a life interest in the manor house and estates at Apethorpe. He inherited nothing more under his father's will. Nor did Lord Westmorland leave anything to his daughters by Sarah Child, each of whom had received a share of the Child inheritance at the time of Sarah Fane's marriage.

Lord Westmorland provided for his son Montagu, who suffered from some disability, by naming his executors as Montagu's guardians and authorizing them to apply the profits from lands already subject to trusts for Montagu for his maintenance, support, benefit, and advantage as they and the trustees thought proper. In addition, Lord Westmorland authorized the expenditure of up to £300 per year for Montagu's maintenance and support, this sum to be a charge against the estates belonging to the Westmorland family in Somerset County. Lord Westmorland left nothing to his son Henry, although he authorized his estate to loan Henry £2,000 interest-free, to be repaid to the estate within six months of the death of Lady Westmorland. The Somerset properties, subject to the charge for Montagu's benefit, went to Georgiana, who, as residuary legatee, also received all the other property that was Lord Westmorland's to give and some that probably was not, including Lady Westmorland's paraphernalia, which, on her husband's death, would have become hers absolutely to dispose of as she liked.[92]

Lord Westmorland did not mention the Prince Edward Island estates in his will, made on 10 July 1840, but in a codicil to the will, made more than a year later, he gave all his rights to any land in the Island previously owned by Charles Saunders or Richard Huck Saunders, along with his rights to all rent and arrears owing with respect to those lands, to his son Henry, subject only to the condition that Henry ratify and confirm any leases made by Lord Westmorland within twelve months of being requested to do so by the executors or residuary legatee. This was the last of four codicils that Lord Westmorland added to his will. The others – two signed the same day as the will and the third signed the following month – provided for money gifts in various amounts to servants and former servants. It is unlikely that Lord Westmorland had forgotten about the Prince Edward Island properties when he made his will, as he had been active in defending landlords' rights from the growing political challenges of the 1830s and had joined with the landlords that FitzRoy criticized in order to do so. As well, Lady Westmorland, as her husband knew, was visiting the Island when he made his will. Lord Westmorland may have believed, correctly, that he had no rights in either Lot 29 or Lot 53 to give to anyone, as Lady Westmorland would resume her right to the Island estates as a widow. The date of the codicil suggests that he changed his mind on this matter, perhaps on learning of the disposition of Lady Melville's share of the Island property. She had died the month before Lord Westmorland made the final codicil.

Lady Westmorland, judging from her response to the Crapaud tenants' requests for a rent reduction, believed herself to be the owner of the Prince Edward Island properties, subject only to the rights that Lord Westmorland enjoyed during his lifetime. While she was in North America and making queries as to the title to the Island lots, her brother-in-law, Lord Melville, recalled that in the marriage settlement between Jane Saunders and Lord Westmorland, Lot 29 and Lot 53 had been handled differently. Jane's share of Lot 29, which was part of Charles Saunders's estate, had been settled on trustees to hold for Lord Westmorland and, on his death, for the eldest surviving son of the marriage. Lot 53, which the Saunders sisters had inherited from their father, was not part of that settlement, so that ownership of Jane's share would revert to her if her husband predeceased her.[93]

After her husband's death, Lady Westmorland continued to assert that both Lot 29 and Lot 53 belonged to her and to try to sort out the source of what she called the "contrived confusion" that led others to believe that this was not the case. She concluded that the estates in the Island were "neither mentioned nor thought of" in the marriage settlements for her and her sister but nonetheless came to be treated as if they had been included in the reference to all the settled estates of Sir Charles Saunders, even though at the time everyone thought only of the estates in Norfolk and Suffolk and not "this wilderness Island, as it was in 1800." Even if what Jane called this "ex post facto" interpretation prevailed, it could not bring Lot 53 into the settlement, because that lot had belonged to her father, not to Charles Saunders. Initially, when Robert Dundas and Lord Westmorland appointed land agents to manage the Island properties, they believed that their wives' title to both lots came from Charles Saunders. Although Dundas realized subsequently that Lot 53 had belonged to Richard Huck Saunders, he was unwilling to substantiate Jane's claims about who should inherit the two lots. In any event, Lord Westmorland had granted 999-year leases and, in Lady Westmorland's view, had thereby alienated the property from her and her heirs.[94]

Henry Fane adopted a more accurate view of the legal effect of the 999-year leases issued by his father: the leases could not have alienated the land because they were in fact invalid. Westmorland had exceeded his legal authority when he unilaterally took unto himself the right of issuing leases on the lot. Henry's solution to this problem was to take unto himself the power of issuing replacement leases containing the same terms.[95] Jane seems to have acquiesced in his acting as proprietor of half of Lot 29. She may have thought the management of the estate would keep him usefully occupied. She also knew that she could not hope for any voluntary recognition of her rights; Henry was already resentful that she had not provided him with a decent allowance.[96] Nonetheless, Jane asserted her rights as owner of one-third of Lot 53 and appointed her own agents to manage it. Her first choice was Charles Worrell, an Island lawyer and politician. At the time of his appointment as Lady Westmorland's land agent, Worrell owned more than 100,000 acres around St Peters Bay in Kings County.[97] After he moved to England, she gave the agency for Lot 53 to Morpeth, Lord Melville's agent, who had escorted her around the Island on her visit in 1839 and 1840.[98]

In the 1840s and 1850s Jane continued to move from place to place, complaining of the undutiful conduct of her children and of the disappointments and vexations they caused her. Her niece Jane, while feeling sorry for her aunt, recognized that there was fault on both sides. In Jane's view, in a family that did things sensibly, Lady Westmorland and Georgiana would live together, but that was "impossible considering the nature of the two individuals. It is, however, a deplorable state of things to exist in a family."[99] Necessity forces compromise though, and by 1856 Lady Westmorland was living with Georgiana at Brympton House, a manor house on the estate in Somerset that Georgiana had inherited from Lord Westmorland. The Dundas children obtained news of their aunt second-hand; in their view, Georgiana deliberately isolated her mother from everyone else, so as to manipulate her into doing as Georgiana wanted.[100]

Jane, Lady Westmorland, died at Brympton House on 26 March 1857, after a fall five weeks earlier. She was buried at Apethorpe. Her nephew Robert Dundas was invited to attend the funeral, but relations between Georgiana and the Dundas family remained difficult. Jane Dundas, reflecting on the differences between her own family life and that of the Westmorlands, provided an apt epitaph for Lady Westmorland: "What a strange tragedy my poor Aunt's history has been!"[101] Jane's will, as the family had feared, favoured Georgiana. Made in September 1856, it was very short, containing only two main clauses. The first released her son Henry from all claims she might have against him for any rents from the Prince Edward Island estates, which Henry had managed as his own after Lord Westmorland's death. The second gave Georgiana all of her mother's property, both real and personal, except for some furniture and household goods that Jane gave to Henry.[102] Her choice of heir set the stage for Georgiana to assume a role as one of the most articulate, strong-willed Prince Edward Island landlords of the second half of the nineteenth century.

4

Georgiana Fane:
Defending Position and Property

Lady Cecily Jane Georgiana Fane, the first child of the tenth Earl of Westmorland and his second wife, Jane Saunders, inherited her mother's property in Prince Edward Island and her mother's determination to make the most of being an Island landlord. After wresting control of the property from her cousin Henry Dundas, she engaged in a lifelong battle against those who wanted to end the proprietorial system of landholding on the Island. Judging from contemporary comments on Lady Georgiana, she was temperamentally suited to this project – earnest, combative, and persistent, with a strong sense of what was due to the ruling class, a facility for political and economic analysis, and considerable leisure for letter-writing. As had her mother, Georgiana visited her Island estate and assisted in providing for schools, churches, improved transportation, a public hall, and prizes to promote agriculture. For this philanthropy, she earned a reputation as "one of the most indulgent and considerate of Island proprietors," letting her land on "very moderate terms ... by no means severe in collecting her rents," and acting toward her tenants "in a noble spirit of justice, of true benevolence and sterling sympathy."[1] But the men of the Colonial Office, to whom she wrote frequently on Island matters, came to regard her as a crank whom they had to placate but not take seriously.

Georgiana was nine when her mother stabbed herself and was sent to an asylum. While Jane was in the asylum, one of Georgiana's younger brothers died. When Lady Westmorland left the asylum and established her own residence, Georgiana and her two surviving brothers remained with their father. Sometimes she accompanied Lord Westmorland on his official appearances at state functions, including the funeral of King George III in 1820, when she was nineteen.[2] She moved back and forth between London and Apethorpe, the Westmorland manor home in Northampton, in accordance with the dictates of the London season. The landed elite usually returned from their country estates for the opening of Parliament, adjourned to Brighton during the Easter recess, and returned to London for the opening of the opera after Easter. The first ball at Almack's Assembly Rooms marked the beginning of the main London season. Almack's, named for its founder, William Almack, offered a Wednesday night ball with supper for those who had been invited to pay the subscription fee. Lady Jersey, Georgiana's half-sister, was on the committee that decided whom to invite; Georgiana was a subscriber. Summer sent people back to the country, and Christmas, too, was usually a quiet time in fashionable London, as people celebrated the season with hunting parties and dances at their country estates.[3] Until Lord Westmorland died, Georgiana played the role of hostess at the family gatherings and parties held every year at Apethorpe to celebrate Christmas and her father's birthday, which was New Year's Day. She went on hunting and boating outings and was among those invited to the "drawing-rooms" of royalty and the galas at the homes of the elite.[4]

Yet as an unmarried female in a world in which men ruled, with "Lady" as a courtesy title only, Georgiana never had the status or the power of her half-sisters, whose husbands had titles, nor of her half-brother, John Fane, who, on her father's death, became the eleventh Earl of Westmorland and possessor of Apethorpe. Georgiana demonstrated neither goodwill nor grace in the necessary arrangements following her father's death. From the perspective of her first cousins, Anne Dundas's daughters, the Westmorland children treated other family members inappropriately. The Dundas sisters regarded Georgiana as a difficult person and despaired of her conduct towards her mother and her brothers, Henry and Montagu, both of whom were partially incapacitated by physical or mental illnesses. When Henry suffered some kind of collapse in 1836 while he was serving with the military in North America, Jane Dundas lamented that Georgiana was too foolish and frivolous to be of any use.[5] Two decades later, at the time of Lady Westmorland's death, Jane contrasted the "union and affection in our family" with "the horrors" in the Westmorland family, saying that it made her unhappy to be "connected with so much wickedness and to feel powerless to make any effect on such minds ... In the midst of all this suffering and misery ... to think that money, money, money is the *only* thing that these creatures *can* think of! It really disgusts one."[6]

From this distance, it is impossible to determine which came first – the difficulties of Lady Georgiana's life or the difficulties of her personality. An intellectually curious person interested in new ideas and new places, she likely felt stifled by the conventions of London society and anxious about whether she had the material resources to sustain her position. She may have been treated with more tolerance had she been a male or even a married woman. Traits that in male members of the elite might have been regarded as appropriate for their role were not necessarily commendable in single women. Some contemporaries linked Georgiana's oddness to her spinsterhood, although remaining single, at least when she was younger, seems to have been a matter of choice, not necessity. One of her suitors was Lord Palmerston, who was notorious both for his many affairs and for his devotion to Lady Cowper, who enjoyed his attentions for many years before they married in 1839, on the death of her husband. It had not always been entirely clear, however, that Palmerston would wait patiently for Lady Cowper. Gossips noted that he spent a great deal of time with Georgiana at dinner parties, at the opera, at dances at Vauxhall, and presumably at Almack's too. By 1824 there was talk that they might marry. Lady Cowper complained that Georgiana hunted Palmerston "up & down the rooms & sits like Patience on a monument ... but I think she will not succeed. If she was handsomer she would have a better chance."[7] According to Harriet Arbuthnot, a prodigious diarist, intimate of the Duke of Wellington, and Lord Westmorland's first cousin, Palmerston proposed to Georgiana twice, but she made herself miserable by refusing him, even though "she liked him very much." Mrs Arbuthnot blamed the lost match, which she favoured, on the interference of Georgiana's half-sister Lady Jersey, who boasted that Palmerston was in love with her.[8] One of Palmerston's biographers concluded that he was probably "well rid" of Georgiana, quoting Sir Robert Peel's description of her as "the most impertinent and odious woman in England."[9] Georgiana was ill with what Mrs Arbuthnot called a "nervous disorder" for more than a year after refusing one of Palmerston's proposals. The illness interfered with the traditional festivities at Apethorpe at year's end both in 1826 and in 1827.[10]

Georgiana's name was also linked with that of the Duke of Wellington. Wellington was certainly a frequent visitor at Apethorpe during Lord Westmorland's lifetime, often in the company of Mrs Arbuthnot. In 1825 he injured Robert Dundas, Georgiana's first cousin, in a hunting accident at Christmas at Apethorpe.[11] Georgiana may have suffered here too from competition with Lady Jersey. In 1823 Lady Cowper had gossiped that Lady Jersey was eager to catch Wellington and wore the diamond ring he had given her constantly on her finger or her neck. Elizabeth Longford, one of Wellington's biographers, described Lady Georgiana Fane as the duke's "most heartless pursuer," leading him to ask others to exclude her from gatherings at which he would be present. When the duke broke with Georgiana in 1851, she consulted her lawyer, who advised her that Wellington's letters to her provided grounds for a suit for breach of promise of marriage. Wellington's death the following year ended the matter.[12] A family connection tells a more flattering but less plausible story, suggesting that Georgiana lost her heart to Wellington but that her father forbade the match because Wellington was an insignificant young soldier. Wellington, who was ten years younger than Lord Westmorland, had married, however, and received his title while Georgiana was still the little girl whimsically portrayed as a peasant child with a laundry tub in a portrait completed by Sir Thomas Lawrence around 1806 (see illus. 4.1).[13] Yet there may be some truth beyond the precise details. The circumstances of her parents' separation and the role that Georgiana assumed as caregiver for her father may have interfered with her opportunities to make a good match.

A contemporary commenting on the Wellington–Georgiana Fane episode described the duke as "brutal" and Georgiana as a "half cracked … tiresome, troublesome, crazy old maid."[14] She was certainly impetuous and litigious, and some of her embarrassments became public knowledge. A couple of years after the Wellington episode, the *Times* reported that Georgiana, in what she described as "a moment of excitement," had laid charges of theft against a Mr Dodimeade and had him taken into custody. The charges were completely unwarranted, and he sued. Georgiana offered to retract the charge and pay compensation of £200. Lord Campbell, hearing the case in the Court of Queen's Bench, so ordered, adding that from what he knew of Lady Georgiana Fane, he believed that she would not willingly do what was wrong.[15]

4.1   Portrait of Georgiana Fane as a peasant girl,
c. 1806. Oil on canvas by Sir Thomas Lawrence.
Tate Gallery, London, N00922

As a single woman, Georgiana had the legal capacity to manage
her own property, and she did so actively. As her father's residuary
legatee, she was entitled to all his personal property, and she
claimed her right to the family plate, linen, pictures, and papers.
When her half-brother, Lord Burghersh, took possession of Apethorpe
as the eleventh Earl of Westmorland, he and his wife dined from
borrowed dishes and silverware, while Georgiana continued to
enjoy weekly deliveries at her London house of vegetables, fruit,

and game from Apethorpe; she even obstructed her mother in her wish to give the earl a pair of coach horses left to her by Lord Westmorland.[16] Lord Melville, Georgiana's uncle, thought that the terms of Lord Westmorland's will were an "atrocious injustice" to his son.[17] He told Georgiana that the will damaged Westmorland's reputation and that when her father made his will, he was not capable of comprehending the state of his affairs or what was required to effect "a just distribution of his property, including a competent provision for his son." In Melville's view, Georgiana could set things right by treating her half-brother with justice, kindness, and liberality, but instead she was acting with unreasonable "rigidity and tenaciousness." In the style of homily his wife had favoured, Melville reminded Georgiana: "Civilized society, especially a Christian society, can only exist by mutual concession and forbearance ... As a general rule in practice, the persons who insist most stoutly on their legal rights are those who in the long run suffer the most by their adherence to such a wayward and unamiable principle."[18]

Lord Melville's sympathy for the eleventh earl was grounded in part in his own experience of inheriting his father's significant debts, as well as obligations to provide for his father's widow and for the next generation. But his appeals to Georgiana's sense of family obligation failed to persuade her that she was wrong. Indeed, they added to her sense that she was being victimized by social and legal conventions that devalued the single female. From her perspective, she had looked after her father and was now expected to do the same for her mother, as well as her ailing brothers, since her mother refused to do anything for them. And yet she had no one to look after her.[19] Georgiana's first cousin Jane shared her father's impatience with Georgiana and sympathy with the eleventh earl, exclaiming that she herself could not "possibly eat my dinner in peace with spoons and forks that ought to be [my brother's], unless he gave them to me."[20]

Lady Georgiana's dispute with her half-brother dragged on for almost three years. At issue was not just the plate and pictures, but the eleventh earl's claim for compensation for the value of timber that their father had harvested from the estate at Apethorpe beyond his entitlement as a life tenant. Georgiana said that he had cut only what was his, but she somewhat weakened her position by adding that, given Lord Westmorland's small income, had he not sold the timber, he would have been reduced to "a mutton chop a day and one horse brougham."[21] As well, Georgiana and her half-brother disputed the ownership of land in Northampton, held in a form of title called copyhold, that she argued was part of the estate left to her. It may have been both parties' lack of funds for lawyers' fees, rather than their aversion to making the dispute even more public, that kept them from litigation. Ultimately, Georgiana agreed to sell some of the land she had inherited to her half-brother, and the two consented to divide the disputed copyholds. Other claims of each against the other, totally about £10,500, cancelled one another out. Among other things, the new Lord Westmorland purchased the family plate and other furnishings at Apethorpe for just under £2,000, and Georgiana was given credit for about £2,800 of the rent owing from the Apethorpe tenants when her father died.[22]

Fortunately for Georgiana, Apethorpe was not the only grand manor in the Westmorland family. She inherited the other one, Brympton d'Evercy, in Somerset, on an estate of about 1,200 acres; annual rent from the farms totalled about £2,600 in 1869.[23] The property had first come into the Fane family in 1731, when it was purchased by Francis Fane (see illus. 4.2). Built as the manor home of the D'Evercys after the Norman Conquest, it had been repaired, rebuilt, modified, and extended many times since. Georgiana added a stone balustrade along the terrace, from which one could view the formal gardens, a pond, and the adjacent church, with effigies and tombs of many of the earlier owners (see illus. 4.3 and 4.4).[24] A descendant of the nephew who inherited the house from Georgiana credited her with planting thousands of oaks on the estate and with furnishing the house with everything "of beauty and good taste that the family now owns."[25] The manor house remained in the Fane family until 1992; the current owners rent it out for movie sets, weddings, and other grand events.[26]

As well as her Somerset estate and the land Georgiana retained in Northamptonshire, she leased a three-storey house in London at 5 Upper Brook Street (see illus. 4.5). In 1957 the US government acquired a large site across from Georgiana's house and built a new, fortress-like embassy that is quite out of character with the late eighteenth-century Georgian houses that still line the other side of the street, Georgiana's among them. Two other Prince Edward Island lady landlords, who were friends of Georgiana's mother, sometimes lived on Brook Street when they were in London. Besides the landed elite, the occupants included professional men and, toward the end of Georgiana's life, at least one foreign legation. To

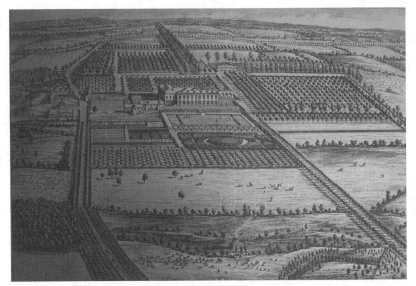

4.2   Plan of Brympton d'Evercy, Somerset, the estate that Georgiana
Fane inherited. Engraving by Johannes Kip, from *Britannia Illustrata*,
vol. 1 (London, 1740)

4.3   Brympton House, Georgiana Fane's country residence, west wing,
and Gothic church. From Tipping, *English Homes*, Periods 1 and 11, 33

4.4 Brympton House, Georgiana Fane's country residence, south front, c. 1680. From Tipping, *English Homes*, Periods I and II, 44

4.5 5 Upper Brook Street, Georgiana Fane's London residence. Photo by authors.

4.6   Georgiana Fane, c. 1860. BL, Babbage
Correspondence, Add. 37/198/202

manage Upper Brook Street, Georgiana probably employed about
six live-in servants, not counting the coachmen and grooms.[27]

Charles Babbage, mathematician and inventor, was a frequent
guest at Lady Georgiana's dinner parties. A widower since 1827,
living on an inheritance from his father, Babbage spent much of his
time and money, as well as funds granted him by the government,
on developing an automatic calculating machine, which, although
never completed, anticipated the modern computer. Georgiana Fane
invited Babbage to Brympton, to rest from work on his machine,
and scolded him excessively when he did not visit. She also provided
him with her photograph (see illus. 4.6). Babbage's biographer

called him "the irascible genius"; he and Georgiana may have
shared personality traits as well as interests.[28] They corresponded
on various subjects, including the English law respecting the pro-
hibited degrees of affinity and consanguinity and the evils of the
modern world. Georgiana noted in one of her letters that the inven-
tion of the railroad had rendered war more horrible by rapidly
bringing together multitudes of men who could then pelt each other
with "murderous missiles." Joseph Howe, journalist and Reform
leader from Nova Scotia, was a guest at one of the dinners to which
Lady Georgiana invited Babbage. She had likely met Howe when
she visited her Island estate in 1860, while Howe was there as the
proprietors' representative on a commission to inquire into the land
question. Georgiana believed that Howe's opposition to Nova
Scotia's entry into the Canadian Confederation of 1867 represented
the sentiments of the majority in Nova Scotia, and she noted that
Prince Edward Island had so far "resisted being tricked" into joining
the union.[29]

Georgiana's household included her mother in the last year of
Lady Westmorland's life, and they spent most of their time at
Brympton. Georgiana's Dundas cousins, Anne and Jane, were sure
that she deliberately kept Lady Westmorland away from other relatives and friends, so that her mother's will would be as Georgiana
wanted it; her cousins believed Georgiana had treated her father
in the same way. Perhaps she had. When Lady Westmorland died
in March 1857, her will left almost everything to Georgiana.[30]
Georgiana's brother Henry survived his mother by only a month,
dying at Georgiana's London house on 7 May 1857; Montagu died
there on 26 June 1857.[31] Henry Fane left all of his property to his
first cousin Henry Dundas, who, with the death of his father in
1851, had become the third Viscount Melville and a proprietor on
Prince Edward Island. Georgiana pursued two claims against her
cousin, one for ownership of her mother's share of Lot 29 and the
other for payment from Henry Fane's estate of £500, which she
said that she had lent her brother in 1854. The available records
do not show what happened with the latter claim. Her cousin
Robert Dundas, who had been brought into the matter while Henry
Fane was still alive, described Georgiana then as "fractious and
unpracticable" and said that the matter would be impossible to
arbitrate.[32] Georgiana succeeded with the claim for the Island property, and Lord Melville acknowledged her title to the western half

of Lot 29. By July 1857 she had secured the services of William
Henry Pope as her land agent on the Island. That fall he notified
the tenants of Lot 29 that Lady Georgiana Fane was their new landlord, "alone entitled" to receipt of their rents, and that they needed
to apply to him for new leases to replace any issued previously by
Lord Westmorland or Henry Fane.[33]

Two years later the *Islander*, a paper edited by Georgiana's land
agent, printed an article, at the request of "friends" of the current
proprietor, defending her actions on Lot 29 as just and generous.
The article explained that any 999-year leases granted by Lord
Westmorland were invalid, as his interest in the property, through
his marriage to its owner, Lady Westmorland, was that of a life
tenant only. Tenants holding land under these 999-year leases were
thus merely tenants at will, subject to eviction at any time. When
Henry Fane took possession of the properties and granted further
leases, he did so without the consent of Lady Westmorland; so
leases that he had granted were also invalid. Georgiana Fane, the
daughter and heir of Lady Westmorland, had offered, at her own
expense, to issue valid leases to all tenants on the same terms as in
the invalid leases granted by her father and brother, with credit to
the tenants for any rent paid. Having waited two years for tenants
to take advantage of an offer made "not so much for the advantage of the proprietor, as for [the tenants'] own security," the proprietor's agent had commenced several ejectment proceedings.
Subsequently, all but one tenant accepted the new leases offered;
whereupon the proceedings were discontinued, without cost to the
tenants. The article offered this concluding summary: "On the whole,
the tenantry of Crapaud have been treated with every consideration
and indulgence they could expect."[34] The tenants whose security of
land tenure had been jeopardized by the complex relations of the
Saunders, Fane, and Dundas families might have described the
situation differently.

Lady Georgiana Fane became a Prince Edward Island landlord
at the beginning of a period of significant economic and political
change for Island residents. The population had grown steadily
across the nineteenth century, and by the mid-1850s, when Georgiana
inherited her lands, it was more than 70,000.[35] Islanders had hoped
that, with the grant of responsible government in 1851, they would
be in a better position to deal with the land question that had been
at the core of colonial political concerns for more than half a

century. The legislature adopted a two-pronged approach in responding to popular pressure for land reform in the 1850s, enacting legislation that facilitated government purchase of landlords' estates for resale to tenants and squatters and legislation to encourage such sales by restricting landlords' property rights and ensuring that they bore a significant share of the costs of public infrastructure development in the colony. Once Georgiana assumed her position as an Island proprietor, she paid close attention to Island events and lobbied the Colonial Office to protect proprietors' rights.

Georgiana made her first appeal to the Colonial Office in 1858, a year after she had inherited her estate, to protest against legislation to assert the Crown's right to the Island's fishery reserves. About two-thirds of the original Crown grants of township lots provided for a reservation of the first 500 feet above the high-water mark along the coast for the support of a fishery. In many parts of the Island, these reserves were the most accessible and, initially, the most valuable lands, and settlement in the colony proceeded as if there were no restrictions on their use. Settlers cut timber, planted crops, and erected fences and buildings close to the shore, within the 500-foot fishery reserves, and proprietors collected rents based on an acreage that included fishery reserve land. Since the 1830s, some tenant leaders had been attempting to reduce the burdens of the tenantry by arguing that they should not have to pay rent to the landlords for fishery reserve land and that any such rent already paid should be applied to offset future obligations. From the perspective of many proprietors, this initiative was potentially fatal to their interests as it might eliminate their ability to collect rents for years to come. The 1858 fishery reserves bill confirmed the right of the colonial Crown to offer leases for land within the fishery reserves and, more importantly, denied the proprietors' right to collect rent on fishery reserve land regardless what their tenants had agreed to in their leases. In order to increase the likelihood that the Colonial Office would approve the bill, the legislature limited its application to thirty-one townships in which the fishery reserve clause in the original Crown grant provided strong support for the claim that such land remained in the hands of the Crown.[36]

Georgiana added her voice to the proprietors' protests even though the bill did not apply to either of her lots. The original Crown grant of Lot 29 did not contain a fishery reserve clause, while the grant of Lot 53 included a clause in language that some legal opinion interpreted as a grant of the land to the proprietor, subject to the Crown retaining a right in the nature of an easement for the benefit of the public. The proprietors, anticipating further anti-landlord legislation, argued that any interference between landlord and tenant was "unconstitutional, contrary to the practice of Parliament, and repugnant to every principle of law, justice, and equity, and if allowed, would form a dangerous precedent in future legislation," especially as proprietors were "virtually unrepresented" in the Island legislature, where "persons having little real estate" were "openly endeavouring to injure the proprietary interests, and to harass the owners of Township lands by passing Bills ... for the avowed purpose of compelling them to dispose of their lands to the local Government at prices far below their real value." Ultimately, the fishery reserves legislation was not confirmed by the imperial government.[37]

Georgiana saw for herself what was happening with her property when she included Prince Edward Island in a North American tour in 1860. She arrived in Halifax on the steamer from Liverpool in August, travelling from there by steamer to Canada East (Quebec) and on to Canada West (Ontario), then east again to New Brunswick and across the Northumberland Strait to Prince Edward Island. She arrived on the Island at the end of September, accompanied by a companion named Mrs Clifford and two servants.[38] Lady Georgiana and Mrs Clifford were guests of Lieutenant-Governor George Dundas and Mrs Dundas at Government House, but they missed the gala dinners given to honour the Prince of Wales, who had visited the Island a month earlier (see illus. 4.7 and 4.8).[39] It is likely that while she was on the Island, Georgiana visited with Robert Bruce Stewart, whose estate, one of the largest on the Island, comprised nearly 70,000 acres spread across seven townships. In subsequent appeals to the Colonial Office, she often presented Stewart's case as well as her own and invoked his story to contradict the idea that the proprietors were all absentees who contributed nothing to the Island's development.

Before leaving the Island, Georgiana executed a new power of attorney for her agent, authorizing him to grant leases not exceeding a term of 100 years. This was a shift from the long-lease policies that land agents acting for her family had followed in the early years of the development of the estate. Georgiana attended to charity as well as business on the Island. She sold a hundred acres on

4.7 Georgiana Fane, far left, with other guests of Lieutenant-Governor Dundas at Government House, Charlottetown, 1860. PARO, Acc. 3466/HF 74.27.3.24

Lot 29 for a nominal consideration to the Incorporated Society for the Propagation of the Gospel in Foreign Parts and authorized her agent to transfer up to three acres to trustees or religious corporations for use for religious or educational purposes. She also authorized the transfer of up to three acres of land at Crapaud to trustees, to be held by them for the erection and maintenance of a public hall, to be used for "the promotion of the moral, intellectual and social improvement" of the inhabitants.[40] Over the next few years, Georgiana assisted with the construction of the hall, named Westmorland Hall, permitting tenants to pay their rent with contributions of labour or materials. She met two of the community's pressing practical needs in the same way by hiring tenants to supply

4.8 Georgiana Fane with other guests of Lieutenant-Governor
Dundas on the grounds of Government House, Charlottetown,
1860. PARO, Acc. 3466/HF 74.27.3.25

the construction materials and labour to build a wharf and also a
bridge over an arm of the sea at Crapaud and applying their contributions to reduce the rent they owed. When the Crapaud community organized a fall fair and industrial exhibition at the new
Westmorland Hall, Georgiana funded prizes for the best farm and
domestic produce, including animals, grains, cheeses and butter,
homespun, shawls, knitted goods, linen sacks, rugs, farm carts,
and tools.[41]

From Prince Edward Island, Georgiana travelled to New York,
Washington, and Albany, leaving for England on 20 January 1861.[42]
In New York, where she spent two months, she attended a great
many parties and balls but proved a disappointment to those

4.9 Water Street, Charlottetown, c. 1860. PARO,
Acc. 3466/HF 74.27.3.223

looking for an exemplar of fashionable British society. As one New
York paper noted, she "cares only for sensible men, and talks politics and political economy most of the time ... Perhaps we learn
what we have to leave off doing, by seeing her, rather than what
we are to do, as reigning belles."[43] Georgiana had visited Prince
Edward Island when the countryside looked its best, with fields
ready for harvesting and the harsh weather of winter still a month
or two away. The cleared land and farm buildings may, however,
have given her a false picture of prosperity. Certainly, a different
picture emerged from some of the testimony of rural residents
speaking before a land commission that had begun public hearings
shortly before Georgiana arrived. The Land Commission of 1860
was presented to the public as an initiative of the Conservative
government that defeated the Reformers in the election of 1859,
but the plan for it had emerged in discussions at the Colonial Office
in the mid-1850s, as proprietors sought to prevent the Island's
Reform government from using its powers in ways that were det-
rimental to proprietary interests. Two bills were particularly wor-
risome. One was an attempt to tax landlords' rent rolls, and the

other was a tenant compensation bill that would have given evicted tenants the right to compensation for any increase in the value of their leasehold during the term of their tenancy.[44]

Faced with colonial legislation that would reduce the value of their holdings, the proprietors expected the imperial government to protect them as it had in the years before the grant of responsible government in 1851. A small cluster of leading non-resident proprietors, all of them men, discussed the matter with the men of the Colonial Office and appear to have come to an understanding that, in exchange for denial of approval of the rent roll tax and tenants' compensation bills, the proprietors would agree to a reasonable exit strategy and thus relieve the Colonial Office of the need to interfere with Island legislation in the future. Key players in these discussions were Samuel Cunard, Laurence Sulivan, and Sir George Seymour, who had recently assumed the position of commander of British naval forces in North America. Collectively, their estates comprised around 300,000 acres.[45] Seymour recommended that the government establish a commission that would "terminate the Questions on the Tenure of Land and Fishery Reserves." From the proprietors' perspective, this meant safeguarding their titles against challenges based on unfulfilled settlement and quit rent obligations and eliminating the Island government's claim to the fishery reserves. Seymour also wanted the proposed commission to value the proprietors' interests in their land. In his view, an independent valuation would lead to the sale of proprietors' estates, since he believed that "there is no indisposition on the part of the latter to dispose of their lands on moderate and reasonable terms if the government desired to obtain control over the lands by purchase ... What the Proprietors do object to is that Legislative Measures should be passed or sanctioned which would have the effect of deteriorating if not destroying their interests."[46] The Land Commission of 1860 had its origins, then, in a gentlemen's agreement hammered out in the corridors of power in London.

With the imperial government's encouragement, the Island government requested a commission on the land question, and not surprisingly, the imperial government acceded to the request, appointing three commissioners from the adjacent Maritime colonies to inquire into "differences prevailing in Prince Edward Island relative to the rights of landowners and tenants, with a view to a settlement of the same on fair and equitable principles." John

Hamilton Gray, from New Brunswick, chaired the commission. Joseph Howe, the nominee of the Island government, was the Reform party leader in Nova Scotia. John William Ritchie, the proprietors' choice, was a Halifax lawyer. The commissioners arrived on the Island in August 1860 and held public hearings in Charlottetown, St Eleanor's, and Georgetown, beginning in early September and concluding in early October.[47]

Georgiana, it seems, did not attend the Land Commission hearings; however, she wrote to the lieutenant-governor to protest against legislation passed by the Island assembly that she feared would make commission rulings binding on her.[48] A decade later she maintained that the commissioners, "on breaking up their court, declared that they had not heard one case of real harshness" in all their weeks of hearings.[49] The Island papers carried full reports of the public meetings held across the Island to determine what position to present to the commissioners, as well as verbatim summaries of the commission proceedings. From these, Georgiana could have learned that proprietors were regarded with considerable hostility by a large proportion of the rural population. At one meeting a speaker denounced the proprietary system as "selfish, soul-harrowing, energy-repressing, and poverty-entailing."[50] She may also have heard of the recent escape from jail of Patrick Hughes, incarcerated for his role the previous November in preventing a sheriff from enforcing payment of rent on Lot 61, in Kings County, owned by Laurence Sulivan. The government offered a £50 reward for Hughes's recapture.[51]

Back again in England, Georgiana reiterated her objections to the Land Commission in a letter to the Colonial Office. After one of the commissioners released what was described as a summary of the commission's report, she complained that government interference between landlords and tenants was destroying "the last chance that there is of coming to a friendly arrangement." In the year since her visit to the Island, her agent had been unable to do anything on either of her estates "owing to the difficulty occasioned by the Land Commission ... I trust your Grace will think that the objections I make to an Award that gives direct encouragement to & holds out inducements to dishonesty – that not only interferes with the rights of a Proprietor but takes from him the right to the possession of his Property & compels him to part with it – are reasonable." An official in the Colonial Office noted that Lady Georgiana Fane had sent "a well-written letter" dealing with one side of the question. Along with other proprietors who were beginning to protest the work of the commissioners, she received a note assuring her that the report was still being considered by the Colonial Office and that her representations would receive every attention.[52]

As rumour circulated on the Island about what was in the report, Georgiana wrote again to the Colonial Office, with apologies for doing so, to provide evidence to support the claims in her earlier letter. Having asked her agent to explain why he could not collect rents on an estate where, when she visited the Island, there had been "no reason to expect any difficulty," he had responded that "the Commission will render the recovery of arrears a very difficult matter ... if the Commission business were disposed of, there would be no difficulty – but so long as it remains uncertain the Tenant will hold back in the hope of gaining by it." In Georgiana's view, the commission recommendations were "based on injustice and spoliation – injustice to the Tenants – as it gives to the dishonest man an advantage over the honest & industrious one who had paid his rent – & spoliation of the landlord as it is an arbitrary seizure of his property."[53]

The final report of the Land Commission, which was not officially released until February 1862, confirmed Georgiana's fears and angered proprietors such as George Seymour, who had hoped for a valuation of his Island property and an offer of purchase based on it. The commissioners recommended that the Island government purchase the proprietorial estates, but they declined to assess their value. Instead, the report urged the imperial government to provide a loan guarantee of £100,000 sterling so that Island authorities might continue to purchase estates, as they had begun doing in the 1850s. Knowing that imperial authorities were unlikely to approve the loan guarantee, the commissioners further recommended that tenants be given the right to purchase their farms from their land- lords, with arbitrators to set the price if the two parties could not agree. They also recommended that landlords forgive all arrears prior to 1858. Georgiana objected vigorously to these recommen- dations, the first because it interfered with landlords' property rights by introducing compulsion in land sales and the second because it rewarded tenants who had failed to pay their rents.[54]

The imperial government had begun withdrawing its support from the Land Commission even before release of the final report. The Conservative government on the Island, however, working with leading proprietors, including members of the Island government and proprietors involved in the gentlemen's agreement that preceded the commission, salvaged parts of the report. The legislature obtained imperial approval for legislation enacted in 1864, applicable only to twelve proprietors who had agreed to be bound by its terms.[55] The legislation, known as the 15 Years' Purchase Act, gave tenants with leases of forty years or more the right, for the next ten years, to buy the freeholds of their farms at a price equal to fifteen years' worth of rent plus any arrears accrued since 1 May 1858, at the highest rate specified in the tenants' lease. The consenting proprietors agreed to give up all claims to arrears prior to 1 May 1858, regardless whether the tenants exercised their right to purchase. In exchange for these concessions, the legislation released the consenting proprietors from any liability for outstanding quit rents specified in the original grants and from any government claims to fishery reserve land. Critics called the legislation "The Proprietors' Bill," not only because the consenting proprietors had helped to draft it but because it gave the proprietors much more than it gave the tenants. The concession on quit rents eliminated a possible weakness in proprietors' titles, and the fishery reserve provisions gave them clear title to valuable shorefront lands. The consenting proprietors, all men, together owned about one-quarter of the Island.[56]

Georgiana did not agree to be bound by the 15 Years' Purchase Act. In her view, the legislation was further interference with landlord-tenant relations that would affect all proprietors, not just those who had helped to negotiate its terms. In writing to protest against the act, she noted the inconsistencies in the argument made in its defence. How, she asked, would giving some tenants the right to buy the freeholds of their farms at less than their value make tenants elsewhere more contented? If the act provided for voluntary sales only, why was it needed? And would the next step be legislation compelling proprietors to sell their land? "The fact is," she declared, "that it is intended by those who have passed this Act to include us all. The organ of the Island government tells the people so. It tells them also that when the Tenants who are best off have bought the lands at the reduced price – & the Landlords have only the poorer Tenants to deal with, they will dislike the trouble of exacting Rent & the expense of paying Agency & will let the Land go for little or nothing."[57] In a subsequent letter, she was able to bolster her arguments by citing a letter in the *Islander* newspaper that gleefully predicted that the land question would be resolved in the way that she had said – by landlords giving up their land when collecting rent became more expensive than it was worth.

Georgiana quite correctly saw the 15 Years' Purchase Act as the beginning of the end for landlordism on the Island, but not just, as she thought, because it would necessarily lead to legislation compelling non-consenting landlords to sell on the same terms. The legislation also permitted the policy-makers in the Colonial Office to divide the proprietors into two groups – the reasonable ones who had consented to the legislation and the others, who, because of their opposition to the legislation, were categorized as "diehard" landlords. Georgiana herself was described, dismissively, as a representative of "the no surrender party in P.E.I., who would like the Imperial Gov't to carry on war with the Tenants ... with the landlords taking the winnings & the Imperial Treasury bearing the loss."[58] The Colonial Office papers, with the notes that officials there made on incoming correspondence, show that over the next decade, as Georgiana and other proprietors responded to further challenges from the Island legislature, official policy was to answer their letters courteously but to pay little attention to their views in making policy.

As Island politicians continued to press for an end to the proprietorial system, Georgiana's protests became more frequent and her rhetoric more extreme, making it ever easier for the Colonial Office to disregard her. A official noted on her final protest against the 15 Years' Purchase Act that she "keeps up a gallant fight to the last, but she does not advance, in this letter, any sufficient reason for diverting this office from the course determined upon"; another official responded to the same note with the suggestion that it be answered "with as much brevity as is compatible with civility."[59] Georgiana's letters reveal her increasing frustration with this kind of treatment. Island residents, however, perceived her as having power to block some of their legislative initiatives. In one of her letters to the Colonial Office concerning the 15 Years' Purchase Act, Georgiana had observed that a proprietor listed in the schedule of consenting proprietors had not actually consented. The delay occasioned while the Colonial Office confirmed that her statement was correct and then sought to obtain the proprietor's consent was the subject of misogynous comment in the Island legislature, with members complaining that the legislature "is not of much account at Downing Street" if a "little pink-edged note" from a "lady" was almost enough to scuttle the Island's legislation.[60]

Passage of the 15 Years' Purchase Act did not quell the unrest on the Island. Indeed, as the only product of the 1860 Land Commission, it fell so far short of popular expectations of a just settlement that it provoked more tenant unrest, both on estates of proprietors who had consented to the legislation and on those of the "diehards" who had resisted it. In March 1864 some of Lady Georgiana's tenants held a public meeting at Crapaud and unanimously resolved to ask her to "grant such concessions to her tenantry as may enable them to convert their Leaseholds into Freeholds on just and moderate terms." They also resolved to withhold payment of rent and arrears until they received a "decisive and satisfactory answer" to their request. The Crapaud meeting, which drew on precedents from the previous decade, preceded the creation of an Island-wide organization to assist tenants in directly resisting the proprietorial system.[61] In May 1864, seventy to eighty people from across the Island met in Charlottetown at the North American Hotel, the Island's largest, to protest against the 15 Years' Purchase Act and to organize a Tenant Union that would assist tenants in purchasing the freehold of the farms they leased. Members of the new organization, which became known as the Tenant League, pledged to withhold payment of rent and arrears and to resist landlords' attempts to enforce payment. Over the summer and fall of 1864, Island newspapers reported on Tenant League meetings and on its success in negotiating the purchase by tenants of a 5,000-acre estate on Lot 49 on terms more favourable than those in the 15 Years' Purchase Act. Many tenants stopped paying rent, and when landlords responded by sending out law officers to seize crops and cattle or to eject tenants from their leaseholds, the officers met armed resistance.[62]

Georgiana's correspondents on the Island kept her informed of the rising violence, and she in turn apprised the Colonial Office, noting that the lawlessness was a predictable consequence of policy choices to which she had objected. In August 1865 she wrote that tenants who a few months ago had been "contented and quiet" had now joined the League, fearing that their houses would be burned if they did not. "The Island is in a dreadfully disturbed state at present. We shall have to send to Halifax for troops, as [tenant activists] threaten to come into town in a body and burn down the jail," in order to free men who had been arrested for their activism. Georgiana accused the Island government of engaging "in a systematic endeavour to incite the tenantry against their landlords" so that proprietors would be forced to sell their land to the "agitators" at less than its value.[63] She wrote again two months later with details she had learned of disturbances on the Island. In one incident the sheriff's wagon was thrown over a bridge, his dog killed, and his horse's tail and mane cut off. In another about thirty men assembled to waylay the sheriff, who, fortunately for him, was home sick in bed. The Colonial Office responded to the first of these letters with a note saying that Island officials were keeping them informed of the situation and to the second by reporting that troops were now on the Island, something that Georgiana already knew, as was clear from her letter.[64]

An official in the Colonial Office advised against answering her second letter "in any detail; for she has the pen of a ready writer and nothing to occupy her at Brympton D'Evercy, and it will require very little provocation to elicit volumes of corresp'ce from her."[65] Georgiana received a bare acknowledgment, nothing more, of a further letter to the colonial secretary pointing out that her earlier letter had complained that the troops sent from Halifax were being kept in Charlottetown to protect the government and town, rather than being deployed in the countryside to prevent outrages. She urged the imperial government to support the Island government in putting down the Tenant League, before the lives of resident proprietors were threatened, and she repeated her observation that tenants had been encouraged in their refusal to pay rent by members of the Island government, who did so for their own advantage.[66] By this time, the troops had ventured out of Charlottetown three times in order to assist sheriffs in arresting Tenant League supporters and serving writs on tenants. With the show of force and subsequent prosecutions, Tenant League activity diminished, and Islanders pursued other means to transform leaseholds into freeholds and to pry the Island's wilderness lands from the grasp of the landlords.[67]

Georgiana correctly recognized that Tenant League activism would decrease the market price of proprietors' holdings, even if she overstated the Island government's agency and culpability in promoting the activism. If proprietors could collect their rents only through the exercise of the coercive power of a government they did not control, the rights were of doubtful value. Prior to the resurgence of Tenant League activism, the Land Commission had warned, presciently, that the imperial government, "having become weary of collecting rents and supporting evictions in Ireland, can hardly be expected to do for the landlords in Prince Edward Island what has ceased to be popular or practicable at home." In later proceedings to determine the compensation to be given proprietors for their estates, the Island government argued that rents which had to be collected at the point of a bayonet did not provide a proprietor with the same security as a mortgage.[68]

Other Island initiatives also diminished the value of proprietors' property rights. In 1866 and 1867 Georgiana wrote repeatedly to the Colonial Office to protest against proposed Island legislation concerning the sale of land for unpaid taxes.[69] Her main complaint, reiterated more vehemently in each succeeding letter, was that the legislation would confirm fraudulent titles. Proprietors had no protection against being required to pay taxes on more acres than they owned and no remedy against agents who did not pay the taxes, even while they assured the proprietors that they had. As the purchasers at tax sales were usually members of the government, "this Act is to confirm to themselves the possession of land of which they have literally robbed the Proprietors."[70] Initially, Georgiana and resident landlord Robert Bruce Stewart were the only proprietors who objected to the legislation, and Colonial Office staff saw no reason to withhold imperial approval for the bill, noting dismissively that, "like all other Acts in relation to landlords' 'interests,' [it] is protested against by Lady Georgina [sic] Fane and Mr. Bruce Stewart."[71] The two organized a proprietors' petition against the bill, signed by both resident and absentee landlords, but the Colonial Office had already decided to confirm the legislation, and it communicated its decision to the Island's lieutenant-governor as soon as the petition arrived.[72] Georgiana responded with "astonishment" and outrage: "I can scarcely believe that such an act can be sanctioned by the English government, as it seems more like the plundering of a province under the sway of a Turkish Pasha than legislation sanctioned by the Government of Great Britain."[73]

Georgiana suffered under several disadvantages in her efforts to persuade the Colonial Office to pay heed to her protests against the actions of the Island government. Despite being the daughter of the

Earl of Westmorland and owner of an estate in Somerset, she was not included in the inner circle of male proprietors who were able to present their petitions to the colonial secretary personally and who would have ample opportunity to meet with government officials less formally as their paths crossed socially and professionally. The men in the Colonial Office recognized that Georgiana made some coherent arguments in her letters, but they decided that she was not "a convincible person" and that it would be "fruitless" to explain why her representations had failed; instead, they communicated explanations orally to her solicitor, leaving it to him to try and convince her.[74] They also recognized her persistence. When Georgiana wrote to recommend the son of a medical man from Brympton for employment in the colonies, the internal memo on her letter suggested that the colonial secretary add the man's name to the patronage list for a clerkship in Hong Kong or some Crown colony, for "she'll bore us both to death until that formality is gone through."[75] Her alliance with Robert Bruce Stewart, her source of news and her ally on the Island, worked to her disadvantage as well. Stewart cultivated and valued the connection with Georgiana, referring to her as "my good and kind friend," and sometimes asked her to forward his letters and petitions to the Colonial Office with her own.[76] Georgiana often linked her protests with his, perhaps believing that the Colonial Office was more likely to listen when the appeal included the voice of an Island-based proprietor who owned more than five times the acreage she did. But Stewart, too, was perceived as a "diehard," and he lacked the class status that might have given his voice more weight.

Georgiana Fane, in common with other non-resident landlords, was also disadvantaged by having to employ land agents of variable competence and honesty to manage her estate. As she correctly reminded the Colonial Office, many land agents were also politicians with the power to ensure that Island legislation would enhance the economic opportunities of members of the Island's commercial class. Island agents did well from the proprietorial system, even if the proprietors did not. Consider the case of William Henry Pope, whom Georgiana had engaged as her agent in 1857. Pope was born on the Island, the son of a shipbuilder and politician. He trained as a lawyer in London and was called to the Island bar in 1847. He was also a land agent, newspaper editor, and Conservative politician. Pope's seventh child, born on New Year's Day

1862, was named Cecily Jane Georgiana Fane Pope, but this gesture did not dispel Lady Georgiana Fane's growing uneasiness with Pope's management of her Island estate.[77] By 1863 she had concluded that Pope was dishonest and had appointed another agent to replace him, but not in time to prevent her losing 400 acres of land because of unpaid taxes. By her account, in six years as her agent, Pope had not remitted a shilling of the rent he received. Worse, he had interfered to prevent one of her tenants from tendering the taxes on the land he occupied, and so the land was lost at a tax sale.[78] Georgiana's allegations against Pope are consistent with his conduct in some of his better-known land transactions. In 1854 Pope acquired the 80,000-acre Worrell estate by questionable means. His father-in-law, empowered to buy land on behalf of the government for resale to tenants, had terminated the negotiations with the owner by deliberately misstating the government's position. Pope then purchased the estate and used the possibility of ejecting tenants who owed back rent to coerce the Island government to buy the property from him, at a profit to himself of more than £10,000.[79]

Suppression of Tenant League activism did not end pressure to resolve the Island's land question, and the government continued its attempts to secure voluntary sales of landlords' estates. When, in June of 1867, the attorney general, Joseph Hensley, asked Georgiana, as he had Charlotte Sulivan, whether she would offer her lands to the government "on generous terms," he suggested that gratifying the "very strong desire" of Island tenants to convert their holdings into freehold was "very essential to the public good." Georgiana refused nonetheless.[80] The government tried again in the fall of 1873, after the Island had become a province of Canada, asking all the proprietors to name the lowest price per acre in cash that they would accept for their land. Some responded with a figure. Georgiana's first cousin, Lord Melville, who, like her, had not consented to the 15 Years' Purchase Act, asked for 20 shillings sterling per acre for his portion of Lots 29 and 53, inclusive of arrears. Others, including Robert Bruce Stewart, refused to name a price. Georgiana's response was described in an Island paper as "somewhat humorous." She wrote: "I do not wish to sell; I am content to remain a P.E. Islander, with my fortunes united with those of the Island. I have no wish to part company with it. I could intimate, if necessary, a price at which I would be willing to do that which I am unwilling to do. What is the price [the government] would offer to induce me to do it?"[81]

In 1871, in order to encourage the proprietors to recognize the advantages of selling their estates and the risks of retaining them, the Island government introduced a bill requiring landlords to compensate their tenants for improvements. Without such legislation, when landlords refused to renew short leases or ejected tenants who were behind in their rent, the landlord obtained all the increase in the value of the land resulting not only from rising land prices but as well from the work and capital that the tenant had invested in clearing and fencing land, erecting buildings, and improving the soil. Legislation to require landlords to compensate evicted tenants for their improvements had been introduced in the late 1840s and again in the 1850s, but the proprietors had protested vehemently against any measures to secure the tenants' rights to their improvements, and the Colonial Office rejected legislation of even quite limited application. Lord Palmerston, who was prime minister from 1855 to 1858 and again from 1859 to 1865, opposed any tenant-right legislation and in the 1850s had been vigilant to ensure that Prince Edward Island did not succeed in enacting tenant compensation legislation that would serve as a precedent for similar legislation for Ireland. By 1871, though, with passage of William Gladstone's Irish Land Act the previous year, the Island government expected the Colonial Office to approve similar legislation for the Island, arguing that it was necessary to protect the tenant who, "after having spent the best years of his life in giving a real value to the property, in his old age finds the results ... pass into the hands of his landlord, who relets the property with its improvements at a high rate to a stranger, and thereby reaps a large profit from the unremunerated labor and industry of the unfortunate tenant." The image was one often invoked in the Island campaign against the proprietorial system. Implicitly and sometimes explicitly, anti-landlord rhetoric suggested that property rights derived from labour, as well as from title, and that proprietors who had done nothing to develop their estates had less right to them than their tenants. The government belittled the proprietors' contributions to the Island as no more than "a few small wooden bridges" that some landlords might have built to give access to a new range of farms, although it noted as an exception the large wooden bridge that Lady Georgiana Fane had paid to have built at Crapaud.[82]

The Colonial Office did not approve the tenant compensation bill, but instead suggested a "more equitable measure" for the Island legislature to consider. Georgiana also objected to the revised bill passed by the Island legislature, describing it as an "iniquitous Act," an act of "spoliation and confiscation," and "a despotic edict of confiscation against loyal subjects of Her Majesty ... whose sole fault ... is that they are owners of property that others wish to obtain."[83] The Colonial Office believed that action on the proposed legislation was best delayed until after Prince Edward Island became a province of the Dominion of Canada, when the Colonial Office would relinquish its supervisory power over the Island's legislation to the Canadian government.[84] In its last session before the Island joined Canada, the legislature passed further amendments to the proposed tenant compensation bill, hoping these would be enough to secure imperial approval. Georgiana denounced this effort as "positive robbery of the property of the landlords." Despite these and other proprietors' objections, the bill was approved, but only after Prince Edward Island joined Canada and a more comprehensive approach to the land question had reduced the bill's significance.[85]

Georgiana did not live to see the denouement of the land question. In the last few months of her life, her letters to the Colonial Office protested against the first version of compulsory land purchase legislation that would ultimately end the proprietary system on the Island. Despite her public profession in 1873 that she was content to remain "a P.E. Islander," her letters to the Colonial Office pleaded for the imperial government to intervene on behalf of proprietors, who otherwise would be victims of "a local Legislature, the members of which are personally interested in passing Acts framed for the purpose of robbing us of our property." When she died on 1 December 1874, she was still awaiting word of the imperial government's decision on whether to approve legislation that would strip her of her Island estate.[86]

Georgiana Fane left all her real property in Somerset and in Prince Edward Island to her nephew and godson, Spenser Cecil Brabazon Ponsonby, the sixth son of the Earl of Bessborough and Georgiana's youngest half-sister, Maria. Ponsonby, cricket enthusiast, collector of shoe buckles, and amateur actor, began a career as a bureaucrat at age sixteen when Palmerston brought him into the Foreign Office. When Georgiana died, he was fifty years old and the father of six sons. She gave him the Prince Edward Island property outright, but the Brympton estate was his for his life only, with the property to go to his male heir on his death and so on down the line of male heirs, excluding any who succeeded to the title of Lord Bessborough. Thus Georgiana attached the same conditions to the gift of Brympton that had deprived her, as a female, of any claim to Apethorpe. The gift was also subject to the condition that whoever inherited the property must take the name of Fane as his surname within twelve months, and if he failed to do so or if he discontinued using the name, the property would go to the next male in the Fane family line. Georgiana gave Ponsonby most of her pictures and engravings, all her china, some of her jewellery, her plate and books, and all the furniture and effects in the manor house at Brympton, as well as the residue of her estate after payment of specific bequests and debts.[87]

According to family tradition, Ponsonby, who duly took the surname Fane, was surprised and entranced by the bequest of Brympton, despite finding that the estate was deeply in debt.[88] The Prince Edward Island property, judging from Georgiana's letters to the Colonial Office, was unlikely to provide him with any immediate income, as her agent had informed her that tenants on the Island, in anticipation of an early resolution of the land question, were not paying any rent.[89] Ponsonby's options regarding his Prince Edward Island estate were limited in any case. The political decision to end landlordism had already been made, although it remained to be seen whether the courts would provide the proprietors with any remedy. The crucial actor in this final chapter of the Island land question was Georgiana's acquaintance and fellow landlord Charlotte Sulivan.

5

Charlotte Sulivan: The Final Defence

Charlotte Antonia Sulivan became an Island landlord in January 1866, following the death of her father, Laurence Sulivan. The Island estate that she inherited had originated with acquisitions made by her great-grandfather, also named Laurence Sulivan, nearly a century earlier. In the late 1760s, almost immediately after the imperial government had decided to distribute Island lands in large lots to men who would promote settlement, an active market developed for titles to these properties. By 1783 Sulivan owned four lots on Prince Edward Island, comprising roughly 80,000 acres (see map 5.1), as well as estates on Grenada. Unlike most of the men who were original grantees, the senior Laurence Sulivan's imperial involvement lay not with the North Atlantic and the Americas but with India, where he had served intermittently as a chairman of the East India Company. It was there that he won, lost, and won back again, with the help of his son, Stephen, the fortune that was the basis of the estate that Charlotte inherited.[1]

Two of the Sulivan lots were in Prince County, in eastern Prince Edward Island. Lot 9 fronted on Egmont Bay on the Northumberland Strait. Crown Surveyor Samuel Holland noted that "the Woods and Lands are both good" and that some river front land near Sandy Cove was "fit for Meadows." Lot 16 had frontage on Richmond Bay, now known as Malpeque Bay, on the north shore of the Island; the Ellis River, now known as Grand River, was its western boundary. Holland described the lands and woods of the lot as "very good" and noted that "having the advantage of Ellis River and Richmond Bay may turn out to Advantage for Fishery and Agriculture." He might also have observed that passage into Malpeque Bay

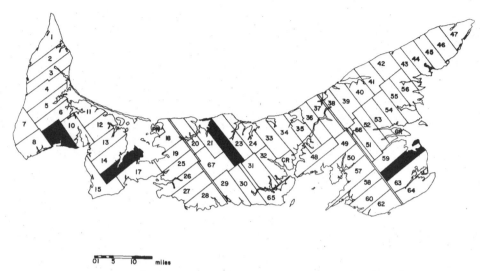

Map 5.1   Lots 9, 16, 20, and 61, the Sulivan lots, Prince Edward Island. Derived from a map drawn by Samuel Holland and reproduced as an insert in United Kingdom, *Acts of the Privy Council of England, Colonial Series, 5.*

could be difficult because of shifting shoals at its entrance. Lot 22, which was in Queens County, faced north as well, fronting on Grenville Bay, now known as New London Bay. The Mi'kmaq name for the bay was Kicheboogwek Booktaba, which meant bay of shoals or enclosed bay. Holland did not praise the land or woods on this lot, but noted that it was well situated for a fishery conducted with small craft. The fourth lot, Lot 61, was in Kings County, in eastern Prince Edward Island, across Cardigan Bay from the Saunders sisters' Lot 53. Holland described the lands on this lot as better than those on adjacent Lot 60, which he called "very bad," and he noted that the coast was "very shallow" and thus "inconvenient." The woods, however, he thought "very good." According to Holland, "being convenient to George Town is [Lot 61's] greatest advantage."[2] In general, the Sulivan estate was not on the best Island lands, in terms of soil and vegetation or locale.

    Charlotte's father, Laurence, was born in Calcutta, where her grandfather, Stephen, was judge-advocate general in Bengal. Educated in Edinburgh and Cambridge, Laurence Sulivan made his career in London, entering employment at the War Office in 1806.

He became deputy secretary of the War Office in 1826 and remained in the post until 1851.[3] Charlotte grew up in the magnificent house that Laurence had purchased in Fulham in 1823, the year before she was born (see illus. 1.1).[4] Broom House, built on spacious grounds fronting on the Thames, was one of many mansions constructed on the western outskirts of London in the second half of the eighteenth century, as nabob wealth funded opulent housing.[5] Like the adjacent Hurlingham House, which persists as the exclusive Hurlingham Club, Broom House was built in the 1760s.[6]

We know little about Charlotte's childhood and schooling and can only speculate about life in the Sulivan household. Born in 1824, she was the youngest of five children. The eldest, Stephen, was twelve in the year that Charlotte was born, and after being educated privately at home, he began study at Cambridge when she was six. Henry, her other brother, was educated at home before leaving for Oxford when Charlotte was nine. She also had two older sisters: Mary Catherine, born in 1820, and Elizabeth, born in 1819. Given their class, the three Sulivan girls were probably educated entirely at home, and much of Charlotte's childhood must have been spent in the company of her sisters.[7] Elizabeth did not marry until 1851, when Charlotte was in her late twenties, and Mary Catherine not until 1865.[8] Charlotte's mother, Elizabeth Temple, was the sister of the third Viscount Palmerston, who after entering the House of Commons in 1802, became one of the leading political figures of his time and prime minister in 1855. His rise was linked with the same political shifts that ended Lord Melville's career in cabinet. Elizabeth's marriage to Laurence in 1811 was a product in part of Laurence's close friendship with Palmerston during their student years at Cambridge.[9] The extensive correspondence between Palmerston and the Sulivan household gives evidence of the strong and enduring friendship between Palmerston and Charlotte's parents and suggests that she grew up immersed in British politics. Local lore has it that Palmerston drew up British plans for the Crimean War at Broom House. He was a frequent guest of the Sulivans, often riding out from London to spend the day; his letters to both Charlotte's mother and her father are rich with the details of political life. Because of Laurence Sulivan's work and his personal connections, Broom House became an important social centre for many of the leading statesmen of the day.[10] After Charlotte's brother Stephen entered the foreign service in 1832, his letters, if not his presence, must have added to her awareness of foreign affairs, as would, of course, her father's work with the War Office in London.[11]

Charlotte's comfortable childhood circumstances were shattered by the death of her mother in 1837, when Charlotte was thirteen. Laurence did not remarry, and he continued to commute to the War Office in London for another fourteen years, before choosing to retire, while Charlotte and her older sisters assumed the responsibilities for managing Broom House and its many servants.[12] Her uncle, Viscount Palmerston, lamented that his bachelor circumstances limited his ability to help fill the domestic void left by his sister's death. Following Palmerston's marriage to the widowed Lady Cowper in 1839, he did his best to remedy this gap, and Charlotte seems to have been a regular guest in their house when she was in her early twenties.[13] Although she did not have a title, her father's prominence ensured that she was among the throngs invited to the "drawing-rooms" at the palace, where Georgiana Fane was also a guest.[14]

Did Elizabeth Sulivan's death blight the marriage prospects of her daughters? And does it help to explain her oldest daughter's marriage at the age of thirty-seven to a widower with a large family, Mary's marriage, at the age of forty-five, to the vicar of Fulham, also a widower, seventy-seven years old, and Charlotte's spinsterhood? Given the expectation in households such as the Sulivans that at least one daughter would remain unmarried and manage the family home for a widowed father, the marriages of Charlotte's sisters left that role to her. Continuing tragedies in the family surely added to the sisters' domestic responsibilities and burdens, as well as possibly deterring suitable suitors. Stephen had serious health problems and an irascible personality. He brought scandal to the family with a series of love affairs, only briefly interrupted by his marriage to a social inferior, his Italian mistress. He was murdered in Lima in 1857 in a dispute over a woman's affections. The other brother, Henry, suffered throughout his life from recurring bouts of mental illness. Ultimately, Charlotte remained at home to care for her father until his death in 1866. She was then forty-one and the only sibling still living at Broom House. Family tragedies and family responsibilities propelled her toward spinsterhood, but the single life may have had attractions as well. For Charlotte, unlike many other women of her generation, economic security and a fulfilling

5.1   The Sulivan family at Broom House, c. 1865. LMA, 77.0, BRO, 80/3108

life were possible without marrying. Despite the difficulties and scandals in the Sulivan family and the challenges that she faced as a young woman, she enjoyed many opportunities and advantages. Laurence Sulivan was, it seems, a kind and decent man. As well, he managed the family's finances prudently, freeing his daughters from the fears of penury that must have haunted many of their peers. When he married Elizabeth Temple, their combined assets were worth around £40,000. At the time of his death, Laurence's estate appears to have been worth nearly £120,000, the result in part of his extensive investments in British railway stock.[15] A photograph of Charlotte, Mary, and Laurence taken in Broom House in the 1860s suggests, as was no doubt intended, the comfortable, stable domesticity that seemed to have prevailed in the household (see illus. 5.1).

Laurence Sulivan was also a charitable man with a concern for public needs. In 1855 he built and endowed schools for the poor on the Broom House estate, naming them the Elizabethan Schools in honour of his late wife. The Tudor Gothic structure built to house

5.2 Elizabethan Schools, founded by Charlotte Sulivan's father and named in honour of her mother. LMA, 77.0, BRO, 60/3887

the Elizabethan Schools was an impressive building. Designed to accommodate 120 students, it included a boys' and a girls' school, two almshouses, and accommodation for a schoolmaster and a schoolmistress (see illus. 5.2).[16] Still standing although a little worse for wear, it has been used as a youth community centre in recent years. The Elizabethan Schools on the Sulivan property were associated with the ragged schools movement in London and elsewhere in Britain that had emerged in the 1840s to provide poor children with a moral and practical education which would keep them from slipping into vagrancy and criminality. The first schools were founded in London and were linked with evangelical efforts to minister to the urban poor.[17]

Laurence Sulivan's charitable initiatives made it easy for Charlotte to assume a public role in education and philanthropy. In the second half of the nineteenth century both these areas provided women, particularly of her class, with opportunities to construct themselves as productive members of society while remaining single, if they chose.[18] Charlotte had helped Laurence to run the schools and almshouses well before formal charge of them passed to her and her sister Elizabeth on their father's death.[19] Accounts of the problems of the ragged schools in achieving their goals suggest that managing the Elizabethan Schools might well have posed significant challenges, as the students the schools sought to help were, by definition, difficult.[20] The ragged schools movement was brought to a close with passage of the Education Act in 1870, four years after Laurence died, and ragged schools were absorbed or superseded by the rise of public education in the following years. The Elizabethan Schools on the Broom House estate, however, persisted within the new structures for more than three decades, before being taken over by London County Council early in the twentieth century.[21] Just before the takeover, seventy students were enrolled in the Elizabethan Schools.[22]

Laurence Sulivan's will gave Charlotte the Broom House property, his interests in the Palmerston estate, shares in the Edinburgh and Glasgow Railway and the Great Western, and the Prince Edward Island lots. In addition, it gave her "immediate possession" of all his "letters, papers and manuscripts of every sort and description" and the exclusive power to use them as she thought fit, excepting documents needed by the executors of his estate. Laurence had given Charlotte management of much of the business of Broom House and its surrounding properties long before his death, as she had proved herself a capable administrator and business person. Now she controlled the core of the Sulivan estate and had the means and capacity to manage it. Laurence's three other living children received substantial legacies, but Charlotte was in a position to maintain the standard of living she had become accustomed to without ever having to marry.[23]

In some areas, Charlotte's stewardship of the Sulivan fortune is consistent with that of her father. Building on Laurence Sulivan's charitable work, she helped to establish schools, churches, libraries, and recreational facilities in Fulham, providing land and money for building costs and maintenance. Philanthropy gave Charlotte the opportunity to become a significant public figure in the community and to influence its development. She established the Ray of Hope Coffee House and the Parsons Green Club and equipped the latter with three billiard tables and a piano, to provide working people with an alternative to socializing in pubs. Her portrait still hangs in the club building (see illus. 5.3).[24] She also funded construction of

5.3   Portrait of Charlotte Sulivan, c. 1883,
hanging in Parsons Green Club, Fulham.
Photo provided by Sue Pierson.

the Parsons Green Mission Hall just to the east of Fulham and a
brick and slate mission house for St Matthew's Church on Rosebury
Road, not far from Broom House.[25] The following decade she provided the land and paid for the construction of a church adjacent
to the mission house, capable of seating more than 800 people.
Charlotte's will reflected these religious and charitable concerns as
well as other local initiatives. She is remembered locally as "a friend
and benefactor of the poor" who lived in and near Fulham and
Parsons Green. Clearly, she was a friend of the pious as well,
provided they were associated with the Church of England.[25]

   As did many other women of her class, Charlotte Sulivan found
opportunities for creative expression in graphic art and gardening,
and she maintained an interest in botany.[26] On her death, she willed
her collection of dried plants to the museum at Eton College and

her paintings and drawings of fungi to the Herbarium at the Royal Botanic Gardens in nearby Kew.[27] Under her management, the Broom House grounds and gardens flourished, in part because she paid the Chelsea Waterworks to install piping and provide a steady supply of water for them.[28] At least four of the more than a dozen servants she employed were charged with managing the nine acres of grounds around Broom House.[29] The beauty of her gardens elicited praise, both locally and more generally, and they became a favoured site for charity functions.[30]

In Charlotte's management of the Sulivan estate on Prince Edward Island, she took at least one initiative not taken by her father, or indeed by any of the Sulivan men who had held the estate before her. After her father's death, she visited Prince Edward Island and inspected the Sulivan estate for herself, as had Lady Westmorland with her estate in 1839–40 and Georgiana Fane with hers in 1860. Charlotte's arrival in Prince Edward Island in the fall of 1867 generated much speculation concerning how she would respond to what she saw and what she might have in mind for the estate; her decisions concerning it would be of central importance to political attempts to resolve land questions in the colony.

Charlotte Sulivan arrived in Charlottetown as the Island legislature was manoeuvring to obtain imperial approval of legislation to finally end landlordism on the Island. The significance of her visit and the great public interest it generated needs to be contextualized in relation to the century-long history of struggle against the proprietorial system in the colony and the place that the Sulivans and their estate held in this history. Charlotte's male ancestors, who had owned the Island estate for three generations, were not among the non-resident landlords celebrated for their active development of Island lots. While James Montgomery and Lord Selkirk, as well as the Melville and Westmorland families, were praised on the Island for the investments and the attention they bestowed on their lots, the Sulivan estate was cited as an example of the worst sort of absentee neglect. The opprobrium may have been as much the product of the needs and intentions of those who constructed the Sulivans in this way as of the actual record of their estate management, though the family certainly provided an easy target. The popular demand in the 1790s for the escheat of proprietorial grants led the assembly to develop a chart purportedly showing the state of settlement on the Island's lots. The Sulivan settlement record was mixed but not one that put the estate among the worst in terms of settlement. Lots 9 and 22 were listed among the many lots having no settlers; Lot 61, however, was among lots that supposedly had, on average, three families settled on them; Lot 16 was listed as having at least a hundred settlers.[31]

Whether the Sulivan estate could have been escheated in the 1790s is an interesting legal question. The terms of the 1767 Privy Council instructions for issuing Island grants required proprietors to have thirty-four settlers per 20,000-acre lot within four years of "the Date of the Grant." If proprietors failed to meet this four-year deadline – and it was this first deadline and not the ten-year deadline of having one hundred settlers per 20,000-acre grant that mattered – "the whole [of their grant] would be forfeited."[32] The language of the grants themselves reflected this requirement. But the Privy Council instructions did not specify when grantees were required to apply for the deeds giving them their grants, although it was the issuing of the deed that started the clock on the four-year settlement requirement. Some applied almost immediately, but others did not. In the case of the Sulivan estate, Charlotte's great-grandfather, Laurence, had his agent apply for the deed of Lot 16 in 1769. Laurence Sulivan had acquired the interests of the three men who had originally received the right to that lot in the Privy Council lottery before they applied and paid to have the colonial governor issue their deed.[33] In the case of Lots 9, 22, and 61, however, it would appear that no one applied until Laurence's heir, Stephen Sulivan, took up the matter in the 1780s. Initially, the governor-in-council on the Island resisted the request to grant lots to Stephen Sulivan, but on instructions from imperial officials in London, Lieutenant-Governor Edmund Fanning ultimately issued them – the last of the original Crown grants of lots – in the spring of 1795.[34] The language of these three Sulivan grants, as in the earlier ones, specified that, to maintain his rights in the property, the proprietor had to establish thirty-four settlers on each lot "within four Years from the Date hereof."[35] Thus three-quarters of the Sulivan estate would have been safe from escheat until the last months of 1799.

When Stephen Sulivan applied for the deeds for Lots 9, 22, and 61, he noted that his family had invested time and money in efforts to settle their Island estate. The Island's receiver general, John Stewart, who knew the Island's history well, did not dispute

Sulivan's claim but noted that "it is much to be lamented that those to whom he entrusted the management of his affairs have not followed up his intentions in any extent." Sulivan's agent in this period, John Patterson, was the brother of the Island's first governor, Walter Patterson, and no friend of Stewart's. Stewart also noted that those who had settled on the Sulivan estate had done so without Sulivan's assistance.[36]

Anne and Robert Dundas might have said, based on their experience with John Stewart as their land agent, that had the Sulivans entrusted their affairs to him, the results would not have been much different. The Sulivan record of quit rent payment certainly does not justify a claim of delinquency. As of 1802, the Sulivans had paid almost £1,200 in quit rents, including payments for Lots 9, 22, and 61, and while the receiver general of quit rents claimed they owed yet more, their record was relatively good. Indeed, given when the last three Sulivan grants were issued, Stephen Sulivan disputed the receiver general's claim that there was a balance owing at the turn of the century.[37] Stewart thought otherwise and subsequently included Sulivan's Lot 9 in a list of properties to be subjected to legal action to enforce quit rent payment.[38]

An 1823 report on the state of settlement on Prince Edward Island, prepared by John Carmichael, the son-in-law of Lieutenant-Governor Charles Douglass Smith, continued to show a mixed record for development on the Sulivan estate. Carmichael reported favourably on the merits of Lot 9, as had Samuel Holland in the 1760s, noting that the woods on the front of the lot were good, the "Soil in general is well calculated for Agriculture," and the marshes of potential value, and that Wolf's Inlet "affords shelter for boats and is full of Trout and Smelts." Despite these advantages, there were "no settlers on this lot." Lot 22 was described in terms of unrealized potential too, with "superior" lands and woods and "two good streams for mills," as well as being "finely situated for carrying on a fishery" within the vessel size limits imposed by shoals at the mouth of Grenville Bay. Lots 16 and 61, which had been among those listed as having settlers in the 1790s, now had 850 cleared acres on the first and 400 on the second.[39]

In the late 1830s Lieutenant-Governor Charles FitzRoy converted this mixed assessment of the management of the Sulivan estate during the six decades since the Island had become a British colony into an unqualified condemnation. When he arrived on the Island in the summer of 1837, he found that rural resistance to landlordism was widespread and growing. He soon decided that one source of rural grievance was the proprietors' failure to develop their estates and provide tenants with long leases and generous terms. From FitzRoy's perspective, while the Melvilles and the Westmorlands were responsible, even benevolent, landlords seeking to develop their properties for the mutual benefit of proprietor and tenant, the Sulivan estate epitomized some of the worst aspects of land acquisition for speculative profits rather than long-term development.

Using returns from the 1833 census, FitzRoy assembled a table showing the extent of settlement and improvement and the nature of land tenure on each lot. For Lot 29, part of the Saunders sisters' inheritance from their great-uncle, Charles Saunders, FitzRoy noted: "The greatest part of the population on this lot has been settled subsequently to 1817 upon the most liberal terms. The people having been allowed to expend a gt. Portion of the Rents in Roads and other improvements." Leases were for 999 years; there were 575 settlers on the lot. FitzRoy noted of Lot 53, which the Melvilles and the Westmorlands shared with Lord Selkirk, that the terms of leases were "liberal," there were 319 settlers on the lot, and the "Population [was] succeeding."[40]

When FitzRoy turned to Sulivan's Lot 9, however, the tone changed. He reported that there were only thirty-three settlers on the lot and that these were tenants at will, as "[t]his proprietor refuses to grant any leases whatever or to sell which accounts for its very scantly Population." FitzRoy offered similar comments regarding the 409 settlers reported on Lot 16. They were "[m]ostly tenants at will ... See Lot 9. The settlers who have titles obtained them from the former Proprietor. The remainder are squatters." FitzRoy recorded 221 settlers on Lot 22 and 231 on Lot 61, the first group all tenants at will and the second mostly so, and noted that his remarks regarding Sulivan's Lots 9 and 16 applied to these lots as well. The lieutenant-governor's assessment of management practices on the Sulivan lots are not supported by the census returns from 1861, which provide data on the length and nature of leases on the Sulivan estate and their date of issue, but accuracy was not his primary concern.[41]

While FitzRoy was decrying Sulivan's failure to invest more energy in developing his estate, others were seeking to engage Sulivan in the campaign to protect Island estates from the threats posed by an increasingly assertive legislature and the rise of the Escheat movement. According to J.B. Palmer, Island politician and land agent for, among others, the Melvilles and the Westmorlands, Laurence Sulivan was ideally situated to assist landed interests on the Island since he could block legislation that was inimical to proprietors simply by appealing to his brother-in-law, Lord Palmerston, who was a member of Lord Grey's cabinet. In Palmer's view, as of the early 1830s, Sulivan had not acted to ensure that royal assent was withheld from bills that threatened landlord interests, because he "always thought, or appeared to think, too little of his landed Estates" in Prince Edward Island.[42] Neither FitzRoy's critique nor Palmer's version of the same position was entirely accurate. In the mid-1820s Laurence Sulivan had appointed John Lewellin to serve as his agent. Lewellin subsequently settled on Sulivan's Lot 61 and, as a member of the legislature, was active in promoting developmental interests.[43] In the 1830s Sulivan began to work with the Prince Edward Island Association, a London-based lobby group that promoted landed interests, and helped to distribute an emigration tract that Lewellin published in 1832 characterizing Prince Edward Island as a good "poor man's country." Through letters from Lewellin and information about the Island that circulated within the Prince Edward Island Association, Sulivan was able to track the growing threats to landlords' interests posed by collectively organized rent resistance and political activism in the 1830s and early 1840s. In the late 1830s he began to work with George Seymour and Samuel Cunard, among others, to formulate policies to protect landed property on Prince Edward Island.[44]

In the 1850s, after Prince Edward Island was granted responsible government, Sulivan, Cunard, and Seymour played a significant role in lobbying the imperial government to continue to protect proprietors from colonial legislation that had the potential to cause enormous damage to their interests, including legislation depriving landlords of the rent they had collected on fishery reserve land, legislation requiring landlords to compensate tenants for improvements they had made to their leaseholds, and legislation to tax the proprietors' rent rolls. Sulivan was part of the negotiations with imperial officials that produced the gentlemen's agreement to the effect that, if the proprietors accepted a reasonable exit strategy, the Colonial Office would continue for a little while to deny approval to Island legislation which would reduce the value of the proprietors' holdings.

The Land Commission of 1860 was one product of this agreement. Although it failed to produce a final solution to the land question, it helped to clarify which proprietors were interested in a negotiated political settlement of the matter and which simply wanted the state to uphold their property rights. Laurence Sulivan, Samuel Cunard, and George Seymour were among the twelve landlords who signed onto the 15 Years' Purchase Act and in so doing, publicly positioned themselves as moderates who were willing to permit leaseholders to buy the freehold of the land they leased, albeit at a price greater than most tenants were willing to pay. Because of Sulivan's prominence among the proprietors who helped to draft the act and because his holdings, next to Cunard's, were the Island's largest, some on the Island referred to the 15 Years' Purchase Act not just as the "Proprietors' Act" but as "Laurence Sulivan's Act."[45] Over the decade during which tenants might take advantage of the provisions of the act, fewer than 7,000 acres changed hands under its terms.[46]

From 1858 on, Cunard made England his permanent home, and he played a significant role in shaping Colonial Office policy toward the Maritimes. Sulivan acted in tandem with Cunard not only on questions of Island legislation but in choosing land agents and in formulating management strategies for their estates. Early in 1865 the agent for Cunard and Sulivan announced that the proprietors would sell unleased land but would not issue any more leases, and he publicized the terms under which they would sell. Neither this announcement nor the purchase terms available to tenants under the 15 Years' Purchase Act addressed the needs and expectations of the Islanders who had anticipated that the 1860 Land Commission would provide a mechanism for ending landlordism on the Island. The Tenant League, which was one rural response to the failure of the commission, was active on Laurence Sulivan's estate, as well as on Georgiana Fane's. Indeed, it was the resistance to a party of law officers who attempted, unsuccessfully, to serve writs on Sulivan's Lot 22 in October 1865 that finally prompted the Island government to deploy troops in aid of the civil power. The use of troops to enforce land law following the Lot 22 incident helped to bring Tenant League activism to a close.[47]

Both Samuel Cunard and Laurence Sulivan died during the years of heightened tenant resistance to proprietorial demands – Cunard in April 1865 and Sulivan in January 1866. Their deaths eliminated the key players in the construction of a moderate landlord position embodied in the gentlemen's agreement of the 1850s, which they had helped to negotiate, and put more than a quarter of a million acres of Island land in new hands. In the case of the Cunard estate, Islanders did not have to wait long to see what the heirs would do. Samuel Cunard's will left his Island property to his son Edward, who was already an Island landlord, and to his other son, William. A year after his death, his heirs agreed to sell all the Cunard lands to the Island government.[48] Laurence Sulivan's will left his four lots to his daughter Charlotte. Her estate was now the largest of those in the hands of non-resident landlords and, with the possible exception of resident landlord Robert Bruce Stewart's estate, which was roughly the same size, the largest remaining in private hands.[49] Stewart was unlikely to part with his estate, but had Charlotte chosen to do so, her decision would have added significantly to the perception that landlordism was waning.

From an Island perspective, there was reason to assume that Charlotte Sulivan might follow the lead of the Cunards and sell the lands that she had inherited on the Island. Samuel Cunard and Laurence Sulivan had adopted the same management strategies since the late 1850s; in the 1860s George W. DeBlois, the agent chosen by both of them, had advised Edward and William Cunard to sell.[50] When Joseph Hensley visited Charlotte in London in July of 1867 to assess the possibilities for purchasing her estate, his visit was part of a broader initiative to query Robert Bruce Stewart and the leading British proprietors, a total of four men and four women, concerning their willingness to sell.[51] Charlotte chose not to give Hensley an answer when he visited her and indicated that she would "decide what course she would pursue" after inspecting her Island estate.[52]

In September 1867 Charlotte arrived on Prince Edward Island to begin the inspection. The Island *Patriot* announced her arrival with a story that highlighted Charlotte's reputation for "philanthropic efforts in the cause of education at home, as well as for her general benevolence." Her good deeds were, the *Patriot* said, "beginning to be everywhere spoken of." As well, the newspaper praised her for her "true desire to look into the condition of her tenantry" and her interest in her estate, noting that her visit was an initiative that "few absentee proprietors have ever taken." It suggested that if Charlotte, after seeing the plight of her tenants, were to "resolve to sell her lands to the local government at a moderate price," it would be very much to her benefit. She would suffer little financial loss and "her name, almost a synonyme [sic] for generosity in certain parts of England, would be embalmed in the hearts of hundreds who now constitute her tenantry in this Island, and be held in grateful remembrance not only by their posterity, but also by those of all classes in the community."[53] In short, the *Patriot* appealed to Charlotte to assume a feminine philanthropic role on the Island comparable to that which it believed she played in Fulham.

The appeal misconstrued the basis of Charlotte's philanthropy. This is understandable, given that she had just acquired sole control of the core of the Sulivan estate in Britain, including the properties in Fulham, as well as the Island holdings. Her philanthropy in Fulham was grounded, as was her father's before her, in strategic land purchases and effective property management. These provided her with the resources to support specific charitable endeavours, even as she enlarged the Fulham estate she had inherited. Even before her father's death, Charlotte had acquired a reputation for her business sense as well as her generosity. To expect her to sell her entire Island estate at a price that would entail some "pecuniary loss" as an act of charity to her tenants was to expect her to act on the Island in ways that were different from her behaviour at home.[54] The *Summerside Journal* also encouraged Charlotte to sell her estate to the government, but with an argument that was better crafted for its audience, as it combined economic calculations with charitable ones. The paper urged her to follow the lead of the Cunard heirs, who, guided by "one of the shrewdest business men in the colony," had decided to sell their estate. As well as making good business sense, such a decision would, the *Journal* suggested, lead to her being "gratefully remembered by her tenants."[55]

While some papers encouraged Charlotte to sell her property, the *Herald* suggested that this had been her intention from the beginning of her trip and that she was "about to offer her lands, either to the tenants or to the government."[56] It soon became clear that such was not the case and that Charlotte really had come, as she had told Joseph Hensley when he visited her at Broom House, to see the estate and make her decision on the basis of what she saw. As Charlotte travelled the Island and viewed her estate, some Island papers began to express concern that her visit was not sufficiently illuminating. The *Examiner* complained in early September that those guiding her on the ground were only taking her for a "flying visit" to the more prosperous parts of her estate.[57] A week later, with Charlotte still on the Island and still inspecting her estate, both the prosperous and the poorer sections, the *Examiner* acknowledged as much and offered the hope that her "generous nature" would lead her to improve conditions for her tenantry.[58]

Island papers had probably been worried that Charlotte would focus her attention on Lot 22 in Queens County, which was the closest part of her estate to Charlottetown. It was also the most settled of her lots, with a population of 1,465 in 1861. Lot 61 in Kings County had 910 inhabitants, and Lots 9 and 16 in Prince County had 262 and 850 respectively. Most of Lot 22 would have shown signs of prosperity. With the exception of some land on the northern part of the lot that had once been pine forest and had burned repeatedly and a few hundred acres of hollows and stony land, the lot as a whole was, according to the 1861 census taker, "of a good quality and will compare favourably with any land in Queens County." That was high praise. New London, on the gulf shore side of Lot 22, was a thriving port with a significant export trade in potatoes and oats. As well, the lot contained good brooks and mill sites. Other parts of Charlotte's estate, however, were less promising. The 1861 census taker had described the land on Lot 9 as, in general, "very bad," with much of it "nothing but barrens." Its main advantage lay in the possibilities for using it as a base to pursue the spring herring fishery. The census taker characterized the land on Lot 16 as primarily "low swampy and barren" and the people as "generally poor." The land on Lot 61 was "generally bad." That which was not "swampy" was either sandy or rocky. The census taker for Lot 61 reported: "When looking at the new fields in the new settler farms I could see flint stones almost as thick as grass over the surface." He "did not see more than 4 or 5 good farms on the whole Township." As well, he drew attention to "40 emigrant Families exiled on the west end of the Lot without even a road to their miserable abodes; of this they complain very much as they have to carry every thing they can get (not what they want) for

10 to 15 miles on their backs." The swamps that he had to cross to get to these settlers were so bad that "I had like to lose my horse."[59]

Island papers not only encouraged Charlotte to sell her estate for her own and her tenants' benefit; some tried to educate her on the difficulties settlers had experienced in farm-making and on the history of the land question as it was understood in the colony. The *Summerside Journal* emphasized the centrality of tenant labour in producing the agrarian landscape that Charlotte viewed. The prosperous farms she inspected had been carved out of wilderness by the unremitting labour of the tenantry and of the tenantry alone. The Island's proprietors had contributed neither "moral nor material aid." She should know that "[t]here is a deeply rooted conviction existing in the minds of our rural population" that landlords had no just claim to ownership of the product of this labour. The paper warned that the only reason Islanders had not rebelled and overthrown the system sustaining this injustice was that the colony was too small to effectively do so.[60] The editor of the *Examiner*, Edward Whelan, a central figure in the Liberal party and an advocate of land reform, predicted that proprietors should expect more resistance like that organized by the Tenant League if they chose not to sell and that the imperial government had made it clear it was unwilling to pay the bill for maintaining troops on the Island. Alternatively, Islanders might opt for annexation to the United States as a strategy for bringing landlordism to a close.[61] By mid-September, Island papers were reporting that Charlotte did not intend to sell her estate.[62] Despite the advice of the local press, appeals to her philanthropic character, vows of undying gratitude, threats of tenant resistance, and the promise of political initiatives that would be inimical to landlord interests, she turned down a government offer of £27,000 in Island currency (the equivalent of $87,500) for the purchase of her estate, both the leased and unleased lands.[63] And she did so in spite of the precedent set by the sale of the Cunard estate in 1866. Why?

No doubt, there were a number of factors in her decision. It is clear from letters she wrote after her visit that she rejected the appeal to sell as an act of charity. Having inspected her estate, she was not persuaded that her Island tenants were oppressed – indeed, to the contrary. As she later noted in a letter to the Earl of Kimberley, she concluded from her visit that her tenants were prospering and had no "cause of complaint."[64] The timing of her visit

– early fall in the aftermath of a good harvest – no doubt helped to produce that perception, but her own knowledge of the condition of the urban poor of London undoubtedly shaped her response to the relative comfort she saw in the countryside. In addition, she believed that her father had already shown great generosity by agreeing to the terms of the 15 Years' Purchase Act, with its provisions for giving up rent arrears prior to 1858 and for tenants to purchase their farms for a sum equivalent to fifteen times the annual rent due on the land.[65] She appears, too, to have formed the opinion that much of the pressure to sell resulted from the politics of the land question and not the legitimate concerns of Island tenants.[66] Although Islanders may have hoped that Charlotte would extend her generosity to Prince Edward Island, she was not persuaded that her Island tenants required charity.

There was also the fundamental business question of what return Charlotte could expect from the sum she was offered for her estate and how this compared with what she was getting in rent. There is no easy answer to this question, which depends in large part on a comparison of the costs, risks, and returns from different kinds of investments. The returns from Charlotte's estate were a matter of dispute when the Prince Edward Island Land Commission of 1875 ultimately determined the price she would receive on the compulsory sale of her estate. In a letter to the London *Times*, Charlotte claimed that the annual rents due to her from leased land on the estate were more than $7,000 and that she had collected almost $5,400 per year from her estate over the period 1870–71.[67] A correspondent from Prince Edward Island, writing as "Colonus," challenged these figures, noting that her land agent on the Island had testified under oath that the "average" gross rental actually received during the six years prior to 1875 was roughly $4,500 and that there were expenses of approximately $1,500 a year in managing the estate. Thus, Colonus argued, Charlotte Sulivan's net annual return from her Island estate was only $3,000.[68] Both sets of figures are inadequate. The net annual return she could expect from the leased lands on her estate was likely around $4,000, a third more than Colonus suggested in his letter to the *Times* but significantly below the gross figures Charlotte provided.[69] Assuming that the Island government offered to pay her a price for her unleased land that was similar to the government's valuation of wilderness land acquired from other proprietors, Charlotte was being offered

$21,500 for her unleased land and $66,000 for her leased land. The main financial question she had to consider, then, was whether she could earn $4,000 annually on $66,000.[70]

According to Charlotte, she could invest money at four per cent interest. At that rate she would receive $2,640 per year from the capital that she was offered for her leased land, less even than Colonus had suggested as her annual returns from her leaseholds. According to Colonus, however, she could expect to earn much more than four per cent on any capital sum. The interest rate for mortgages on the Island, he noted, ranged from seven and one half to ten per cent. Colonus also asserted that Charlotte's father, Laurence Sulivan, in agreeing to the fifteen years' purchase arrangements, must have assumed a six and two-thirds per cent return on cash in calculating a fair price for his leased land.[71] At six and two-thirds per cent, the lowest of the interest rates Colonus thought reasonable to assume, rather than four per cent, the Island government's offer becomes more attractive, as it would yield roughly $4,400 per year, a figure ten per cent higher than what Charlotte had reason to expect as a net return from her leased land. That would enable her to replace the loss of income from rents with an extra $400 per year which might begin to compensate for giving up more than $30,000 in rent arrears. If she could have counted on the higher rates of interest, her decision not to sell looks increasingly irrational from an economic perspective. A.B. Warburton, who wrote to the London *Times* from Prince Edward Island to dispute Charlotte's figures, focused on this issue as well, arguing that she could expect to receive a return of seven and a half per cent from "safe" Island investments.[72]

But were Colonus's and Warburton's claims reasonable? Some of the evidence presented to the 1875 commission to determine the price for purchasing the proprietors' estates corroborated their claims concerning interest rates demanded by moneylenders on the Island.[73] One flaw with this evidence, though, is that, much like Charlotte's evidence concerning the book value of her rent rolls, it ignores the costs of management and any losses from bad debts.[74] Other testimony indicated that savings account investments at Island banks typically returned four per cent and sometimes five; these were net returns.[75] The Island government's strategies for financing land purchases provide a useful context for considering Charlotte's financial options. The government financed the 1866

Cunard purchase by making twice-yearly payments at six per cent interest, with the balance at five per cent payable ten years from the date of purchase.[76] Subsequent government purchases of estates in the 1860s were financed in part by offering the vendors debentures of up to ten years at six per cent interest.[77] Clearly, Charlotte might have obtained five or six per cent interest on some of the purchase price for her estate, had she been willing to accept Island debentures in payment. A six per cent return on $66,000 would have been $3,960, close to replacing her net annual rental returns, although with no compensation for the loss of outstanding arrears. This was not an unreasonable offer, provided that Island debentures were as secure an investment as Island real estate or off-Island investments. The Island government in other contexts acknowledged that the investing public perceived a difference in the relative safety of colonial, as compared to imperial, debentures. The government issued debentures paying six per cent interest to raise capital for land purchases in the late 1860s and again to finance railway construction in the early 1870s, but only after failing to obtain imperial guarantees for its debentures; debentures backed by imperial guarantees, the Island government argued, would sell even if they paid only four per cent interest.[78]

The government's offer of Island debentures would, from a financial point of view, appeal most to proprietors, such as the Cunards, who were willing to invest in a speculative money market. Charlotte's circumstances, though, were not those of the Cunard heirs, who accepted a similar offer for their Island estate. Under the terms of Sir Samuel Cunard's will, the estate had to generate £20,000 for each of Cunard's six daughters.[79] In this context, the government's offer may have been particularly attractive. There were no similar pressures on Laurence Sulivan's estate. Men such as Samuel and Edward Cunard, too, had other advantages. Because they had direct access to the corridors of male power at the Colonial Office, they had insider knowledge of the risks involved in attempting to retain an Island estate and, indeed, a hand in formulating policy. Samuel Cunard had been told privately that the Colonial Office intended to stop protecting landlords from Island legislation and was advised to "make whatever terms you can."[80] No doubt, man-to-man advice of this sort figured into Edward and William Cunard's subsequent decisions to sell their Prince Edward Island estate.

There were other significant differences between Charlotte's circumstances and those of the Cunards, as a result of the gendering of opportunities for using cash to generate an income. Many of the men who testified at the 1875 commission on the returns available from lending money were politicians, businessmen, or lawyers who had an active hand in shaping the environment that determined whether these investments would prove profitable. As well, they had inside knowledge of the investment world gained from filling roles that were reserved for males. Shifting investment from land to more liquid property was likely more attractive to business-oriented male proprietors such as the Cunards than to women such as Charlotte Sulivan. On her death in 1911, the majority of her assets, other than those in real property, were investments in Consols, British government annuities that provided a safe but modest return.[81] Given that Prince Edward Island's offer would provide her with the equivalent of her annual rentals only if she could benefit from relatively risky investment opportunities, her gender may well have factored into her decision, as well as that of other proprietors. As of 1874, none of the Island's women proprietors were among those who had agreed to sell their estates to the Island government.[82]

Events following Charlotte's decision not to sell her estate ultimately drew her into a central role in the defence of landlordism on Prince Edward Island. It is not clear whether the Island officials who offered her $87,500 for her estate thought they were making an attractive offer. The sum works out to 5 shillings sterling per acre, the maximum the government could offer under land purchase legislation enacted in 1853. Subsequently the government raised this ceiling and successfully negotiated purchases from proprietors resident on the Island who had not been included in the first round of offers in 1867.[83] Making offers that landlords rejected, however, did not necessarily represent a failure of the Island government's political strategy for resolving the land question. It could then blame proprietor intransigence for any impasse and appeal to the imperial government for support in forcing the landlords to relinquish their holdings. In January 1868 the government did just that, asking for Colonial Office support for legislation to compel proprietors to sell their estates. The request noted that "every effort has been exhausted to obtain the desired result by voluntary agreement with the remaining proprietors" and provided as evidence the offers recently rejected by Robert Bruce Stewart and proprietors resident in Britain.[84] The government acknowledged that in some cases proprietors had said that they would sell at a price higher than the 5 shillings sterling per acre the government offered.

The official response of the Colonial Office indicated that the imperial government was not persuaded by the Island government's arguments.[85] Behind the scenes, however, officials at the Colonial Office were coming to accept the necessity of a legislative resolution of the land question.[86] The following year the Island government pressed again for compulsory land purchase legislation, but its initiative was soon overtaken by other events, as the imperial government chose to link resolution of the land question with the Confederation issue. The Island had remained outside the Dominion of Canada, created in 1867 by a confederation of some of the British North American colonies, but the imperial government did not see this as a viable option for the long term. Given that it was possible that Prince Edward Island might soon join Canada and that the Colonial Office was doing its best to encourage this move, the colonial secretary suggested that it would be inappropriate for London to make policy decisions that might better be left to federal Canadian politicians.[87] The queries and responses of the late 1860s concerning compulsory land purchase legislation produced, in time, the understandings among officials in Charlottetown, London, and Ottawa, the Canadian capital, that facilitated passage of compulsory purchase legislation in 1875, after the Island had become a Canadian province. By deferring resolution of the land question, London was of course increasing its pressure on Prince Edward Island to join the Dominion. As well, the delay meant that it would be Canadian politicians in Ottawa, rather than the Colonial Office in London, which would bear the responsibility for vetting the Island legislation that brought landlordism to a close.

Landlords, such as Charlotte Sulivan, Georgiana Fane, and her first cousin, Lord Melville, who chose not to sell in the late 1860s and early 1870s, faced a rapidly changing context. Legislative initiatives on the Island threatened to undercut the value of their estates and, ultimately, separate them from their holdings altogether. As well, the imperial government was proving increasingly unwilling to defend landlord interests in Ireland and in the colonies. Added to these problems were the structural and constitutional changes brought by Prince Edward Island's reluctant entry into Confederation on 1 July 1873, putting another layer of government between the imperial centre and events in the Island. Landlords, though, continued to respond to colonial legislation that challenged their interests as they always had, by appealing to the Colonial Office for protection. On the Island, Georgiana Fane's ally, Robert Bruce Stewart, assumed the central role in drafting individual and collective petitions to the Colonial Office in the late 1860s and early 1870s to oppose Island legislation and in rallying landlords and land agents in the colony to protect landlord interests.[88] He and his father and uncle before him had been leaders in the collective defence of landlordism for four decades. In Britain, though, there was little continuity in landlord leadership in the Confederation period. The two elder Stewarts had provided effective leadership from their Bloomsbury residence in the 1830s and 1840s.[89] Samuel Cunard and Sir George Seymour subsequently became central players in the defence of landlord interests through the mid-century.[90] After Cunard's death in 1865, Laurence Sulivan's in 1866, and Seymour's in 1870,[91] Charlotte Sulivan might have been the most likely person to step into the breach. She possessed the largest estate of any of the non-resident proprietors, had recently been to the Island, and was knowledgeable concerning the situation there. She held her father's papers documenting a century of Sulivan involvement in the Island's land question. And she lived on the outskirts of London, close to the Colonial Office.

Charlotte joined in proprietor protests against the tenants' compensation legislation in the early 1870s, citing the similar protest by Georgiana Fane, but she did not become the leading British player in landlord opposition until after the death of Lady Georgiana in December 1874.[92] Perhaps this delay reflected Georgiana's longer history as an Island proprietor; she acquired her property nearly a decade before Charlotte did. Georgiana was also more than twenty years older than Charlotte and senior, as well, in rank and status, although Charlotte did not lack in wealth and connections. These factors, coupled with Georgiana's forceful personality, ensured that she would be at the forefront of landlord protests to the Colonial Office. It would seem, too, that Charlotte's travelling sometimes distracted her from paying close attention to Island affairs. For good reason, her will included a clause specifying where she should be buried "if I shall happen to die in Great Britain or Ireland."[93] In June of 1869 Georgiana noted, in one of her many letters to the Colonial Office to protest the evil intentions of the Island legislature, that Charlotte Sulivan might not have heard of the latest "injustice" as "she is I believe at present in Italy."[94] Later, during the final phase of the land question, Charlotte wrote from Algiers to object to the compulsory sale of her lands.[95] On another occasion, though writing from Broom House, she used Montreal stationery.[96]

Charlotte was not as persistent as Georgiana in informing the Colonial Office of her opposition to the Island's legislative challenges to landlordism, but she wrote cogent letters to the Colonial Office asking that royal assent be withheld from legislation prejudicial to landlord interests, signed numerous landlord petitions, and authorized her land agent to sign landlord petitions on her behalf. In her own letters to the Colonial Office, Charlotte drew on her understanding of imperial policy in the past and her personal knowledge of the Island. As well, she spoke of herself as "a large landowner" who, she believed, had been promised security in her property in exchange for the concessions her father had made in the 1860s concerning arrears.[97] In general, Charlotte's letters were much more temperate than Georgiana Fane's or those of Georgiana's first cousin, Lord Melville, who, in common with other proprietors, condemned Island politicians as knaves and tried to raise the alarm at what they saw as the rise of socialist and communist principles on the Island. Charlotte also contributed her name to petitions that sought to damn land reform initiatives on the Island by suggesting they had the same ideological base as the Paris Commune.[98]

Charlotte Sulivan's refusal to sell her estate and her defence of landlord interests made her an object of attack on the Island. Indeed, in the years after her visit, she came to feature in an evolving popular narrative concerning the evils of landlordism. In arguing against proprietorial appeals to the Colonial Office to stop the tenant compensation legislation of the early 1870s, the Executive Council offered a long recital of the history of the land question that concluded with a rhetorical question concerning who most deserved legal protection. Was it "the toiling men and women whose constancy and courage have claimed her Majesty's Island of Prince Edward from its primeval forests, and converted it into fertile cornfields and smiling meadows" or "the proprietor, living … in luxury on the banks of the Thames"?[99] The men in the Colonial Office came to share this view of the "diehard" landlords. When one of the officials at the Colonial Office considered the issue of compulsory land sales in the late 1860s, he noted that some of the proprietors were "idle non-residents who merely cumber the Earth and deserve little money."[100] The many male proprietors who served the public in Parliament, the civil service, or the business world could not be included in this group, but it was almost inevitable that women proprietors, who were excluded from these male roles, would be seen as idlers, especially if, as spinsters, they were neither raising children nor providing support to an active male.

Female proprietors, it seemed, had difficulty gaining the respectful attention of officials at the Colonial Office. Georgiana Fane and Charlotte Sulivan were both skilled writers who knew how to present their positions effectively. Both had been to the Island and possessed extensive papers concerning the history of the land question. And both had powerful friends in and out of government. The official Colonial Office replies to their appeals on various Island issues are, understandably, prompt and civil. They were not women to be trifled with. Yet the private exchanges within the Colonial Office reveal a different reaction to their appeals. Georgiana Fane was described as not convincible, and instructions were left to answer her letters as briefly as possible, with enough to "keep her quiet for a time" but not enough to encourage her to use her ample leisure time to write more.[101] An internal memo concerning proprietors' resistance to imperial and colonial pressure to sell their estates noted that some refused to do so because they were "obstinate" or "half crazy."[102] The latter label was probably meant for Georgiana rather than Charlotte, although Charlotte too was considered one of the "diehard" landlords – as were all who decided not to sell except on their terms. Charlotte could be described as inflexible, but there is a gendered aspect to the internal male correspondence with its dismissive assessments of these women, in keeping with the comment on Lady Westmorland's Island report that it was "one of the cleverest ever written by a woman."

For a variety of reasons, proprietors by the early 1870s could no longer permanently block tenant compensation and compulsory land purchase legislation by appealing to the Colonial Office to withhold royal assent. The political context for defending landlordism had changed; the best that proprietors could hope for in the political arena was modifications that would reduce the negative effect of the legislation. The outcome of an appeal to the courts, however, had yet to be tested. Powerful political leaders on both sides of the Atlantic might have decided to sacrifice proprietors' interests in order to resolve the land question on Prince Edward Island and smooth the way for the Island's entry into Confederation, but it did not necessarily follow that the courts would agree. It was in this forum that Charlotte Sulivan assumed a leadership role in the landlords' final struggles to assert their property rights.

In 1875 Governor General Lord Dufferin, a landlord in Ireland, reluctantly gave royal assent to the Island's Land Purchase Act, enabling the Island government to compel proprietors to sell their estates. The legislation provided for a three-member Land Commission to determine the price the government would pay for expropriated land. The commission was chaired by Hugh Culling Eardley Childers, a British politician, friend of Lord Dufferin's, and his appointee.[103] The Prince Edward Island government appointed the second commissioner, and each proprietor chose a third commissioner to decide his or her case. Many of the proprietors, including Charlotte Sulivan and Georgiana Fane's heir, Ponsonby, who had inherited her property when she died in December 1874, agreed to select Nova Scotia lawyer Robert Haliburton, who had been counsel for the proprietors at the 1860 Land Commission.[104] The commissioners held hearings in August 1875 in Charlottetown and released their decisions, called "awards," for the first nine estates, Charlotte Sulivan's and Ponsonby Fane's among them, in early September. By the terms of the award, Charlotte was to receive $81,500 for her estate, $6,000 less than she had been offered in 1867.[105] She, Ponsonby Fane, and Robert Bruce Stewart joined in challenging these awards in the Supreme Court of Prince Edward Island. The applicants failed to persuade the court to rule that the Land Purchase Act was unconstitutional, but they succeeded in obtaining a unanimous judgment striking down the awards.[106]

Island papers expressed shock at this outcome, in part because the Land Purchase Act had been carefully crafted to minimize opportunities for legal challenge. As well as delaying resolution of the land question, the Supreme Court's decision raised the question of whether the province would be willing to undertake the potentially costly task of redoing the work of the Land Commission. There was suggestion in the press that perhaps the Island government's best response would be to return to the tactic of attempting voluntary purchase of proprietors' holdings.[107] The government, though, chose to appeal the decision to the newly established Supreme Court of Canada. In the time between the Island court decision and the hearing in Ottawa, Robert Bruce Stewart and Ponsonby Fane negotiated out-of-court settlements with the province. Had Georgiana Fane been alive for the Land Commission proceedings, she likely would have joined Charlotte Sulivan in the final defence of landlords' rights in the Supreme Court of Canada, but Ponsonby Fane, as he said to his friend, Lord Dufferin, was "sorely in want of the money." He would not have challenged the award even in the Island court, but his agent and lawyer had done so without his authorization.[108] In the event, Charlotte stood alone to contest the constitutionality of the Land Purchase Act of 1875 and the validity of the commissioners' awards under the act.

The Supreme Court of Canada rejected Charlotte Sulivan's challenge to the expropriation of her estate. In making its decision, the court dealt with arcane legal issues such as the structure and authority of the courts in Prince Edward Island, the division of powers between the federal government and the provinces, and the scope of judicial review of the decisions of a tribunal created by statute to perform a specific function. It considered these issues, though, in the context of a much larger policy question: whether concerns about the public good justified an admitted interference with private rights. Noting the difficulties experienced for many years in collecting rents in the province and noting, as well, that the proprietors would receive compensation for the lands, Chief Justice William Richards concluded that, although the Land Purchase Act, 1875, might work "harshly," it was aimed at settling a "question of great moment to the community" and could not be judged in the same way as "ordinary legislation." Like the recent settling of the land question in Ireland and the earlier conversion of seigneurial tenure in Lower Canada, the purchase of the proprietors' estates was necessary to ensure the peace and prosperity of the population at large. Having upheld the legislation, the Supreme Court also upheld the awards made in individual cases. It pointed to the privative clause in the Land Purchase Act barring any legal challenge to the Land Commission's awards. This clause meant what it said: there could be no appeal to the courts against the awards of the commission.[109] In short, the defence of landlordism was over, unless Charlotte Sulivan appealed to the Judicial Committee of the imperial Privy Council. Her counsel filed for leave to appeal, but she ultimately chose not to contest the Supreme Court decision.[110]

6

Differences That Matter

Anne and Jane Saunders, Georgiana Fane, and Charlotte Sulivan had much in common as members of elite society in nineteenth-century Britain, enjoying personal wealth and family and social connections to politically powerful men. All shared the experience of being Island landlords, but this experience differed for each of them, as did their responses to the challenges and opportunities of owning large estates in a small British colony. These differences, and ultimately the place of these women in the evolving history of landlordism in Prince Edward Island, were shaped by many factors, including the timing of their assumption of ownership and the particularities of their private lives.

Anne and Jane Saunders appear to have become aware of their Island inheritance around the time of their marriages in 1796 and 1800 respectively. For many Island proprietors, this was a period of crisis, as political developments on the Island and changes in imperial policy raised questions about the security of landlords' titles and about the costs of maintaining colonial estates. Many Island landlords chose to sell their properties rather than assume the risks of managing them, but the Melvilles and the Westmorlands were not among these proprietors. Instead, they paid the quit rents owing on their shares of Lots 29 and 53 and invested in the development of the estate, hiring land agents to manage the properties and providing resources to construct infrastructure and assist new settlers. Anne and Robert Dundas's approach to the management of their Island estate paralleled that of the family of their fellow Scot and friend, the fifth Earl of Selkirk, who became a major Island landlord in this period. Both the Melvilles and the Selkirks assumed that estates required active management and capital investments, and that long leases and security of tenure were important facets of effective estate development. Anne and Robert thus came to participate in a new period of Island landlordism in the early nineteenth century marked by significant shifts in the ownership and management of estates and as well by sustained population growth.

An important choice that affected Anne's estates was her decision to marry Robert Dundas, as his character and their relationship shaped the handling of her Island inheritance. Crucially, both viewed the Island lands that Anne brought into the marriage as assets of their partnership, and the couple worked together to achieve constructive, purposeful management of their property and the debts that Robert inherited. Despite their shared belief in the prudent use of property and their strong managerial skills, events on their Island estates did not unfold as they wished. The investments they made to develop Lots 29 and 53 appear primarily to have benefited the land agents they appointed to act on their behalf, and the estates were a drain on their resources.

Jane Saunders's marriage to the tenth Lord Westmorland was never a true partnership, and ultimately it failed altogether. Lord Westmorland communicated with Robert Dundas, his political ally as well as his brother-in-law, on decisions concerning the management of the Island properties, and for the most part they adopted similar strategies, but residents on Jane's portions of Lots 29 and 53 had different experiences of landlordism from those on the portions allocated as Anne's share. Tensions and conflicts within the Westmorland family undermined the security of tenure that the tenants thought they had gained by signing leases offered by Lord Westmorland's land agent. The powers of attorney granted by Lord Westmorland and Robert Dundas to their land agents began with recitals recognizing that they held their shares in Lots 29 and 53 in right of their respective wives and restricted the agents to granting leases for such terms as did not exceed the husband's interest.[1] Without access to the wills whereby Jane and Anne had inherited the property and the marriage settlements defining their husbands' rights in their wives' inheritances, however, land agents could not know what terms they could legally grant. Lord Westmorland, who held only a life interest in his wife's Island estates, could not authorize any leases for a term longer than his own lifetime, yet his agent granted terms of 999 years. Tenants with these leases faced the possibility of Georgiana Fane taking legal action to evict them, despite their holding their farms under leases issued by agents acting for her father and brother, unless they signed new leases recognizing her as their landlord. Security of tenure on Prince Edward Island was thus subject to the intricacies of English property law and the ways in which elite families employed the law's arcane doctrines to provide for the transmission of property from generation to generation, preferably from one male heir to the next.

Jane's separation from her husband isolated her from her children, her sister, and her social networks, and in this context, her ownership of an Island estate came to mean something quite different for her from what it meant for her sister. In Anne's case, the estate was a vexatious managerial problem, a liability that was unlikely ever to become an asset, and at best a landscape for dreams of escape from the problems of Britain. Jane, however, came to regard her colonial estate as an asset. She travelled to the Island, living there for nearly a year, and directly assumed the role of lady bountiful with her tenants and other Island residents. As Lady Westmorland, wife of the tenth earl, she had formal rank and status above that of most Island landlords and even above that of most of the men who received appointments as lieutenant-governors of the Island. Her marriage to Lord Westmorland had put her at the centre of Britain's political and social elite, but the subsequent separation left her in the uncomfortable position of a wife who was excluded from social functions hosted or attended by her husband. In the ten months that she spent on Prince Edward Island, Jane was free to claim the status of the wife of the Earl of Westmorland without having to worry about the social constraints of her ambiguous position. Her Island properties, having come to her from her great-uncle and her father, were important to her as a source of prestige independent of her husband. From her rented house on Queen Street in Charlottetown, Jane played the role of the grand lady, enlivening the social functions at Government House, visiting her tenants, dispensing charity, and receiving addresses of thanks from a grateful public. When tenants raised their concerns about the fundamentals of the landlord-tenant relationship, however, she evaded any responsibility to act by alluding to her helplessness as a married woman, subject to the dictates of her husband.

In some ways, Jane's responses to the opportunities of owning an Island estate prefigured those of Georgiana Fane and Charlotte

Sulivan, neither of whom chose to marry. Both Georgiana and Charlotte acquired ownership of their Island estates in a period when increased demand for land created more opportunities for proprietors to lease or sell to their advantage. With Britain's grant of responsible government to the Island in 1851, however, land policy on the Island would come to be determined by the men who controlled the Island legislature, rather than the men of the Colonial Office in London, to whom Georgiana and Charlotte addressed their petitions. Georgiana, as had her mother two decades earlier, played the grand lady when she visited the Island, being entertained at Government House and doing good works by providing support for a church, a public hall, a bridge, and a wharf. Island maps and road signs attest to her lasting reputation for benevolence. A road and a settlement are called Lady Fane, to recognize the proprietor who is said to have devoted all her rents to the improvement of Lot 29.[2] It may have helped Georgiana's reputation that it was her heir, Ponsonby Fane, rather than she, who resisted the Island government's final resolution of the land question. In testimony before the 1875 Land Commission, Robert Bruce Stewart described the late Lady Georgiana Fane as one of the "kindest, noblest, and best women that ever lived."[3] It appears that no one was willing to speak ill of the dead to contradict his claim. Georgiana, had she been alive, might have had the grace to demur at the use of the superlative, but she would have not have disputed any claims that she was a diligent and just landlord.

Charlotte, too, visited Prince Edward Island and directly managed her estate there, as she did her properties in Britain. While she was on the Island, she enjoyed celebrity status as the owner of the largest Island estate remaining in the hands of a non-resident proprietor. In the context of heightened pressure on proprietors to sell their land to their tenants or to the Island government, and with the government seeking imperial approval for compulsory sale legislation, Charlotte's celebrity status, though, was of a different sort from that of Lady Westmorland and Lady Georgiana Fane. Although she inherited much more land than the Saunders sisters or Georgiana Fane, the Sulivan record as landlords is not honoured in Island place names.

For Jane, Georgiana, and Charlotte, owning Island estates provided the opportunity for purposeful travel. Clearly, all three were intrepid travellers. Lady Westmorland's peregrinations took her to Europe as well as the United States and British North America, and Georgiana Fane travelled elsewhere in North America when she came to inspect her Island properties. Charlotte Sulivan's travels included parts of North America, Europe, and North Africa.[4] Their interest in travel was consistent with choices made by other women of their class background at this time. No doubt all three of these women wished to see their Island properties and evaluate their potential for themselves, but possession of a colonial estate added a solid business justification for travels that appealed to them for other reasons as well.[5]

All four of the lady landlords profiled here were intelligent and thoughtful women who followed and participated in debate on the political and social questions of the day. Jane was the first of them, however, to engage directly with the politics of the Island land question. She arrived on Prince Edward Island in October 1839 during a period of crisis in landlord-tenant relations and in the administration of the lieutenant-governor, Charles FitzRoy, who had to manage an Island assembly dominated by an Escheat majority. Jane wrote directly to the Colonial Office to convey her analysis of the situation on the Island at the time of her visit and, it seems, harmed her relations with FitzRoy by making her own investigation into the situation and then critiquing his policies.

The Escheat movement failed to eliminate landlordism in the colony in the 1840s. Nonetheless, its activities ushered in a period during which landlords increasingly found themselves responding to existential challenges. As Island governments employed various strategies to limit proprietorial power and to encourage proprietors to sell their Island estates, Georgiana and Charlotte assumed prominent roles in the defence of landlords' interests. To a limited extent, they were effective in their political interventions, although their opportunities for shaping policy were constrained because, as women, they had limited access to some of the crucial forums for political discussion and deal-making. Certainly, Georgiana and Charlotte were able to highlight and frame issues by letter and petition and to command the attention of imperial and colonial officials. As well, they elicited respectful responses, at least in the correspondence that they actually saw. Being colonial landlords did not, however, give them the political power necessary to protect their interests. In this, women landlords were not, of course, alone; they simply bore an additional disadvantage.

The Supreme Court of Canada's rejection of Charlotte Sulivan's arguments provided a formal conclusion to the final defence of landlords' interests, ending the century-long struggle over land ownership on Prince Edward Island. A system of land distribution that began with imperial rewards for prominent men ended with a single woman challenging the Island government in the Colonial Office, the London *Times*, and the highest judicial forum in the new Canadian federation. That women had assumed, over time, a significant profile among Island landlords had much to do with the vicissitudes of marriage and succession, as well as with laws that recognized that widowed and unmarried women had the legal capacity to own and manage property, and even that married women could retain some rights in property they brought to the marriage if these rights were preserved for them through a marriage settlement. The chance circumstances of family formation, procreation, and inheritance, though, do not entirely explain the high proportion of women among the landlords whose lands were expropriated under the Land Purchase Act, 1875, or women's prominent role in the concluding struggle to maintain landlordism. A variety of forces, including women's limited access to informal sources of information about investment possibilities and government policy and their exclusion from formal roles in business and government, created gender-based differences in their economic and social opportunities and in the decisions that women and men made.

In its ruling in Charlotte Sulivan's case, the Supreme Court in Ottawa validated the often-articulated claim of tenants and their supporters that large proprietorial estates threatened the peace and prosperity of the Island. In the early days of the colony, the opponents of landlordism had grounded their demands for an escheat of the proprietors' grants in a specific critique of the legitimacy of proprietors' titles, arguing that the landlords had forfeited their rights because of their failure to meet settlement and quit rent conditions. This claim was linked to a much broader critique, which contrasted the rights of the actual settler, whose work had made the land valuable, with the claims of non-resident landlords who lived in idle luxury in their grand establishments in the imperial centre, where they could easily influence the colonial administrators to protect them against the efforts of honest Islanders who merely sought ownership of what was justly theirs. The image of the absentee landlord as a parasite or drone lying on a gilded couch resonated with tenants on the Island, and it was invoked by journalists, politicians, witnesses before the 1860 Land Commission, and counsel for the Island government in their arguments before the 1875 Land Commission, whose decisions were upheld by the Supreme Court of Canada after being set aside by the Island Supreme Court.

Derogatory characterizations of landlords were as old as the land struggle, and as women acquired a greater profile among proprietors, some of these charges became more difficult to refute. From an Island perspective, titled landlords who had never visited the Island could easily be pilloried as idle members of a distant aristocracy, sustained in their privileged existence by the labour of those they considered their inferiors. But in a British context the charge was less effective. Men such as the tenth Earl of Westmorland or the second Lord Melville were active servants of the Crown who used their landed wealth to sustain their contribution to managing the affairs of the state. This defence of the value of holders of landed wealth was less apt once these estates passed into the hands of widows or unmarried daughters, who were excluded from assuming the public roles at home that might have provided some justification for their existence. The logic of changing constitutional arrangements – responsible government for Prince Edward Island in 1851 and then the Island joining Confederation in 1873 – created pressure within the Colonial Office to abandon landlords to the mercies of the Island legislature. It became easier for the Colonial Office to act in accordance with this logic when the landlords to be abandoned were not well-connected and powerful men such as Lord Westmorland, Laurence Sulivan, or Samuel Cunard.

The Land Purchase Act, 1875, under which the provincial government acquired the estates of the remaining proprietors, applied to all estates of over 500 acres, although proprietors could retain up to 1,000 acres if they actually occupied the land. Non-resident proprietors, of course, could not retain anything. Women owned at least twenty-four of the fifty-seven estates acquired under the Land Purchase Act, individually, as co-owners with other women and men, or as the guardian for children. These figures do not include Georgiana Fane's property on Lots 29 and 53, which her nephew, Ponsonby Fane, inherited on her death in 1874. Excluded as well is a 4,192-acre estate owned by Mrs W. Sydney Smith, née Anne Winsloe, not purchased by the government until 1895.[6] Including Mrs Smith, at least thirty-five females received compensation as owners or co-owners of Island properties. Excluding land owned by a married couple or co-owned with a male, women owned twenty-eight per cent of the roughly one-third of a million acres that the government expropriated after passage of the 1875 act, and they received just under one-quarter of the money paid in compensation (see appendix).

The commissioners appointed to determine the compensation due to the proprietors received little guidance from the Land Purchase Act on the specifics of their task. According to the act, proprietors were to receive "a fair indemnity or equivalent for the value of [their] interest and no more," taking into consideration the price the government had previously paid to proprietors who had sold voluntarily and without allowing any extra compensation because the sale was compulsory rather than voluntary. The act also instructed the commissioners to consider the quality of the land in making their estimate of its value, as well as the number of acres unoccupied or occupied by squatters; the contractual rent for leased land; net returns from rent actually paid, after deducting the expenses of collection; the extent of arrears and likelihood of their collection; and whether the proprietors had complied with the settlement and quit rent conditions of the original grants. The latter issue had been regularly raised by tenants' advocates as justification for limiting proprietors' compensation for surrendering their estates; it was in the legislation at the insistence of Louis Davies, leader of the Island Reformers, who was one of the lawyers representing the Island government at the Land Commission hearings.[7]

Much of the evidence at the hearings concerned how much land the proprietors had lost to squatters, who through long possession unchallenged by the landlord had acquired title to the land by adverse possession. The lawyers for the Island government also introduced evidence that the landlords' returns from leased land were minimal, given the extent of the arrears and the high costs of collecting rents. The lawyers for the proprietors countered with arguments that the squatters could not prove their right to the land and that rent arrears had accumulated, not because tenants were unable to pay, but because politicians had encouraged tenants to withhold their rent and proprietors had been unwilling to press for payment. The evidence to support these claims, however, was equivocal.[8]

In Charlotte Sulivan's case, the second heard by the commission, her lawyers asked for a total of $239,185 for her estate, including

$36,304 for arrears owing, the value of the rents capitalized at five per cent, and $2.43 per acre for the unleased land. The government lawyers argued for a much lower figure, citing the poor quality of much of the unleased land, the extent of land held by squatters, who could not be evicted except at greater cost than the land was worth, and the prices paid for comparable land under voluntary sales. Witnesses for the government, noting that the best land on Lot 16 had already been sold, placed little value on what remained, with $1.25 per acre being the top estimate for the best land on the other three lots.[9]

George W. DeBlois, who had been the Sulivan agent since 1860 at an annual salary of £200 sterling plus expenses, testified that he "could easily collect by harsh measures; but when we use harsh measures, we are abused by everyone." DeBlois also said that he had attempted to collect back rents by using distraint proceedings to seize tenants' goods, such as cattle or crops, but a great many of the tenants had nothing to seize. In his assessment, the farms were worth "infinitely more than the rent due upon them." He testified that the proprietor could recover back rent and expenses by evicting a tenant for non-payment of rent and regaining possession of the leasehold with the improvements.[10] Louis Davies, arguing for the Island government, responded by invoking rhetoric refined in the long struggle against the proprietary system, telling the commissioners that DeBlois's description of his estate management "grated on my ears and heart ... Mr. De Blois says that if he finds a farm upon which a poor widow lives who is unable to pay, he does not press her for the rent. He allows the arrears to accumulate. Year by year he sees the young children growing up. He sees them expending their labour on the farm, and he stands waiting by until that labour has made the farm worth the arrears, and then he comes down ... It is a terrible picture to see [the widow and children] by their hard labour gradually improving the farm, with the agent all the while watching for his opportunity to pounce upon it."[11]

Despite the many things that the Land Purchase Act directed the commissioners to consider, their award simply stated the total, $81,500, to which Charlotte was entitled. It did not specify how many acres were included in calculating the compensation, whether it included any sum for arrears, or how it was apportioned between leased land and unleased land. Nor did the award state whether the commissioners had made deductions for land lost to squatters or for the proprietor's failure to comply with the terms of the original grants. Robert Haliburton, Charlotte's appointee on the commission, did not sign the award, but that did not affect its validity. The provincial government's report on land acquired under the Land Purchase Act gave $1.29 per acre as the price per acre that the government paid for Charlotte's estate, much less than she had demanded but more than Islanders' estimates of the value of her best land.[12] Of the ten awards made while Governor General Lord Dufferin's friend Hugh C.E. Childers chaired the Land Commission, only Robert Bruce Stewart received less per acre – $1.14. Of all the estates purchased between 1875 and 1880, only one other proprietor, holding about 2,200 acres, received less per acre (see appendix).

Childers chaired the hearings for the larger estates, including Ponsonby Fane's. The rent rolls listed 7,765 acres under lease on the Fane half of Lot 29 but only 888 acres under lease on Lot 53. Total arrears on the two lots were $5,482. DeBlois, agent for Georgiana Fane since 1868, testified that, but for her leniency and kindness, the arrears could have been reduced by taking legal action against the tenants. Louis Davies, for the government, called several witnesses who testified that most of Lot 53 and some of Lot 29 had been lost to the proprietor through adverse possession. The commissioners' award for the Fane estate, as for the others, simply stated the total compensation payable. Ponsonby Fane was awarded $21,200 for his share of Lots 29 and 53. Lord Melville was awarded $34,000 for what should have been roughly the same quantity of land; it appears that his land agent, Francis L. Haszard, was able to persuade the commissioners that more of the estate was under lease and less had been lost to squatters.[13]

In the final compulsory sale of their estates, as in their attempts to profit from leasing them, what proprietors obtained depended in large part on how well the estates had been managed, and that in turn depended on the skill and honesty of their land agents. Many agents did quite well out of the proprietorial system – some better than the landlords who employed them. In 1895, reform politician Benjamin Davies, Louis's father, recounting the history of the Escheat movement, reported as "uncontradicted" the claim that land agents, lawyers, and bailiffs consumed three-quarters of the rent paid by the tenants, leaving only one-quarter for the proprietors.[14] Using the local knowledge and capital that they acquired as land agents, some became proprietors themselves. Subsequent sales of these estates were on terms that were particularly advantageous to their owners. Between 1868 and 1871 the Prince Edward Island government acquired five estates totalling almost 60,000 acres, purchased at an average price of $2.07 per acre, from men who had been land agents before becoming proprietors; three of them were also prominent Island politicians.[15]

Men as well as women were vulnerable to being taken advantage of by their agents, and some women, as well as some men, avoided the costs of employing agents by managing their estates themselves. Eliza Cundall, for example, a spinster whose estate was among those subject to compulsory sale, had managed her 1,455 acres without an agent, although her brother, also a proprietor, spoke for her before the 1875 Land Commission.[16] Women, however, were precluded by custom and law from the opportunities that land agents, lawyers, and politicians could exploit to ensure that they obtained maximum returns from tenants, proprietors, and the government.

Given the quite different circumstances of single and married women and the quite different opportunities for resident and non-resident proprietors, it is not possible to assess whether female proprietors managed their estates differently from male proprietors. Judging from the treatment of women landlords in the Island press, though, it seems that women were expected to act differently. Some of the pressure on Charlotte Sulivan to enhance her reputation as a philanthropist by selling her estate at a low price was surely gendered. Her response must have been disappointing. As a single woman with considerable experience in managing property, she made her own assessment of whether her tenants could meet their legal obligations and based her decisions about what to do with her estate on what returns she might reasonably expect from various kinds of assets. Some of those returns she might dedicate to charitable purposes of her choosing, but she would not have based a business decision on specious claims about an obligation to be charitable. A quarter of a century earlier Lady Westmorland had responded more magnanimously to appeals to act charitably toward her tenants, but her situation was different from Charlotte Sulivan's.

In writing to the Colonial Office, Georgiana Fane blamed her problems with rent collection on the unprincipled agitation of the Island politicians who hoped to force the proprietors to sell for prices well below the value of the land. During the proprietors' campaign against legislation requiring landlords to compensate tenants for the value of improvements that tenants had made to their leaseholds, she complained that the Island legislature was dominated by tenants' representatives and that Island legislation made it difficult for landlords to collect their rent. She asserted that her tenants could not complain of harsh treatment and protested that she "should not be subjected to a confiscation of my property without even knowing what I have done to deserve it."[17] The complaint was repeated frequently at the 1875 Land Commission hearings, as the commissioners oversaw the dismantling of a system of land distribution that had been at the centre of Island politics from the creation of the colony. Women did not constitute the majority of landholders whose estates were expropriated under the Land Purchase Act. They did, however, form a significant minority, in large part because no female proprietors voluntarily sold their estates to the government in the decades between 1853, when the Island legislature first passed legislation to facilitate the purchase of proprietorial estates, and 1873, when Confederation cleared the way for compulsory sale legislation.

The initial distribution of Island land in large lots implemented a decision of the imperial authorities for the benefit of those men whom the Crown wished to reward for their contribution to the military effort in British North America. The Escheat movement contested the validity of the proprietors' titles in order to secure a more egalitarian distribution of land. After responsible government gave more power to the elected Island assembly and then Confederation transferred supervisory authority for Island legislation from the imperial government to the governor general in Ottawa, the imperial authorities were no longer willing to protect Island proprietors, female or male, from reform of a land distribution system that had proved unacceptable to the new polities which emerged from the territories that Britain acquired in 1763. Not surprisingly, democratic land reform was of most benefit to the men who promoted it.

During the century following the distribution of the spoils of the Seven Years War, British women had come to participate directly in the development of Prince Edward Island, through their ownership and management of Island estates and through their attempts to ensure that Island law and policy supported their interests as landlords. Empire transformed the lives of British women in ways that mirrored and that differed from how it transformed the lives of men. For the four women that are the focus of this book, the incorporation of Prince Edward Island within the British imperial sphere broadened the possibilities available for them to construct meaningful and interesting lives. The final success of the hard-fought struggle for land reform on the Island, which came with passage of the Land Purchase Act of 1875 and the expropriation of proprietorial estates, marked the closure of some of the varied opportunities that colonial estate ownership had once provided for elite British women such as Anne and Jane Saunders, Georgiana Fane, and Charlotte Sulivan.

Proprietors' Estates Purchased by the Prince Edward Island Government, 1875–1880

	Estate	Acres	Arrears due to prop. ($)	Gross annual rental under leases ($)	Amount paid to prop. by gov't[1] ($)	Price per acre paid to prop. ($)	Average price per acre paid by tenants to gov't ($)
1	Bellin, Agnes C. and Robert[2]	740	–	–	2,300	3.10	1.33
2	Bourke, J.R.	3,114	2,066	536	5,402	1.73	1.33
3	Brenan	1,378.5	–	–	5,878	4.27	1.65
4	Crookes, Mary and Frances	2,131.75	712	389	5,500	2.58	1.80
5	Cumberland, Col., and wife	6,216.5	4,624	1,920	30,900	5.13	2.66
6	Cundall, Henry J.	1,886.5	456	335	5,149	2.73	2.17
7	Cundall, H.J., guardian of four children of Alfred Winsloe[3]	7,590	248	1,422	22,300	2.93	2.02
8	Cundall, Mary Eliza	1,455	2,086	266	4,450	3.05	2.07
9	Cundall, Wm	2,844	1,188	530	9,200	3.23	2.12
10	Cunningham	2,188	–	–	2,055	0.94	–
11	Douse, Arabella	410.5	–	–	1,437	3.50	1.88
12	Douse, Esther	2,039.5	414	544	7,525	3.68	2.16
13	Douse, Henry C.	733.5	–	169	3,010	3.78	3.10
14	Douse, James B.	423	–	–	1,197	2.83	2.35
15	Douse, Jane B.	402	–	–	1,407	3.50	2.20
16	Douse and Strong[4]	809.5	–	–	6,080	7.52	2.14
17	DesBrisay, Theo.	5,200	–	–	16,375	3.14	1.94
18	Earle, Samuel N.	384	–	–	1,383	3.34	2.20
19	Evans, Arthur W.	997.5	–	–	2,954	2.96	2.12
20	Evans, Sydney T. and Amelia	4,598	927	865	11,452	2.48	1.96

	Estate	Acres	Arrears due to prop. ($)	Gross annual rental under leases ($)	Amount paid to prop. by gov't[1] ($)	Price per acre paid to prop. ($)	Average price per acre paid by tenants to gov't ($)
21	Fane, Spencer Ponsonby	13,000	5,482	1,298	21,200	1.63	1.84
22	Fanning, Maria S.M.	8,469	7,818	1,194	20,200	2.40	1.56
23	Fanning, W.W., and two others[5]	10,000	17,854	1,753	25,250	2.52	1.07
24	Hodgson, Daniel, trustee of Charles Wright	4,736	1,737	1,104	21,700	4.63	2.01
25	Hodgson, Edward J.	1,751	292	343	4,800	2.74	1.93
26	Holland, A.E.C., and wife	4,846	1,556	841	11,734	2.42	1.70
27	Holland, F.F.	615	106	103	1,450	2.36	1.57
28	Irving, P.F., and G.W. DeBlois	928.75	209	136	2,572	2.77	1.52
29	Lawson (Lauton), Anna Maria, and four others[6]	2,131	878	278	4,222	1.98	1.33
30	MacDonald, Helen Jane[7]	1,630	451	249	6,000	2.32	0.95
31	MacDonald, Rev. John A.S.	21,779	–	3,944	38,880	1.78	1.06
32	MacDonald, William C.	10,435	–	–	25,154	–	–
33	MacMillan, Mrs, guardian of Henry, Stanley, and Agnes Winsloe	2,994.5	295	603	10,247	3.42	2.07
34	MacNutt, G.A., trustee of Mrs Stephens	3,382.75	1,066	584	9,239	2.62	1.65
35	McDonnell, John A.	2,400	125	625	7,592	3.16	1.79
36	Melville, Lord	11,309.75	13,702	2,104	34,000	3.26	1.52
37	Montgomery, Sir Graham	5,610	6,021	878	12,400	2.21	1.48
38	Montgomery, James F.	5,678.5	1,028	969	16,900	2.89	1.63
39	Montgomery, Louisa[8]	1,362.5	598	253	4,569	3.35	2.06
40	Palmer, Henry	1,800	–	–	4,952	2.75	1.56
41	Ramsay, A.A., and others	1,763.5	–	–	3,350	1.90	1.41
42	Rennie, Robert (trustee)	10,220	8,485	2,554	33,000	3.22	1.99
43	Stewart, Margaret	3,235.5	713	561	9,241	2.85	1.41
44	Stewart (Gibson), Mary	592	–	–	1,776	3.00	–
45	Stewart, Robert Bruce	66,727	32,103	6,471	76,500	1.14	1.27
46	Sulivan, Charlotte A.	66,937	36,304	7,290	84,107	1.29	1.03

| | | Arrears due to prop. ($) | Gross annual rental under leases ($) | Amount paid to prop. by gov't[1] ($) | Price per acre paid to prop. ($) | Average price per acre paid by tenants to gov't ($) |
Estate	Acres					
47 Thompson, Eliz., and three others[9]	7,140	9,173	1,434	10,700	1.50	1.58
48 Traverse, Mary Ann, and Jane H.[10]	1,246.5	–	–	3,700	–	–
49 Wiggins, Helen Diana, and two others[11]	1,004	304	314	4,890	4.87	2.00
50 Winsloe, John	2,016	–	–	6,328	3.13	–
51 Wright, George	492	–	–	1,476	3.00	2.43
52 Wright, Lemuel	856	–	–	2,568	3.00	–
53 Wright, Thomas, and wife	1,103.5	96	172	3,066	2.78	2.75
54 Yates, A.H., and wife	611	–	83	1,493	2.45	2.02
55 Yeo, estate of the late Hon. James	17,202	13,243	1,895	37,000	2.15	1.06
56 Yeo, estate of, willed to John Inge and others	679	–	–	2,283	3.30	1.62
57 Yeo, estate of, willed to J. Yeo and others	996.5	–	–	3,195	3.20	1.62
Totals	343,222			713,688		

SOURCES: Based on table in PEI, JHA, 1881, Appendix K, with additional information on names of estate owners from PEI, JHA, 1877, Appendix E; MacGowan, *Report of the Proceedings*, 669–9; PEI, JHA, 1879, Appendix F. Table includes estates purchased under the act and smaller estates sold voluntarily.

1 Amounts paid for seven estates exceeded the commissioners' award. Sydney and Amelia Evans, G.A. McNutt (trustee of Mrs Stephens), and Margaret Stewart were allowed interest on the sum awarded because of the delay in perfecting their title of $545, $364, and $741 respectively. William C. MacDonald and Helen J. MacDonald received additional sums for dower interests not considered by the commission. Charlotte Sulivan received an additional $2,607 for rent. James F. Montgomery obtained an order in the Island Supreme Court referring his case back to the commissioners, but he settled with the province for an additional $1,700 for accruing rents and costs. John A.S. Macdonald obtained an order in the Island Supreme Court setting aside the award in his case, but he settled for an additional $4,880 for his costs and interest on the award.

2 Bellin and Traverse estate, below, treated as single estate in table in PEI, JHA, 1881, Appendix K.

3 Children were Amy, Isabel, and Arthur Winsloe and Alice Hyndman.

4 This estate is listed in MacGowan as "William Cundall and others, Trustees of late William Douse."

5 Others were Sylvester Hodges Fanning and Edmund Frederick Augustus Fanning.

6 Others were Margaret G. Lauton, Catherine Lauton, Mary B. Lauton, and Nancy Lauton Clarke.

7 Includes dower rights identified in PEI, *JHA*, 1879, as having been acquired by voluntary purchase in 1878.
8 This estate is listed in MacGowan as "H.J. Cundall, Trustee of Mrs. Montgomery."
9 Others were Edward Selby Smith, Frederick Gordon Thompson, and Gordon Augustus Thompson.
10 Included with Bellin estate in table in PEI, *JHA*, 1881, Appendix K.
11 Others were Caroline M. Wiggins and Flora Townshend Wiggins.

Notes

BL	British Library
CO	Colonial Office
CAS(CRO)	Cumbria Archive Service (Carlisle Record Office)
HA	Hammersmith Archives
HALS	Hertfordshire Archives and Local Studies
LAC	Library and Archives Canada
LMA	London Metropolitan Archives
NA	National Archives (Kew)
NAS	National Archives of Scotland
NLS	National Library of Scotland
NRO	Northamptonshire Record Office
NSCLRC	Nova Scotia Crown Lands Record Centre
OUBL	Oxford University Bodleian Library
PARO	Prince Edward Island Public Archives and Record Office
PRONI	Public Record Office of Northern Ireland
PEI, *JHA*	Prince Edward Island, *Journals of the House of Assembly*
RHP	Register House Plans
SARS	Somerset Archive and Record Service
YPR	York Probate Registry

CHAPTER ONE

1 "Report of the Honourable Joseph Hensley," *Royal Gazette*, Extra, 14 Nov. 1867.

2 Bird, *The Englishwoman in America*, 38–40; Saunders, *The Economic History of the Maritime Provinces*, 103, 105.

3 The island was called Île Saint-Jean at the time of its conquest by the British, who renamed it St John's Island. In 1799 it was renamed Prince Edward Island.

4 Robertson, *The Tenant League of Prince Edward Island*, 10–12.

5 Blakeley, "Cunard, Sir Samuel," 184; PEI, *JHA*, 1875, Appendix E, Commissioner of Public Lands Department, Statement Showing the Number of Acres of Land Purchased by the Government of Prince Edward Island, 15 May 1874. There is a typographical error in the date of the Selkirk purchase. The table shows it as December 1874, rather than 1854, but it is listed in the correct chronological order before another purchase in 1856.

6 Bittermann and McCallum, "Upholding the Land Legislation of a 'Communistic and Socialist Assembly.'"

7 Mackay, "Keppel, Augustus, Viscount Keppel (1725–1786)"; Nelson, "Fraser, Simon (1729–1777)"; Laughton, "Saunders, Sir Charles (c. 1713–1775)."

8 United Kingdom, *Acts of the Privy Council of England, Colonial Series*, 5: 62–4, 13 April 1767.

9 Ibid., 62.

10 Ibid., 56.

11 Bumsted, *Land, Settlement, and Politics on Eighteenth-Century Prince Edward Island*, 29–30.

12 PARO, RG 16, Land Registry Records, Grant of Governor's Island to Torriano, 1 Oct 1774, Liber 1^1/143.

13 Bumsted, *Land, Settlement, and Politics on Eighteenth-Century Prince Edward Island*, 33, 44. The Island's name originated during the French regime. See Rayburn, *Geographical Names of Prince Edward Island*, 57.

14 Holman, "William Townshend"; Bumsted, "Peter Stewart."

15 PARO, RG 16, Land Registry Records, Indenture, Flora Townshend to Charles Worrell, 13 Sept. 1834, Liber 4^1/401.

16 Bittermann, "Women and the Escheat Movement"; Bittermann, *Rural Protest on Prince Edward Island*, chap. 5.

17 Bumsted, "Fanning, Edmund"; PARO, Smith, Alley Collection, Acc. 2702, series 12, vol. 116, Will of Governor Fanning, 24 Feb. 1818.

18 United Kingdom, *Acts of the Privy Council of England, Colonial Series*, 5: 60, 8 July 1767.

19 Ibid.

20 Bittermann, *Rural Protest on Prince Edward Island*, chap. 1; Bumsted, *Land, Settlement, and Politics on Eighteenth-Century Prince Edward Island*, chap. 10.

21 Clark, *Three Centuries and the Island*, 40. Earle Lockerby argues that even with the addition of Acadian refugees, it is "improbable" that the Island population exceeded 5,000 at the time of deportation. See Lockerby, "The Deportation of the Acadians from Ile St.-Jean," 70.

22 PARO, Crown Lands Office, Quebec, transcript, Acc 2324/8a, 94, Commission of George III to Samuel Holland (1764), 16 Nov. 1760.

23 White, ed., *Lord Selkirk's Diary, 1803–1804*, 40.

24 PARO, Smith, Alley Collection, Acc. 2702/684, [Joseph Robinson], *To the Farmers in the Island of St. John, in the Gulf of St. Lawrence.*

25 Stewart, *An Account of Prince Edward Island in the Gulph of St. Lawrence, North America*, 137–43. The Island's surveyor general, Charles Wright, reported in 1814 that, on average, settlers who had been on the land for twelve years had cleared and were cultivating twelve acres. NA, CO 226/29/116, 14 March 1814, "Return of the Number of Families Settled on Each Township in PEI."

26 PARO, Smith, Alley Collection, Acc. 2702/684, [Joseph Robinson], *To the Farmers in the Island of St. John, in the Gulf of St. Lawrence.*

27 McNutt, "Fanning's Regime on Prince Edward Island," 53; Clark, *Three Centuries and the Island*, 263–9, provides a partial list of changes in lot owners to 1806.

28 NA, CO 226/ 22/ 68; Clark, *Three Centuries and the Island*, 66, 237; Saunders, *The Economic History of the Maritime Provinces*, 105.

29 Bittermann, "Rural Protest on Prince Edward Island in Transatlantic Context."

30 Clark, *Three Centuries and the Island*, 52.

31 PEI, *JHA*, 1876, Appendix E.

32 Robertson, *The Tenant League of Prince Edward Island*, 236.

33 The current legislation sets a limit of 1,000 acres for individuals and 3,000 acres for corporations. See Lands Protection Act, PEI, *Statutes of Prince Edward Island*, chapter L-5.

CHAPTER TWO

1 Webb, "Saunders, Richard Huck (1720–1785)"; NAS, Bonar,
  Mackenzie and Kermack Collection, GD 235/10/40/19, Licence
  Granted by King George the Third to permit Richard Huck of
  Spring Gardens, Westminster, Doctor, to take the Surname
  and Crest of Saunders; NAS, Melville Castle Muniments,
  GD 51/11/20/2, Case: 30 Aug. 1799.
2 Laughton, "Saunders, Sir Charles (c. 1713–1775)."
3 NSCLRC, Grant of Lot 29 to Sir Charles Saunders, 22 May 1769,
  8/53, 9/93; United Kingdom, *Acts of the Privy Council of England,
  Colonial Series,* 5: 70, 26 Aug. 1767.
4 Lockerby, "The Deportation of the Acadians from Ile St.-John,
  1758."
5 Webb, "Saunders, Richard Huck (1720–1785)"; "A Short Account
  of the Late ... Dr. Richard Huck Saunders, Physician, London,"
  Edinburgh Medical Commentaries 10 (1786): 322.
6 PARO, RG 16, Land Registry Records, Grant of Lot 53 to Huck,
  Williams and Macleane, 5 Oct. 1769, Liber 1^1/13; United
  Kingdom, *Acts of the Privy Council of England, Colonial Series,*
  5: 76, 26 Aug. 1767.
7 Laughton, "Saunders, Sir Charles (c. 1713–1775)"; NAS, Bonar,
  Mackenzie and Kermack Collection, GD 235/10/39, An Account
  Touching the Fortunes of the two Miss Saunders and of the Application of the Money allowed for their Maintenance to the time of
  the Marriage of Rob't Dundas, Esq., with Miss Saunders.
8 Thompson, *Hampstead,* 26–30.
9 NAS, Bonar, Mackenzie and Kermack Collection, GD 235/10/13/4,
  Dr Richard Huck Saunders to Anne Saunders, 19 March 1783.
10 Ibid., Dr Richard Huck Saunders to Anne Saunders, 28 Oct. 1783.
11 NAS, Melville Castle Muniments, GD 51/11/20/1/9, Will of
  Dr Richard Huck Saunders, 13 Sept. 1872.
12 NA, Chancery Records, *Saunders v. Kinsey, Saunders v. Dent,*
  C33/494/42, 1 Dec. 1795, C33/494/386, 18 March 1796.
13 Published in 1853, the novel begins with a description of an
  afternoon's sitting in the Court of Chancery, amid the mud and fog
  of November in London. One of the matters for the Court to decide
  is the appointment of a guardian for two orphans who might be
  entitled to an inheritance under a will the interpretation of which is
  being contested in the Court of Chancery in the decades-old suit of

Jarndyce v. Jarndyce. The novel follows the fortunes of the orphans and others associated directly and indirectly with the suit. At its conclusion, the suit is abandoned, all the estate assets having been consumed by the endless Chancery proceedings.

14 NA, CO 226/18/5, Draft of Quit Rent Scale and Amounts.

15 PEI, *JHA*, 1797, 14. The assembly's report, as Bumsted has noted, was compiled for political purpose and should be read accordingly. See Bumsted, "The Land Question on Prince Edward Island and the Quitrent Controversy of 1802–1806."

16 PEI, *JHA*, 1797, 15.

17 White, *Lord Selkirk's Diary, 1803–1804*, 26.

18 Bumsted, "The Land Question on Prince Edward Island and the Quitrent Controversy of 1802–1806."

19 McNutt, "Fanning's Regime on Prince Edward Island."

20 Doubleday and Howard de Weldon, *The Complete Peerage*, 8: 652–4; Fry, *The Dundas Despotism*, 108–9, 288–9.

21 NAS, Bonar, Mackenzie and Kermack Collection, GD 235/10/13/22, Robert Dundas to Anne Saunders, 3 June [?].

22 *Times*, 31 Aug. 1796.

23 On the law of married women's property and of marriage settlements, see Staves, *Married Women's Separate Property in England, 1660–1833*; Simpson, *An Introduction to the History of the Land Law*; Holcombe, *Wives and Property*; and Stone, *The Family, Sex and Marriage in England, 1500–1800*, 87–8, 156–7, 195–6, 242–4, 330–3.

24 NAS, Bonar, Mackenzie and Kermack Collection, GD 235/10/13/39, Henry Dundas to Anne Saunders, 6 May [1796]; Fry, *The Dundas Despotism*, 157.

25 NAS, Bonar, Mackenzie and Kermack Collection, GD 235/10/12/6, Short Heads of the Proposed Settlement; GD 235/10/13/43, 13 January [?], Robert Dundas to Anne Dundas; NAS, Melville Castle Muniments, GD 51/11/20/1, Attested Copy, Marriage Articles, 29 Aug. 1796, Robert Dundas, Esq., to Miss Anne Saunders.

26 See Stone and Stone, *An Open Elite*, 126–39, for a discussion of surrogate heirs who adopt the family name of their benefactor in order to prevent it from dying out. As the Stones point out, the problem arises because of the "peculiar English habit of wholly obliterating the wife's maiden name at marriage."

27 NAS, Melville Castle Muniments, GD 51/11/20/2, Case, 30 Aug. 1796.

28 NAS, Bonar, Mackenzie and Kermack Collection, GD 235/10/39,
An Account Touching the Fortunes of the two Miss Saunders;
GD 235/10/12/1, Miss Saunders' Fortune.

29 Ibid., GD 235/10/12/6, Short Heads of the Proposed Settlement;
NAS, Melville Castle Muniments, GD 51/11/20/1, Attested Copy,
Marriage Articles, 29 Aug. 1796, Robert Dundas, Esq., to Miss
Anne Saunders. For an explanation of the rise and fall of this kind
of arrangement, called a strict settlement, see Habakkuk, *Marriage,
Debt and the Estates System*, chaps. 1 and 2. For details on suffer-
ing a recovery, see Simpson, *An Introduction to the History of the
Land Law*, 121–2.

30 NAS, Bonar, Mackenzie and Kermack Collection, GD 235/10/39,
Account from Greene and Tennant of Purchase Money received
from sale of the Estates of Stokesby, Fishley and Gunton in
Norfolk and Suffolk; GD 235/10/12/11, The Melville Trusts.

31 NAS, RHP 6699/1–89, Plans for Melville Castle; Fraser, *The
Melvilles, Earls of Melville*; Fry, *The Dundas Despotism*, 22, 60,
108; Leach, "Playfair, James (1755–1794)."

32 NAS, Bonar, Mackenzie and Kermack Collection, GD 235/10/12/6,
Short Heads of the Proposed Settlement; GD 235/10/13/102,
Robert Dundas to Anne Dundas, 10 Jan [179?]; NAS, Melville
Castle Muniments, GD 51/11/20/1, Attested Copy, Marriage
Articles, 29 Aug. 1796, Robert Dundas, Esq., to Miss Anne
Saunders; GD 51/10/16/251–63, Robert Dundas to Anne Dundas,
Dec. & Jan. [179?]. For pictures of Melville Castle today, see
http://www.melvillecastle.com, the website for Melville Castle
Hotel.

33 Burke and Burke, *A Genealogical and Heraldic History of the
Peerage and Baronetage*, 1589; *Scotsman*, 18 Sept. 1841; Fry,
"Dundas, Robert Saunders, second Viscount Melville (1771–
1851)"; Fry, *The Dundas Despotism*, 320, 350.

34 Hewitt, "Scott, Sir Walter (1771–1832)"; Anderson, *The Journal of
Sir Walter Scott*, 4n3, 8, 11, 18, 172, 200, 203, 235, 240, 326,
346–7, 376, 381–2, 458, 477; NLS, Scott Papers, Ms. 3884/20–2,
Anne Melville to Scott, 13 Jan. 1813. Teaching "through bass" in
this context meant instructing her daughter in keyboard harmonic
bass-line improvisation.

35 *Scotsman*, 24, 31 Aug. 1822; *Gazette*, 10, 14, 21 Aug. 1822;
Observer, 8, 21, 26, 27, 28 Aug. 1822; Prebble, *The King's Jaunt*,

62–3, 166, 179, 214–15, 232, 242, 252, 276, 282, 331–2; Fry, *The Dundas Despotism*, 347–8.

36 NAS, Melville Castle Muniments, GD 51/7/2/25, Anne to Robert, 2 Nov. 1821.

37 Ibid., GD 51/8/7/30, Anne to Robert, 24 April 1838; GD 51/8/7/31, Anne to Robert, 3 Oct. 1838.

38 Ibid., GD 51/8/7/23, Anne to Robert, 28 Feb. 1834.

39 Ibid., GD 51/8/7/30, Anne to Robert, 24 April 1838.

40 Ibid., GD 51/8/7/27, Anne to Robert, 17 Oct. 1836; GD 51/8/7/34, Anne to Robert, 30 July 1840.

41 Ibid., GD 51/8/7/29, Anne to Robert, 2 Nov. 1837.

42 Stuart, "Gardens," 148.

43 NAS, Melville Castle Muniments, GD 51/8/7/26, Anne to Robert, 7 Sept. 1836.

44 Ibid., GD 51/8/7/32, Anne to Robert, 24 July 1839; Goody, *The Culture of Flowers*, 161n156.

45 NAS, Melville Castle Muniments, GD 51/8/2/2, Richard to Anne, 2 Feb. 1840; GD 51/8/7/33, Anne to Robert, 4 June 1840.

46 Ibid., GD 51/8/7/31, [?] to Robert, 17 Dec. 1838.

47 Ibid., GD 51/8/7/26, Anne to Robert, 13 Aug. 1836.

48 NAS, Bonar, Mackenzie and Kermack Collection, GD 235/10/13/71, Robert to Anne, 7 April [1800?]; GD 235/10/13/135, Robert to Anne, 28 March 1800; GD 235/10/13/131, Robert to Anne, 16 March [1800?].

49 Ibid., GD 235/10/22/20, Anne to Robert, 20 Feb. 1802; Campbell, "The Landed Classes," 103–4.

50 NAS, Melville Castle Muniments, GD 51/8/7/23, Melville to Robert, 13 April 1834; Anderson, *The Journal of Sir Walter Scott*, 326–7.

51 NAS, Melville Castle Muniments, GD 51/8/7/24, Melville to Robert, 4 Jan. 1835.

52 Ibid., GD 51/8/7/31, Anne to Robert, 17 Dec. 1838, emphasis in the original.

53 Ibid., GD 51/8/7/30, Anne to Robert, 12 Feb. 1838.

54 Ibid., GD 51/8/7/33, Anne to Robert, 3 Feb. 1840; GD 51/8/7/34, Anne to Robert, 10 Dec. 1840.

55 NAS, Bonar, Mackenzie and Kermack Collection, GD 235/10/10/11, Melville to Sir John Hope, 3 July 1811; Fry, *The Dundas Despotism*, 313.

56 Bumsted, *Land, Settlement, and Politics on Eighteenth-Century Prince Edward Island*, 51–5; Clark, *Three Centuries and the Island*, 52.

57 NAS, Bonar, Mackenzie and Kermack Collection, GD 235/10/39, Account to Michaelmas 1808 to the Right Honourable Robert Dundas from G. Tennant; Account to Christmas 1805 to the Right Honourable Robert Dundas; GD 235/10/22/211, Mary Stewart to Melville, 23 March 1827.

58 Bumsted, *Land, Settlement, and Politics on Eighteenth-Century Prince Edward Island*, 51–5; NAS, Bonar, Mackenzie and Kermack Collection, GD 235/10/18/1, Regulations & Conditions to be Observed by the Tenant and Possessors of the Estate of Penicuik and Lasswade; PARO, RG 16, Land Registry Records, Power of Attorney, Robert Dundas & Earl of Westmorland to John Stewart, 20 July 1805, Liber 19/237; Power of Attorney, Viscount Melville & Earl of Westmorland to William Johnston, Liber 23/10, 30 July 1813.

59 White, *Lord Selkirk's Diary, 1803–1804*, 35–9; LAC, Selkirk Papers, MG 19/E1/74/19320; NAS, Bonar, Mackenzie and Kermack Collection, GD 235/10/39, J. Stewart to Melville, 27 April 1827; Clark, *Three Centuries and the Island*, 67; NA, CO 880/8/3, "Memorandum Respecting the Land Tenure Question in Prince Edward Island," Appendix, Map of Prince Edward Island.

60 White, *Lord Selkirk's Diary, 1803–1804*, 1–43.

61 NAS, Bonar, Mackenzie and Kermack Collection, GD 235/10/37/45, Melville to Henry, 15 May 1834.

62 PARO, RG 16, Land Registry Records, Power of Attorney, Robert Dundas & Earl of Westmorland to John Stewart, 20 July 1805, Liber 19/237; Pigot, "Stewart, John"; Bumsted, "The Land Question on Prince Edward Island and the Quitrent Controversy of 1802–1806," 8–14.

63 Bumsted, "Stewart, Charles"; White, *Lord Selkirk's Diary, 1803–1804*, 5–6; NAS, Bonar, Mackenzie and Kermack Collection, GD 235/10/22/221, Mary Stewart to Melville, 23 March 1827; PARO, RG 16, Land Registry Records, 1769–1872, Substitute Power of Attorney, John Stewart to Charles Stewart, 31 Aug. 1807, Liber 19/242.

64 NAS, Bonar, Mackenzie and Kermack Collection, GD 235/10/22/221, Mary Stewart to Melville, 23 March 1827; NAS, Melville Castle Muniments, GD 51/11/40/2, Mary Stewart to Westmorland and

Melville, 19 July 1814; NA, Chancery Records, Master Rose's
Exhibits, C-112/5/3, Letter Book of William Gosling and Gosling
and Sons, 1802–1810, Gosling & Son to Joseph Browne, 7 April
1809. Our thanks to Dr Beverly Lemire for bringing this last
source to our attention.

65 Taylor, "Johnston, William"; PARO, RG 16, Land Registry Records,
Power of Attorney, Viscount Melville & Earl of Westmorland to
William Johnston, 30 July 1813, Liber 23/10; NA, CO 226/34/69,
Johnston to Smith, May 1818; LAC, Selkirk Papers, MG 19/E1/73/
19169, Colville to Johnston, 15 April 1823; 19/E1/73/19173,
Colville to Johnston, 19 June 1823.

66 Holman, "Palmer, James Bardin"; PARO, RG 16, Land Registry
Records, Power of Attorney, Viscount Melville and Earl of
Westmorland to J.B. Palmer and J.N. LePage, 3 Sept. 1817, Liber
25/41; Substitute Power of Attorney, Viscount Melville and Earl of
Westmorland to Ewen Cameron, 21 April 1818, Liber 25/85.

67 NAS, Bonar, Mackenzie and Kermack Collection, GD 253/10/16/
174–5, Palmer to Westmorland, 27 Nov. 1817.

68 Ibid., GD 253/10/16/174–5, Palmer to Westmorland, 27 Nov. 1817.
On Charles Stewart, see White, *Lord Selkirk's Diary, 1803–1804*,
5–6; Bumsted, "Stewart, Charles."

69 NA, CO 226/34/61, Palmer to Smith, 3 Feb. 1818.

70 NA, CO 226/34/72, Johnston to Smith, May 1818.

71 NA, CO 226/34/61, Palmer to Smith, 3 Feb. 1818.

72 NA, CO 226/34/76, Minute of Council.

73 NA, CO 226/34/66–75, Johnston to Smith, May 1818.

74 Bolger, "Land and Politics, 1787–1824," 85.

75 NA, CO 226/37/49–51, Smith to Bathurst, 1 May 1821, Roads of
Prince Edward Island.

76 PARO, RG 15, 1543, Land Records, Rent Book and Day Book or
Diary (1832–34), Melville Estate.

77 NA, CO 226/34/66–75, Johnston to Smith, May 1818.

78 NLS, Cochrane Papers, Ms. 2275/279–83, Anne Melville to
Sir Thomas Cochrane, 24 Dec. 1834.

79 PARO, RG 16, Land Registry Records, Power of Attorney, Viscount
and Viscountess Melville to John Stewart, 8 June 1826, Liber
33/406.

80 NAS, Bonar, Mackenzie and Kermack Collection, GD 235/10/16/207,
J. Stewart to Melville, 9 Feb. 1827; GD 235/10/16/196–7,
J. Stewart to Melville, 27 April 1827.

81 Ibid., GD 235/10/22/221–2, Mary Stewart to Melville, 23 March
    1827; NAS, Melville Castle Muniments, GD 51/11/40/8,
    George Tennant to Westmorland and Melville, 17 March 1830;
    GD 51/11/40/9, Tennant to Westmorland and Melville, 8 Oct.
    1830; GD 51/11/40/10, Tennant to Westmorland, [1830]; PARO,
    RG 6, Supreme Court Case Papers, 1827, M. Stewart vs. J. Earl &
    R. Viscount; Attachment, 2 March 1827.
82 NAS, Bonar, Mackenzie and Kermack Collection, GD 235/10/18/3–4,
    Westmorland to Melville, 13 Sept. 1833.
83 NAS, Melville Castle Muniments, GD 51/8/7/23, Anne to Robert,
    3 Sept. 1834.
84 NAS, Bonar, Mackenzie and Kermack Collection, GD 235/10/21/2,
    Henry to Melville, 13 Aug. 1834.
85 NLS, Cochrane Papers, Ms. 2275/279–83, Anne Melville to
    Thomas Cochrane, 24 Dec. 1834.
86 NAS, Bonar, Mackenzie and Kermack Collection, GD 235/10/37/45,
    Melville to Henry, 15 May 1834, emphasis in original.
87 NAS, Melville Castle Muniments, GD 51/8/7/23, Melville to Robert,
    15 March 1834.
88 Bittermann, Rural Protest on Prince Edward Island, 30–3, 35, 39–40.
89 Taylor, "Johnston, William"; Buckner, "Smith, Charles Douglass."
90 Bittermann, Rural Protest on Prince Edward Island, 36–42.
91 NAS, Bonar, Mackenzie and Kermack Collection, GD 235/10/16/40–1,
    Westmorland to Melville, 16 Nov. 1831.
92 Ibid., GD 235/10/16/25, Palmer to Westmorland, 22 May 1832.
93 Royal Gazette, 7 Aug. 1832.
94 NAS, Bonar, Mackenzie and Kermack Collection, GD 235/10/16/23–4,
    Westmorland to Melville, 22 June 1832.
95 Ibid., GD 235/10/21/14, Henry to Melville, 5 March 1836.
96 Ibid., GD 235/10/21/15, Henry to Melville, 14 Nov. 1836.
97 Ibid., GD 235/10/21/19, Henry to Melville, 25 Dec. 1837.
98 NLS, Cochrane Papers, Ms. 2269/24–30, Anne to Thomas
    Cochrane, 15 Feb. 1826; Thompson, "Cochrane, Sir Thomas John."
99 NLS, Cochrane Papers, Ms. 2269/183–9, Anne to Thomas
    Cochrane, 12 March 1827, emphasis in original.
100 Ibid., Ms. 2271/91, Anne to Thomas Cochrane, 1 Aug. 1829.
101 Ibid., Ms. 2273/134–7, Anne to Thomas Cochrane, 6 Oct. 1831.
102 Ouellet, "Lambton, John George, 1st Earl of Durham"; NAS,
    Melville Castle Muniments, GD 51/8/7/30, Anne to Robert, 8 April
    1838.

103 Canada, General Commission of Enquiry for Crown Lands and Emigration, *Minutes of Evidence*; Bittermann, *Rural Protest on Prince Edward Island*, 226–9.

104 "A Proprietor," *Facts versus Lord Durham.*

105 NAS, Melville Castle Muniments, GD 51/8/7/31, Anne to Robert, Dec. 1838.

106 Ibid., GD 51/8/7/35, Anne to Robert, 4 Jan. 1841.

107 Ibid., GD 51/8/7/35, Anne to Robert, 17 March 1841.

108 Ibid., GD 51/8/7/35, Jane Dundas to Robert Dundas, 23 July 1841; *Gentleman's Magazine*, Oct. 1841, 445.

CHAPTER THREE

1 NA, Chancery Records, *Saunders v. Kinsey, Saunders v. Dent*, C33/498/383, 24 May 1797, C33/499/623, 11 Aug. 1797.

2 The title of Earl of Westmorland had previously belonged to the Neville family, having been granted to Ralph Neville in 1397. The Nevilles lost the title and estates by the Act of Attainder, 1571, as punishment for the sixth earl's support for Mary, Queen of Scots, and the re-establishment of Roman Catholicism as the religion of England. The title was granted to Francis Fane in 1624; children who did not inherit the title used the family name of Fane. See White and Lea, *The Complete Peerage*, 577–8; *Times*, 17 Dec. 1841.

3 Walker, *A Legal History of Scotland*, 6: 631, 633. The Marriage (Scotland) Act 1856 reduced the possibilities for Gretna Green marriages by providing that no irregular marriage was valid unless one of the parties had his or her usual residence in Scotland for twenty-one days prior to the ceremony.

4 Borer, *Mayfair*, 130; Ditchfield, *London's West End*, 138.

5 Thus Westmorland's eldest son, who would become the eleventh Earl of Westmorland, received nothing from his grandfather's estate. Sarah, Lord Westmorland's eldest daughter, was Child's heiress. See LMA, Jersey Family Papers, Acc. 1128/11, Will of Robert Child.

6 NAS, Bonar, Mackenzie and Kermack Collection, GD 235/10/22/198/105, Lady Westmorland to Robert Dundas, 5 Dec. 1810; GD 235/10/13/106, Robert Dundas-Saunders to Anne Dundas-Saunders, 15 Jan. [1800].

7 NAS, Melville Castle Muniments, GD 51/8/7/34, Anne Melville to Robert Dundas, 6 Dec. 1840; Thompson, *English Landed Society in the Nineteenth Century*, 19.

8 NA, Chancery Records, *Saunders v. Kinsey, Saunders v. Dent*, C33/
   510/346, 17 March 1800; NAS, Bonar, Mackenzie and Kermack
   Collection, GD 235/10/12/2, Heads of Settlement directed by the
   Lord Chancellor to be made on the Marriage of the Earl of
   Westmorland and Miss Saunders. See also Habakkuk, *Marriage,
   Debt and the Estates System*, 79–89, and Staves, *Married Women's
   Separate Property in England, 1660–1833.*

9 Tipping, *English Homes*, Period III, 2: 1–20, quotation at 1;
   Serjeantson and Adkins, *The Victoria History of the Counties of
   England: Northamptonshire*, 2: 543–8.

10 White and Lea, *The Complete Peerage*, vol. 12, part 2: 579; NAS,
   Bonar, Mackenzie and Kermack Collection, GD 235/10/15/12–16,
   Lady Westmorland to Melville, Feb. 1811.

11 LMA, Jersey Family Papers, Acc. 1128/16, Declaration of Trust on
   the Intended Marriage of Viscount Villiers and Lady Sarah Fane
   dated 23 May 1804; Acc. 1128/17, Articles for a Settlement of the
   Real and Personal Estate of Lady Augusta Fane on her Marriage to
   John, Lord Borington, dated 20 June 1804; Acc. 1128/18, Articles
   of Agreement dated 16 Nov. 1805, Intended Marriage of Maria
   Fane and Viscount Duncannon; Mosley, *Burke's Peerage and
   Baronetage*, 1: 73; 2: 1996, 2990; Reynolds, "Villiers, Sarah
   Sophia Child-, countess of Jersey (1785–1867)"; McCord, "Taming
   the Female Politician in Early-Nineteenth-Century England"; Rigg,
   "Paget, Sir Arthur (1771–1840)."

12 Burke and Burke, *A Genealogical and Heraldic History of the
   Peerage and Baronetage*, 2379; *Gentleman's Magazine*, Feb. 1842,
   207–8; NRO, MSS W(A) 1/IV/2, Baptism Certificate of Cecily Jane
   Georgiana Fane.

13 NAS, Bonar, Mackenzie and Kermack Collection, GD 235/15/12–16,
   Lady Westmorland to Melville, Feb. 1811; GD 235/10/22/160x,
   Lady Jersey to Robert Dundas, [Nov. 1810].

14 Ibid., GD 235/10/13/78, Robert Dundas to Anne, 27 April [1799].

15 NLS, Melville Papers, Ms. 9734, Melville to Robert Dundas,
   21 Nov. 1810.

16 Comments quoted in White and Lea, *The Complete Peerage*, 12,
   part 2: 578–9, note (e); see also Bury, *The Diary of a Lady-in-
   Waiting*, 1: 271–2, 403–4.

17 NAS, Bonar, Mackenzie and Kermack Collection, GD 235/10/22/
   105–8, Lady Westmorland to Robert Dundas, 16 Oct. 1810.

18 Ibid., GD 235/10/22/122, Lord Westmorland to Robert Dundas,
   23 July 1810; GD 235/10/15/10, copy, Willis to Lord Westmorland,
   23 Aug. 1810; GD 235/10/15/34–6, Lady Westmorland to
   Anne Melville, no date, with enclosure dated 28 Nov. 1810;
   GD 235/10/36/154–5, Anne Dundas to Melville, 16 Jan. [1811];
   GD 235/10/15/7, Copy, Drs Reynolds, Halford, and Willis to
   Westmorland, 16 Feb. 1811; GD 235/10/36/158–9, Anne Dundas to
   Melville, 26 Jan. 1811; NLS, Melville Papers, Ms. 9735, f. 37–40,
   Melville to Robert Dundas, 21 Nov. 1810.

19 The doctors were Dr John Willis, who had assisted his father,
   Francis Willis, in treating King George III during his first attack of
   mental instability in 1788–89, Dr Henry Revell Reynolds, and
   Dr Henry Halford. Dr Willis Sr received a pension of £1,000 per
   year for treating the king, and Dr John Willis received £500 per
   year. The third of the king's attacks, which led to the installation in
   February 1811 of the Prince of Wales as Regent, coincided with
   Lady Westmorland's crisis. See Trench, *The Royal Malady*, 2, 95,
   96, 97, 117, 118; Hibbert, *George IV, Prince of Wales, 1762–1811*,
   80–1, 87, 187, 279, 287; Porter, *Mind-Forg'd Manacles*, 206, 210.

20 NAS, Bonar, Mackenzie and Kermack Collection, GD 235/10/22/116,
   Westmorland to Robert Dundas, Aug. 1810; GD 235/10/22/105,
   Lady Westmorland to Robert Dundas, 16 Oct. 1810;
   GD 235/10/36/182, Halford to Anne Dundas [undated].

21 Ibid., GD 235/10/22/117–18, Lady Westmorland to Robert Dundas,
   22 Feb. 1811, emphasis in original.

22 Ibid., GD 235/10/36/157, Anne Dundas to Melville, 15 Jan. 1811.

23 Ibid., GD 235/10/22/198, Lady Westmorland to Robert Dundas,
   5 Dec. 1810, emphasis in original.

24 Ibid., GD 235/10/22/196x, Lady Jersey to Robert Dundas, [Nov.
   1810]; GD 235/10/22/164; Lady Jersey to Robert Dundas, 1811.

25 Ibid., GD 235/10/15/5, Robert Dundas to [?], 18 Feb. [1811].

26 Ibid., GD 235/10/15/8–9, Robert Dundas to Westmorland, 6 Sept.
   1810; GD 235/10/22/197, Robert Dundas to Westmorland, 14 Sept.
   1810; GD 235/10/15/78–81, Robert Dundas to Westmorland,
   16 Jan. 1811.

27 Kurata, "Wrongful Confinement."

28 NAS, Bonar, Mackenzie and Kermack Collection, GD 235/10/36/
   154–5, Anne Dundas to Melville, 16 Jan. 1811; quotation from
   GD 235/10/36/156–7, Anne Dundas to Melville, 15 Jan. 1811.

29 Ibid., GD 235/10/36/180–1, Anne Dundas to Melville, 25 March
   [1811]; GD 235/10/15/81–2, Melville to Lady Jersey, 29 June 1811;
   GD 235/10/15/41, Melville to Tennant, 14 Oct. 1811; quotation
   from GD 235/10/5/81–2, Melville to Lady Jersey, 29 June 1811.

30 Ibid., GD 235/10/22/149x, Lady Westmorland to Earl of Lonsdale,
   [1811]; quotation from GD 235/10/15/76, Lady Westmorland to
   Robert Dundas, 31 Jan. 1811.

31 Ibid., GD 235/10/22/127–8, Lady Westmorland to Robert Dundas,
   20 Feb. 1811.

32 Horstman, *Victorian Divorce*, 42; Staves, *Married Women's
   Separate Property in England, 1660–1833*, 160–95; Moore,
   "Common Sense and Common Practice."

33 NAS, Bonar, Mackenzie and Kermack Collection, GD 235/10/15/37,
   copy, Lord Melville to Lord Jersey, 10 Sept. 1811.

34 Ibid., GD 235/10/36/180–1; Anne Dundas to Lord Melville,
   25 March [1811].

35 The maintenance sum was calculated by taking the pin money of
   £800 per year provided in the marriage contract, adding the jointure of £4,000, and subtracting the income tax that Jane would
   have had to pay on the jointure and the Westmorland share of
   annuities created by Sir Charles Saunders's will. See NAS, Bonar,
   Mackenzie and Kermack Collection, GD 235/10/16/29, [undated],
   Memorandum for a letter which Lord Westmorland is to write to
   Lord Melville as establishing the separate settlement of Lady
   Westmorland; GD 235/10/15/40, Melville to Lady Westmorland,
   10 Sept 1811; GD 235/10/15/133, John Leach to Tennant, 13 Jan.
   1813.

36 Horstman, *Victorian Divorce*, 4–5, 13, 16, 20, 23–4; Staves,
   Married Women's Separate Property in England, 1660–1833, 18.

37 NAS, Bonar, Mackenzie and Kermack Collection, GD 235/10/36/157,
   Anne Dundas to Melville, 15 Jan. 1811; GD 235/10/16/44–6, Anne
   Dundas to Melville, 18 Feb. 1811; GD 235/10/22/130, Lady Jersey
   to Robert Dundas, Feb. 1811; GD 235/19/36/180–1, Anne Dundas
   to Melville, 25 March 1811; GD 235/10/15/81–2, Melville to Lady
   Jersey; 29 June 1811; GD 235/10/15/37, Melville to Jersey, 10 Sept.
   1811. The separate maintenance contracts reviewed by Staves in
   Married Women's Separate Property in England, 1660–1833, 63,
   provided for annual sums ranging from £12 to £3,000.

38 Douglass, *Lady Caroline Lamb*, 104, 153.

39 *Brighton as It Is, 1834*; Musgrave, *Life in Brighton*, 85, 93, 96, 124–5, 203–5, 223–5. The word "shampoo" is derived from the imperative form of the Hindi verb *champna*, "to knead and press the muscles with the view of relieving fatigue, etc." See Rushdie, "Hobson-Jobson."

40 NAS, Bonar, Mackenzie and Kermack Collection, GD 235/10/15/32, Lady Westmorland to Melville, 4 Oct. 1811.

41 Bury, *The Diary of a Lady-in-Waiting*, 1: 252–3, 271–2, 396; 2: 26.

42 Reeve, *The Greville Memoirs*, 1: 308.

43 Blessington, *The Idler in Italy: New Series*, 35–6.

44 Ilchester, *The Journal of Hon. Henry Edward Fox, 1818–1830*, 158–61, 266–8, 281.

45 Ibid., 279–80; NLS, Stuart de Rothesay Papers, Ms. 21301/112, Bentinck to Stewart, 16 Nov. 1828; Ms. 21301/114–15, Georgiana Fane to Stewart, 13 Nov. 1828; Ms. 21301/118–19, Georgiana Fane to Stewart, 27 Nov. 1828.

46 Ilchester, *The Journal of Hon. Henry Edward Fox, 1818–1830*, 9–10, 15, 228, 237, 240, 242, 244–50, 257, 261, 266–8, 273–4, 279, 281–2, 286–94, quotation at 293–4, emphasis added.

47 Ibid., 300–1, quotation at 306.

48 Blessington, *The Idler in Italy*, 353–4.

49 Ilchester, *The Journal of Hon. Henry Edward Fox, 1818–1830*, 229.

50 NAS, Melville Castle Muniments, GD 51/8/7/27, Anne Melville to Robert, 11, 18 Oct., 13, 30 Dec. 1836, 30 April 1838; GD 51/8/7/28, Anne Melville to Robert, 20 March 1837; GD 51/8/7/30, Anne Melville to Robert, 28 March 1838.

51 Ibid., GD 51/8/7/23, Melville to Robert Dundas, 15 March 1834, Anne Melville to Robert, 3 Sept. 1834; NAS, Bonar, Mackenzie and Kermack Collection, GD 235/19/15/105–7, Lady Westmorland to Melville, 13 April 1839.

52 NAS, Bonar, Mackenzie and Kermack Collection, GD 235/10/21/120, Henry Dundas to Anne Melville, 7 Dec. 1838.

53 Ibid., GD 235/10/15/108–10, Melville to Lady Westmorland, 14 Feb. 1839; GD 235 10/21/120, Henry Dundas to Anne Melville, 7 Dec. 1838.

54 *Royal Gazette*, 22 Oct. 1839, 3; Rogers, *Charlottetown*, 239; Sobey, "Prince Edward Island in 1840," part 1: 28; part 2: 6.

55 Johnstone, "A Series of Letters, Descriptive of Prince Edward Island," 118; Census of the Population, and Statistical Return of Prince Edward Island, 1841, *Royal Gazette*, Supplement, 19 Jan. 1842.

56 Sobey, "Prince Edward Island in 1840," part 1: 28; Laughton, "Seymour, Sir George Francis (1787–1870)"; Buckner, "FitzRoy, Sir Charles Augustus."

57 PARO, Correspondence of Lady FitzRoy, Acc. 3876/18, Lady FitzRoy to her mother, 14 Oct. 1849; Acc. 3876/19, Lady FitzRoy to her mother, 12 Nov. 1839.

58 Rogers, *Charlottetown*, 238–41.

59 PARO, H.D. Morpeth fonds, Acc. 2794/1, Morpeth to Melville, 11 Aug. 1840

60 Bittermann and McCallum, "When Private Rights Become Public Wrongs"; Vass, "Ready, John"; NAS, Bonar, Mackenzie and Kermack Collection, GD 235/10/16/40-1, Westmorland to Melville, 16 Nov. 1831; CO 226/50/321-4, "The humble memorial of the undersigned and others ..." [14 Sept. 1833].

61 PARO, Correspondence of Lady FitzRoy, Acc. 3786/19, Lady Fitzroy to her mother, 12 Nov. 1839.

62 Rayburn, *Geographical Names of Prince Edward Island*, 40.

63 Johnstone, "A Series of Letters, Descriptive of Prince Edward Island," 119.

64 PARO, RG 16, Land Registry Records, Deed of Gift, Viscount Melville to John Lane and others, Trustees, 8 Aug. 1839, Liber 47/268.

65 *Royal Gazette*, 26 Nov., 17 Dec. 1839; *Colonial Herald*, 28 Dec. 1839.

66 *Colonial Herald*, 14 Dec. 1839.

67 *Colonial Herald*, 28 Dec. 1839, 18, 26 Jan., 1 Feb., 18 July 1840.

68 *Colonial Herald*, 29 June 1840; PARO, Diocesan Church Society Records, Acc. 1005/4, "Report of the Diocesan Church Society of Prince Edward Island, 1841–42."

69 Bittermann, *Rural Protest on Prince Edward Island*, 67.

70 *Royal Gazette*, 26 Nov. 1839.

71 PARO, H.D. Morpeth fonds, Acc. 2794/1, Morpeth to Melville, 11 Aug. 1840.

72 Lawson, *Letters on Prince Edward Island*, 36.

73 Census of the Population, and Statistical Return of Prince Edward Island, 1841, *Royal Gazette*, Supplement, 19 Jan. 1842; *Royal Gazette*, 7 July, 4 Aug. 1849.

74 *Royal Gazette*, 12 Nov. 1839, 24 Nov. 1840; PARO, Correspondence of Lady FitzRoy, Acc. 3786/18, Lady FitzRoy to her mother, 14 Oct. 1839; Blakeley, "Cunard, Sir Samuel."

75 NAS, Melville Castle Muniments, GD 51/8/7/34, Anne Melville to Robert Dundas, 18 Aug. 1840.

76 PARO, H.D. Morpeth fonds, Acc. 2794/1, Morpeth to Lord Melville, 11 Aug. 1840.

77 Bittermann, *Rural Protest on Prince Edward Island*, 197–216.

78 Ibid., chap. 9.

79 Ibid., chap. 10.

80 PARO, H.D. Morpeth fonds, Acc. 2794/1-2, Morpeth to Melville, 11 Aug. 1840; Morpeth to Henry Dundas, 2 Sept. 1840; Bittermann, *Rural Protest on Prince Edward Island*, 197–8.

81 *Royal Gazette*, 18 Aug. 1840.

82 *Royal Gazette*, 1 Sept. 1840.

83 *Colonial Herald*, 15 Aug. 1840.

84 *Royal Gazette*, 17 Nov. 1840.

85 *Royal Gazette*, 18 Aug. 1840, 3; 13 Oct. 1840, 3; NAS, Bonar, Mackenzie and Kermack Collection, GD 235/10/21/137, Henry Dundas to Melville, 19 Aug. 1840; GD 235/10/21/136, Henry Dundas to Melville, 22 Sept. 1840.

86 NAS, Melville Castle Muniments, GD 51/8/7/35, Anne Melville to Robert, 4 Jan. 1841.

87 NAS, Bonar, Mackenzie and Kermack Collection, GD 235/10/21/138, Henry Dundas to Melville, 21 May 1840; *Royal Gazette*, 17 Nov. 1840.

88 NAS, Melville Castle Muniments, GD 51/8/7/34, Anne Melville to Robert, 18 Aug., 16, 28 Nov., 6, 10 Dec. 1840; CAS(CRO), Lonsdale Papers, DlonsL1/12/65, Melville to Lonsdale, 27 Nov. 1840, 15 July 1841.

89 NAS, Bonar, Mackenzie and Kermack Collection, GD 235/8/7/34, Anne Melville to Robert, 16 Nov. 1840; GD 235/10/37/11, Anne Melville to Richard, 26 Nov. 1840; NAS, Melville Castle Muniments, GD 51/9/7/34, Anne Melville to Robert, 28 Nov., 6 Dec. 1840.

90 *Times*, 17 Dec. 1841. Lord Westmorland had not outlived the scandal of his elopement with Sarah Child. It is not mentioned in his obituary, but the *Times* reprints an account of the story on 30 Dec. 1841.

91 *Brighton as It Is*, 76; Bury, *The Diary of a Lady-in-Waiting*, 1: 252–3n.

92 NA, Probate Records, Will of John, Earl of Westmorland and First
and Second Codicils, 10 July 1840; Third Codicil, 19 Aug. 1840;
Fourth Codicil, 7 Oct. 1841.

93 Henry Dundas believed that all of Lady Westmorland's share of the
Prince Edward Island properties had been settled on the eldest son
on Lord Westmorland's death. See NAS, Melville Castle Muni-
ments, GD 51/8/4/148, Henry Dundas to Jane, [1857]. Lord
Westmorland may have come to think so too. See NAS, Bonar,
Mackenzie and Kermack Collection, GD 235/10/15/100–2, draft,
Melville to Lady Westmorland, 16 May 1839.

94 NAS, Bonar, Mackenzie and Kermack Collection, GD 235/10/18/
18–20, Lady Westmorland to Melville, 25 June 1842; GD 235/10/
15/137, Melville to Lady Westmorland, 19 May 1842; PARO,
RG 16, Land Registry Records, Power of Attorney, Robert Dundas
and Earl of Westmorland to John Stewart, 20 July 1805,
Liber 19/237.

95 NA, CO 226/66/104–7, Henry Fane to Colonial Office, [Account of
State of Prince Edward Island, 1843].

96 NAS, Bonar, Mackenzie and Kermack Collection, GD 235/10/18/
18–20, Lady Westmorland to Melville, 25 June 1842; NAS, Melville
Castle Muniments, GD 51/8/7/38, Henry Fane to Robert Dundas,
13 Jan. 1843.

97 PARO, RG 16, Land Registry Records, Power of Attorney, Dowager
Countess of Westmorland to Charles Worrell, 8 July 1842,
Liber 50/422; Taylor, "Worrell, Charles."

98 PARO, RG 16, Land Registry Records, Power of Attorney, Dowager
Countess of Westmorland to H.D. Morpeth, 5 Jan. 1850,
Liber 61/225.

99 NAS, Melville Castle Muniments, GD 51/8/7/38, Jane Dundas to
Robert, 12 March, 11 May 1843.

100 Ibid., GD 51/8/4/130, Henry Dundas to Jane, 12 Sept. 1849;
GD 51/8/7, Jane Dundas to Robert, 24 March 1857; Anne Dundas
to Robert, 28 March 1857; GD 51/8/4/148, Henry Dundas to Jane,
[1857].

101 Ibid., GD 51/8/7, Jane Dundas to Robert and Richard, 8 May
[1857].

102 Jane made no other financial provision for Henry or for her
younger son, Montagu. She named Lord Lonsdale as her executor,
but he agreed to renounce the appointment, and Georgiana was
appointed the administrator of her mother's estate. See NA,

Probate Records, Will of Jane, Countess Dowager of Westmorland, 20 Sept. 1856; NAS, Melville Castle Muniments, GD 51/8/4/150, Henry Dundas to Jane, 12 Sept. 1849; GD 51/8/7, Jane Dundas to Robert, 24 March 1857; Anne Dundas to Robert, 28 March 1857; GD 51/8/4/148, Henry Dundas to Jane, [1857].

CHAPTER FOUR

1 *Patriot*, 4 Sept. 1875; *Examiner*, 19 Nov. 1860.

2 Bamford and Wellington, *The Journal of Mrs. Arbuthnot*, 1: 3.

3 Sheppard, *Survey of London*, part 1, 39: 90; Grant, *The Great Metropolis, 2nd Series*, chap. 1; Bourne, *Palmerston*, 191.

4 Bamford and Wellington, *The Journal of Mrs. Arbuthnot*, 1: 61–2, 134–6, 279, 371, 408; 2: 1, 71, 157, 229, 322, 410, 439; *Times*, 14 May 1852, 8 Jan. 1854, 28 May 1856, 2 March 1863.

5 NAS, Melville Castle Muniments, GD 51/8/7/28, Jane Dundas to Robert Dundas, 25 Feb. 1837.

6 Ibid., GD 51/8/7, Jane Dundas to Robert Dundas [1857], emphasis in original.

7 Bourne, *Palmerston*, 222. Lady Cowper (Emily Lamb) was the sister of Lord Melbourne, who was prime minister when Victoria came to the throne.

8 Bamford and Wellington, *The Journal of Mrs. Arbuthnot*, 1: 405–6, 409, 424; 2: 1.

9 Bourne, *Palmerston*, 224.

10 Bamford and Wellington, *The Journal of Mrs. Arbuthnot*, 1: 419; 2: 35, 51, 71, 157.

11 Ibid., 1: 61, 132, 136, 279, 353; 2: 1, 51, 71, 229, 308, 322, 410; NLS, Cochrane Papers, Ms. 2269, Anne Melville to Thomas Cochrane, 15 Feb. 1826.

12 Airlie, *Lady Palmerston and Her Times*, 2: 49–50; Longford, *Wellington, Pillar of State*, 385–6; Bourne, *Palmerston*, 224; Wilson, *The Greville Diary*, 2: 344–5.

13 Clive-Ponsonby-Fane, *We Started a Stately Home*, v–vi. The portrait was painted while the artist was working on two conventional portraits of Lord Westmorland. Georgiana bequeathed it to the National Gallery; it is now in the Tate Gallery collection.

14 Wilson, *The Greville Diary*, 2: 344–5.

15 *Times*, 8 Dec. 1853.

16 NAS, Bonar, Mackenzie and Kermack Collection, GD 235/10/15/ 142–6, Robert Dundas to Melville, 29 March 1842.

17 NAS, Melville Castle Muniments, GD 51/8/7/35, Melville to Robert Dundas, 20 Dec. 1841.

18 NAS, Bonar, Mackenzie and Kermack Collection, GD 235/10/18/ 16–17, Melville to G. Fane, 26 July 1842.

19 Ibid., GD 235/10/15/117, G. Fane to Melville, 7 July 1842; GD 235/10/18/228, G. Fane to Melville, 1 Aug. 1842; GD 235/10/18/127–9, G. Fane to Melville, 12 Aug. 1842.

20 NAS, Melville Castle Muniments, GD 51/8/7/36, Jane Dundas to Robert Dundas, 9 April 1842.

21 NAS, Bonar, Mackenzie and Kermack Collection, GD 235/10/15/ 139–41, copy of Berkley to G. Fane, 15 March 1842 enclosing extracts from Fane's letters to Berkley.

22 NRO, Westmorland (Apethorpe), 9/XII/1, Parkinson to Frere, 5 Sept. 1844; Parkinson to Frere, 2 Aug. 1844; Indenture between the Earl of Westmorland and Lady Georgiana Fane, 4 May 1842; Memorandum, 4 May 1842; Misc. 48.M.1., Heads of a Proposed Agreement ... between the Earl of Westmorland and Lady Georgiana Fane ..., 18 July 1844.

23 SARS, Records of Bennett and Co., DD/BT 1411 C/1531, copy, Survey and Valuation of the Brympton Estate ... belonging to Lady Georgiana Fane, 1842; Statement Showing the Alterations and Increase of Rents on the Farms Belonging to the Brympton Estate; Numerical Survey of the Brympton Estate, 1868.

24 Tipping, *English Homes*, Periods I and II, 31–50.

25 Clive-Ponsonby-Fane, *We Started a Stately Home*, vi.

26 See Wedding Venues Limited at www.weddingvenues.co.uk; The DiCamillo Companion: The Database of Houses at dicamillocompanion.com.

27 Sheppard, *Survey of London*, 39, part 1: 40, 96; part 2: 169, 199–201; *Times*, 8 July 1859, 13 May 1872; NA, CO 226/51/ 376–8, Lady Wood to Stanley, 21 Jan. 1834.

28 Swade, "Babbage, Charles (1791–1871)"; BL, Babbage Correspondence, Add. 37.198/316, G. Fane to Babbage, 4 May 1862; Add. 37.199, 481–5, G. Fane to Babbage, 19 Sept. 1869.

29 BL, Babbage Correspondence, Add. 37.197/494–6, G. Fane to Babbage, 6 Feb. 1860; Add. 37.199, 512–14, G. Fane to Babbage, 12 April 1870; Add. 37.200/199–200, G. Fane to Babbage [1866 or 1867]; Beck, "Howe, Joseph."

30 NA, Probate Records, Will of Jane, Countess Dowager of Westmorland; NAS, Melville Castle Muniments, GD 51/8/4/130, Henry Dundas to Jane Dundas, 12 Sept. 1849; GD 51/8/4/148, [Henry Dundas] to Jane Dundas, [1857]; GD 51/8/7, Jane Dundas to Robert Dundas, 24 March 1857; GD 51/8/7, Anne Dundas to Robert Dundas, 28 March 1857.

31 *Gentleman's Magazine*, June 1857, 74; Aug. 1857, 229.

32 NAS, Bonar, Mackenzie and Kermack Collection, GD 235/10/381, J.W. Gregory to Robert Dundas, 24 Dec. 1858; GD 235/10/22/190, Robert Dundas to C.F. Skirrow, 28 Feb. 1854.

33 *Monitor*, 15 Oct. 1857.

34 *Islander*, 18 May 1860.

35 Saunders, *The Economic History of the Maritime Provinces*, 105.

36 *Royal Gazette*, 23 April 1858, reproduced in NA, CO 226/89/490–1. The relevant clause reserved 500 feet above the high-water mark along the coast "for the disposal of His Majesty, His Heirs and Successors ... to erect stages and other necessary buildings for carrying on the fishery." On the significance of this wording and on the fishery reserves issue generally, see Bittermann and McCallum, "The One That Got Away."

37 NSCLRC, Crown Grants, 8/53, 9/93, Grant of Lot 29, Campbell to Saunders, 22 May 1769; PARO, RG 16, Land Registry Records, Grant of Lot 53 to Huck, Williams and Macleane, 5 Oct. 1769, Liber 1¹/13; NA, CO 226/89/402, "The Humble Petition and Memorial of the Undersigned Proprietors of Land in Prince Edward Island"; "Opening of the Legislature," *Royal Gazette*, 19 April 1859.

38 *Royal Gazette*, 14 Aug. 1860; *Islander*, 24 Aug., 5 Oct. 1860; *Monitor*, 12 Sept. 1860.

39 *Royal Gazette*, 21 Aug. 1860.

40 PARO, RG 16, Land Registry Records, Power of Attorney, Lady Fane to William Henry Pope, [?] Nov. 1860, Liber 78/428; Deed, 12 Oct. 1860, Liber 78/448; NA, CO 226/54/267–9; "Return of Township Lands in Prince Edward Island ..."

41 PARO, RG 15, Land Records, Rent Books, vol. 1486, Fane, Lot 29, 1853–1872; *Islander*, 30 Aug. 1867.

42 *Islander*, 1 Feb. 1861.

43 *Royal Gazette*, 12 March 1861.

44 NA, CO 226/86/179–96, Samuel Cunard to Russell, 13 June 1855; CO 226/86/217–21, Melville et al. to Russell, 21 June 1855.

45 Blakeley, "Cunard, Sir Samuel"; NA, CO 226/54/267–9, "Return of Township Lands in Prince Edward Island ..."

46 NA, CO 226/86/244, Seymour to Molesworth, 4 Sept. 1855.

47 PEI, JHA, 1875, Appendix E, [32]; Robertson, *The Prince Edward Island Land Commission of 1860*, xix–xx; *Examiner*, 4 Sept., 2 Oct. 1860; *Monitor*, 12, 19 Sept., 3 Oct. 1860.

48 *Royal Gazette*, 19 March 1861, reprinting dispatch from Dundas to Newcastle, 12 Nov. 1860.

49 NA, CO 226/111/359–63, G. Fane to Kimberley, 29 March 1873.

50 *Examiner*, 11 Sept. 1860.

51 *Islander*, 11 Nov. 1859, 9 Dec. 1859; *Monitor*, 12 Sept. 1860.

52 NA, CO 226/94/431–6, G. Fane to Newcastle, 26 Nov. 1861, Minutes and Draft Response dated 31 Dec. 1861.

53 NA, CO 226/320–2, G. Fane to Newcastle, 13 Jan. 1862.

54 The full text of the report is reprinted in PEI, JHA, 1875, Appendix E. Robertson provides an edited version with an introduction in *The Prince Edward Island Land Commission of 1860*.

55 Robertson, *The Tenant League of Prince Edward Island*, 36–8; PEI, JHA, 1864, Appendix F.

56 An Act for Settling Differences between Landlord and Tenant, and to enable Tenants on Certain Townships to purchase the fee simple of their Farms, PEI, *Statutes of Prince Edward Island*, 1864 (27 Vic.) c. 2; "The Proprietors' Bill – End of the Delegation Humbug," *Examiner*, 29 Feb. 1864. On the complex negotiations behind the bill, see NA, CO 880/8/3, "Memorandum Respecting the Land Tenure Question in Prince Edward Island, Colonial Office, April 1875."

57 NA, CO 226/100/547–50, G. Fane to Cardwell, 13 June 1864.

58 NA, CO 226/101/ 688–90, Minutes on Fane to Cardwell, 18 Oct. 1865. Robertson, *The Tenant League of Prince Edward Island*, 214, attributes the comment to Frederic Rogers.

59 NA, CO 226/567–689, Minutes on Fane to Cardwell, 29 Aug. 1864.

60 *Examiner*, 24 April 1865.

61 *Examiner*, 4 April 1864, 12 May 1851; *Islander*, 1 Aug. 1851.

62 Robertson, *The Tenant League of Prince Edward Island*, 63–5, 74–5, 89–92.

63 NA, CO 226/101/689–2, G. Fane to Cardwell, 19 Aug. 1865.

64 NA, CO 226/101/686–8, G. Fane to Cardwell, 18 Oct. 1865; CO 226/101/682–3, Elliot to G. Fane, 25 Aug. 1865 (draft); CO 226/101/688–9, Elliot to G. Fane, 28 Oct. 1865 (draft).

65 NA, CO 226/101/690. Robertson, *The Tenant League of Prince Edward Island*, 214, attributes this comment to Arthur Blackwood, Georgiana's neighbour on Upper Brook Street.

66 NA, CO 226/101/691–3, G. Fane to Cardwell, 15 Nov. 1865; CO 226/101/633, Elliot to G. Fane, 23 Nov. 1865, draft.

67 Robertson, *The Tenant League of Prince Edward Island*, 228–32, 237, 245–57.

68 Quotation from Robertson, *The Prince Edward Island Land Commission of 1860*, 196; MacGowan, *Report of Proceedings before the Commissioners appointed under the Provisions of the "Land Purchase Act, 1875,"* 352. See also McCallum, "The Sacred Rights of Property," 376–9.

69 NA, CO 226/102/248–52; Dundas to Cardwell, 5 July 1866 and draft response; CO 226/102/327–34, Dundas to Cardwell, 11 Sept. 1866; CO 226/102/541–3, G. Fane to Cardwell, 13 June 1866; CO 226/103/573, G. Fane to Carnarvon, 29 Jan. 1867; CO 226/103/574, G. Fane to Carnarvon, 23 Jan. 1867; CO 226/103/588, G. Fane to Carnarvon, 25 Feb. 1867; CO 226/103/592, G. Fane to Addesley, 13 March 1867.

70 NA, CO 226/102/541–3, G. Fane to Cardwell, 13 June 1866.

71 NA, CO 226/102/406–9, Notes on Remarks of the Attorney General of Prince Edward Island on the Acts of ... 1866.

72 NA, CO 226/103/573, G. Fane to Carnarvon, 29 Jan. 1867; CO 226/103/584–7, Memorial from Proprietors, Sept. 1866; CO 226/103/589–90, Minute, 13 March 1867.

73 NA, CO 226/103/574–5, G. Fane to Carnarvon, 23 Jan. 1867.

74 NA, CO 226/103/576–7, Minute re Fane to Carnarvon, 23 Jan. 1867.

75 HALS, Bulwer-Lytton Papers, DE/K/024/98/4, G. Fane to Arthur Blackwood,[?] December [1858], and memo on letter. Our thanks to Dr Ged Martin for bringing this source to our attention.

76 PEI, *JHA*, 1876, Appendix E, R.B. Stewart to Robinson, 25 Nov. 1873.

77 Robertson, "Pope, William Henry"; Beck and Townshend, "The Island's Florence Nightingale."

78 PARO, RG 16, Land Registry Records, Power of Attorney, Lady Fane to Henry Palmer, 26 June 1863, Liber 82/308; NA, CO 226/103/588, G. Fane to Carnarvon, 25 Feb. 1867; CO 226/103/592–3, G. Fane to Addesley, 13 March 1867.

79 Robertson, "Pope, William Henry."

80 *Islander,* 15 Nov. 1867, "Report of the Honorable Joseph Hensley, Attorney General ..."
81 *Patriot,* 21 March 1874; PEI, JHA, 1874, Appendix 1, Copy of Correspondence between the Colonial Secretary and Certain Proprietors.
82 Steele, *Irish Land and British Politics,* 44, 69, 74; Steele, "Ireland and the Empire in the 1860s"; McCallum, "The Sacred Rights of Property," 371–9; PEI, JHA, 1873, Appendix N, Copy of Correspondence relative to the "Tenants' Compensation Act, 1872," Extract from Minutes of Executive Council, Prince Edward Island, [2?] Dec. 1872.
83 PEI, JHA, 1873, Appendix N, Copy of Correspondence Relative to the "Tenants' Compensation Act, 1872," G. Fane to Kimberly, 29 March 1873.
84 NA, CO 227/12/46–8, Granville to Hodgson, 13 March 1869.
85 PEI, JHA, 1876, Appendix E, "Copies of Correspondence Relative to the Land Tenure Question in Prince Edward Island," Holland to G. Fane, 26 April, 1873; Kimberley to Dufferin, 12 Feb. 1874; G. Fane to Kimberley, 26 Jan. 1874.
86 Ibid., G. Fane to Carnavon, 25 Nov. 1874; Malcolm to Frere and Co., 19 Jan. 1875.
87 YPR, Will and Codicil to Will of Cecily Jane Georgiana Fane, 1 June 1870; *Times,* 10 Feb. 1875; Ponsonby, *The Ponsonby Family*; Bourne, *Palmerston,* 224, 430; Mosley, *Burke's Peerage, Baronetage and Knightage,* 1: 361.
88 Clive-Ponsonby-Fane, *We Started a Stately Home,* vi.
89 PEI, JHA, 1876, Appendix E, "Copies of Correspondence Relative to the Land Tenure Question in Prince Edward Island," G. Fane to Carnarvon, 17 Oct. 1874.

CHAPTER FIVE

1 *Gentleman's Magazine,* Feb. 1866, 274; NA, CO 226/3/7, John Stewart to Lord North, 29 June 1783. Laurence Sulivan acquired three of these lots, as well as the Grenada estates, as securities from Lauchlin Macleane, a political agent and speculator who was among the original Island grantees. See McGilvary, *Guardian of the East India Company,* 195, 242; Marshall, "Macleane, Lauchlin ... (1728/9–1778)"; Marshall, "Sulivan, Laurence (c. 1713–1786)"; *Fulham Chronicle,* 7 April 1911.

2 PARO, RG 16, Land Registry Records, Grant of Lot 16 to Lawrence Sulivan [sic], 5 Oct. 1769, Liber 1¹/114; Grant of Lot 9 to Stephen Sulivan, 18 May 1795, Liber 8²/57; Grant of Lot 22 to Stephen Sulivan, 18 May 1795, Liber 8²/55; Grant of Lot 61 to Stephen Sulivan, 18 May 1795, Liber 8²/58; United Kingdom, *Acts of the Privy Council of England, Colonial Series*, 5: 66–9, 78, 26 August 1767; Rayburn, *Geographical Names of Prince Edward Island*, 57–8, 80, 92.

3 *Gentlemen's Magazine*, Feb. 1866, 274; OUBL, Letters from Laurence Sulivan, 1764–84, Ms. Eng. his.b. 190/57, Dugald Stewart to Stephen Sulivan, 9 Dec. 1799; Bourne, *The Letters of the Third Viscount Palmerston*, 6–7, 18–19, 67.

4 Whitting, *A History of Fulham to 1965*, 98–9.

5 Thorold, *The London Rich*, 184–5.

6 Hasker, *The Place Which Is Called Fulhanham*, 64.

7 Peterson, *Family, Love, and Work in the Lives of Victorian Gentlewomen*, 35–57. Jalland, *Women, Marriage and Politics, 1860–1914*, 10, 16, notes that women from upper-class families such as the Sulivans benefited, too, from access to their fathers' libraries.

8 Bourne, *The Letters of the Third Viscount Palmerston*, 22–7; Whitting, *A History of Fulham to 1965*, 99.

9 Bourne, *The Letters of the Third Viscount Palmerston*, 5–8.

10 *West London and Fulham Times*, 7 April 1911; Feret, *Fulham, Old and New*, 3: 248; *Fulham Chronicle*, 7 April 1911.

11 Jalland, *Women, Marriage and Politics, 1860–1914*, 16–17, notes the significance of visitors in providing educational opportunities for daughters in political families, such as the Sulivans.

12 Whitting, *A History of Fulham to 1965*, 153; BL, Sulivan Mss. 59783, ff. 85–6, Sulivan to Fox Maude, 5 July 1857.

13 Bourne, *The Letters of the Third Viscount Palmerston*, 270, 282, 293, 295, 297.

14 *Times*, 14 May 1852, 2 March 1863.

15 Roberts, "The Paterfamilias of the Victorian Governing Classes," 63–4; *Times*, 6 October 1857; Bourne, *The Letters of the Third Viscount Palmerston*, 21–6; YPR, Will of the Right Honorable Laurence Sulivan.

16 Feret, *Fulham, Old and New*, 3: 251; Hasker, *The Place Which Is Called Fulhanham*, 92.

17 Schupf, "Education for the Neglected."

18 Prochaska, *Women and Philanthropy in Nineteenth-Century England*, 5, 41, 222; Vicinus, *Independent Women*, 5–7, 21–2.

19 Whitting, *A History of Fulham to 1965*, 201. Laurence Sulivan's will gave control and management of the schools to Charlotte and her sister Elizabeth, but it appears that Charlotte actually managed them; they were within sight of her house, whereas her sister lived in Berkshire.

20 Schupf, "Education for the Neglected."

21 Whitting, *A History of Fulham to 1965*, 202.

22 Feret, *Fulham, Old and New*, 3: 252.

23 *Fulham Chronicle*, 7 April 1911; YPR, Will of the Right Honorable Laurence Sulivan.

24 HA, Parsons Green Club, 736.06, Official Opening of the Memorial Bowls Green; *Fulham Observer*, 19 Dec. 1902; *Fulham Chronicle*, 5 July 1974.

25 Pierson, *St. Matthew's, Fulham, 1895–1995*, 1–7; *Fulham Chronicle*, 7 April 1911; Feret, *Fulham Old and New*, 3: 81, 118; Whitting, *A History of Fulham to 1965*, 99; YPR, Will of Charlotte Antonia Sulivan.

26 These were all zones of opportunity for Victorian women, though the professionalization of botany during Charlotte's lifetime increasingly marginalized women's contributions to plant science. See Shteir, "Gender and 'Modern' Botany in Victorian England," and Peterson, *Family, Love, and Work*, 46–8.

27 YPR, Will of Charlotte Antonia Sulivan.

28 HA, Sulivan Papers, A, contract dated 20 April 1877.

29 *Fulham Chronicle*, 7 April 1911; YPR, Will of Charlotte Antonia Sulivan. Three gardeners are among the seven servants listed by name, as opposed to position, in her will.

30 *Country Life Illustrated*, 4 May 1901; *Fulham Chronicle*, 7 April 1911.

31 PEI, *JHA*, 1797, 14–15.

32 United Kingdom, *Acts of the Privy Council of England, Colonial Series*, 5: 60, 26 August 1767.

33 PARO, RG 16, Land Registry Records, Grant of Lot 16, 5 Oct. 1769, Liber 1^1/114.

34 NA, CO 226/19/239–41, report of John Stewart, 17 April 1803; CO 226/19/242, extract of a letter of John Patterson to Sulivan, 12 Oct. 1788.

35 PARO, RG 16, Land Registry Records, Grant of Lot 9 to Stephen Sulivan, 18 May 1795, Liber 8^2/57; Grant of Lot 22 to Stephen

Sulivan, 18 May 1795, Liber 8²/55; Grant of Lot 61 to Stephen
Sulivan, 18 May 1795, Liber 8²/58.

36 NA, CO 226/19/239–41, Report of John Stewart, 17 April 1803.

37 NA, CO 226/18/5, Scale of Composition in lieu of the Arrears of
Quit Rent; CO 226/19/241–2, Stephen Sulivan to Right Honourable
Lords Commissioners of His Majesty's Treasury.

38 NA, CO 226/20/5, 3 March 1804, notice regarding enforcement of
quit rents.

39 NA, CO 226/39/61, 68, 81, 103, Statistical Report of Prince
Edward Island, 1823.

40 NA, CO 226/54/267, "Return of Township Lands in Prince Edward
Island …"

41 Ibid.; PARO, Census, 1861, Lots, 9, 16, 22, and 61.

42 NAS, Bonar, Mackenzie and Kermack Collection, GD 235/10/16/25,
copy of letter from J.B. Palmer to Lord Westmorland, 22 May
1832.

43 Holman and Greenhill, "Lewellin, John Lewellin."

44 Lewellin, *Emigration: Prince Edward Island*; Bittermann, *Rural
Protest on Prince Edward Island*, chap. 6, 251.

45 Robertson, *The Tenant League of Prince Edward Island, 1864–
1867*, 221, notes that this was the term for the act used by Louis
Henry Davies in 1875, when he represented the Island government
at the commission hearings into the price the proprietors would
receive on the compulsory sale of their estates.

46 PEI, *JHA*, 1875, Appendix E, Commissioner of Public Lands
Department, Statement Showing the Number of Acres of Land
Purchased by the Government of Prince Edward Island under the
Act 28 Vic., Cap. 5, 15 May 1874.

47 Robertson, *The Tenant League of Prince Edward Island, 1864–
1867*, 122, 222–35; Blakeley, "Cunard, Sir Samuel."

48 Blakeley, "Cunard, Sir Samuel," 184.

49 Stewart, "Robert Bruce Stewart and the Land Question," provides
a useful overview of the man and his estate.

50 Gordon and Laird, *Abstract of the Proceedings of the Land
Commissioners' Court*, 33–5; MacGowan, *Report of Proceedings*,
88–97, 228.

51 NA, CO 226/104/14, Dundas to Buckingham, 11 Jan. 1868.

52 Report of the Honourable Joseph Hensley, *Royal Gazette*, extra,
14 Nov. 1867.

53 *Patriot*, 7 Sept. 1867.

54 Ibid.

55 *Summerside Journal*, 26 Sept. 1867.

56 *Herald*, 4 Sept. 1867.

57 *Examiner*, 9 Sept. 1867.

58 *Examiner*, 16 Sept. 1867.

59 PARO, Census, 1861, Lots, 9, 16, 22, and 61.

60 *Summerside Journal*, 26 Sept. 1867.

61 *Examiner*, 9 Sept. 1867; Robertson, "Whelan, Edward."

62 *Herald*, 11 Sept. 1867.

63 *Examiner*, 13 April 1868. The currency-to-sterling rate of exchange used by government officials on Prince Edward Island at this time was 3 to 2. See NA, CO 226/103/213, Dundas to Chandos, 5 June 1867. Charlotte Sulivan calculated dollars to pounds sterling at a rate of 4.86 to 1. See *Times*, 5 Oct. 1875.

64 PEI, *JHA*, 1876, Appendix E, Charlotte Sulivan to Kimberley, 31 March 1873.

65 PEI, *Statutes of Prince Edward Island*, 27 Vic, c. 2. The Sulivan rent rolls show that Laurence Sulivan had all the appropriate arrears struck off his books with a recalculation of tenant debts. See PARO, RG 15, Land Records, Rent Books: 1836–1876, vols. 1516–18.

66 PEI, *JHA*, 1876, Appendix E, Charlotte Sulivan to Kimberley, 31 March 1873.

67 *Times*, 5 Oct. 1875.

68 Colonus's figure of "roughly" $1,500 per year was based on sworn testimony that Charlotte's agent received $1,263 per year on average in the six years prior to 1875. Colonus then rounded this figure up to $1,500. A fairer assessment of management costs would round down rather than up, as the fees Charlotte's agent received were to manage the one-third of her estate that was not under lease as well as that which was rented. Her land agent, G.W. DeBlois, sought to clarify some of this for the readership of the *Times*, but the editors chose not to publish his letter. See PRONI, Dufferin and Ava Papers, D 1071/H/B/S/684/1, Charlotte Sulivan to Lord Dufferin, 13 March 1876.

69 As Charlotte acknowledged with her own calculations, landlords could not assume that they would realize the full sum of the rents owed to them. But the ratio of gross returns to the amount owed according to rent rolls varied from year to year, depending on factors such as agricultural returns, the state of the larger economy, and the political situation. Charlotte picked good years, from a

proprietor's perspective, for making her case for returns of $5,400 per year. Colonus used evidence from a less favourable period for his $4,500 figure. A sum halfway between these two positions, or roughly $5,000 per year, is probably a more reasonable figure for the gross rental returns she could anticipate from her estate. Her letter to the *Times* also failed to acknowledge the management costs of obtaining these returns. Colonus exaggerated them. A figure of $1,000 a year for the management of the leasehold portion of Charlotte's estate, 20 per cent of her gross rental receipts, fits best with the available evidence.

70 This figure assumes a 6 shillings per acre (currency) valuation of the 22,000 acres of unleased land on the Sulivan estate, the lowest rate at which the province valued wilderness land. See NA, CO 226/103/220, Report of John Aldous, Commissioner of Public Lands, 3 June 1867.

71 There are problems with Colonus's claim that Laurence Sulivan, by accepting the terms of the 15 Years' Purchase Act, had implicitly accepted six and two-thirds per cent as an appropriate figure for calculating the return on capital. From Charlotte's perspective, her father's willingness to sell at fifteen years' purchase was an act of generosity. Nonetheless, tenants wishing to take advantage of this offer, which was open for ten years from 1864, had to pay all accrued arrears since 1858. Depending on the amount of arrears, Laurence Sulivan had agreed to terms that ranged from fifteen years' to twenty-one years' purchase. Given that the arrears on his estate at the time averaged about five times the annual rents, the financial reality of the offer for the leased portion of the estate as a whole was twenty years' purchase based on the annual rent rolls. Thus a fairer overall assessment of the interest rate assumption that informed his offer was not six and two-thirds per cent but five per cent. For the arrears on the Sulivan estate, see MacGowan, *Report of Proceedings*, 97.

72 *Times*, 27 Nov. 1875.

73 MacGowan, *Report of Proceedings*, 47, 126, 140, 339.

74 Warburton acknowledged the issue to some extent, suggesting a management fee that amounted to one-third of one per cent for the expense of collecting these investment returns.

75 MacGowan, *Report of Proceedings*, 50, 75, 127, 319, 321, 339–40.

76 NA, CO 226/103/213–14, An Act to Authorize the Government to Raise a Loan of Money for the Public Service of this Island, 1 June 1867.

77 NA, CO 226/105/53, Hodgson to Granville, 15 Feb. 1869;
    CO 226/105/254–5, Hodgson to Granville, 25 July 1869;
    CO 226/105/399–400, Hodgson to Granville, 21 Dec. 1869.
78 NA, CO 226/110/69, Robinson to Dufferin, 16 Nov. 1872;
    PEI, *JHA*, 1875, Appendix E, Executive Council to Granville, 6 Feb.
    1869.
79 Blakeley, "Cunard, Sir Samuel," 184.
80 NA, CO 226/105/59, Minute paper.
81 The return on the nearly £22,000 worth of Consols (Consolidated
    Annuities) that Charlotte owned at the time of her death was two
    and a half per cent. See HA, Sulivan Papers, Miss C.A. Sulivan,
    Probate Affidavit, Estate and Succession Duty Accounts, Legacy
    and Other Receipts, and Residuary Account.
82 PEI, *JHA*, 1875, Appendix C.
83 PEI, *JHA*, 1875, Appendix E, Commissioner of Public Lands
    Department, Statement Showing the Number of Acres of Land
    Purchased by the Government of Prince Edward Island, 15 May
    1874, [6].
84 NA, CO 226/104/13, Executive Council Minutes, 9 Jan. 1868.
85 NA, CO 227/11/240–1, Buckingham and Chandos to Dundas, 3
    March 1868.
86 NA, CO 226/104/32, marginal note on Executive Council Minutes.
87 NA, CO 227/12/23–4, Granville to Hodgson, 13 March 1869.
88 NA, CO 226/107/335–40, Memorial of the Proprietors of Township
    Lands in Prince Edward Island, 10 June 1871; CO 226/110/172–6,
    Memorial of the Proprietors of Township Lands in Prince Edward
    Island, 1872; CO 226/110/199–200, R.B. Stewart to Robinson,
    30 July 1872.
89 Bittermann, *Rural Protest on Prince Edward Island*, chap. 6.
90 Blakeley, "Cunard, Sir Samuel"; MacGowan, *Report of
    Proceedings*, 235.
91 Laughton, "Seymour, Sir George Francis (1787–1870)."
92 PEI, *JHA*, 1876, Appendix E, Sulivan to Kimberly, 31 March 1873;
    Sulivan to Under-Secretary of State, 20 Dec. 1873.
93 YPR, Will of Charlotte Antonia Sulivan.
94 NA, CO 226/105/522–3, Fane to Granville, 3 June 1869.
95 PRONI, Dufferin and Ava Papers, D 1071/H/B/S/684/1, Charlotte
    Sulivan to Dufferin, 13 March 1876.
96 Ibid., D 1071/N/B/S/684/2, Charlotte Sulivan to Dufferin, 9 March
    1877.

97 NA, CO 226/108/368–9, Sulivan to [CO], no date; PEI, *JHA*, 1876, Appendix E, Charlotte Sulivan to Kimberley, 31 March 1873; Charlotte Sulivan to Under-Secretary of State, 20 Dec. 1873.

98 NLS, Ms. 9819, folio 90–3, Henry, 3rd Lord Melville to Earl Grey, 25 June 1851; PEI, *JHA*, 1875, Appendix E, Petition of the Proprietors of Land in Prince Edward Island, [1874].

99 NA, CO 226/110/149, Executive Council comments on petition of proprietors against Tenant Compensation Act of 1872.

100 NA, CO 226/105/59, Minute paper.

101 NA, CO 226/103/576–7, Minute paper; CO 226/103/594, Minute paper.

102 CO 226/105/59, Minute paper.

103 Land Purchase Act, 1875, PEI, *Statutes of Prince Edward Island 1875*, 38 Vic., c. 32; Childers, *The Life and Correspondence of the Right Hon. Hugh C.E. Childers*, 1: 231–5; Bittermann and McCallum, "Upholding the Land Legislation of a 'Communistic and Socialist Assembly.'"

104 PRONI, Dufferin and Ava Papers, D 1071/H/B/F/24/1, Ponsonby Fane to Dufferin, 13 July 1875.

105 PEI, *JHA*, 1877, Appendix E, No. 7, Report by the Crown Officers … of Proceedings before the Commissioners under Land Purchase Act, 1875 … , [6, 11].

106 *Kelly v. Sulivan and Others* (1875), Haszard and Warburton, *The Prince Edward Island Reports*, 2: 34–107.

107 *Patriot*, 12 Feb. 1876.

108 PRONI, Dufferin and Ava Papers, D 1071/H/B/F/24/4, Ponsonby Fane to Dufferin, 17 Feb. 1876.

109 *Kelly v. Sulivan* (1877), Canada, Registrar of the Supreme Court, *Supreme Court Reports*, 1: 3–64, quotation at 35.

110 LAC, RG 125, Supreme Court Case Files, *Kelly v. Sulivan* case file, Notice of Motion for leave to appeal.

CHAPTER SIX

1 PARO, RG 16, Land Registry Records, Power of Attorney, Robert Dundas and Earl of Westmorland to John Stewart, 20 July 1805, Liber 19/237; Power of Attorney, Viscount Melville and Earl of Westmorland to William Johnston, Liber 23/10, 30 July 1813.

2 Rayburn, *Geographical Names of Prince Edward Island*, 72.

3 MacGowan, *Report of Proceedings*, 262.

4 NA, CO 226/105/522–3, Fane to Granville, 3 June 1869; PRONI, Dufferin and Ava Papers, D 1071/H/B/S/684/1&2, Charlotte Sulivan to Dufferin, 13 March 1876 and 9 March 1877.

5 Foster, *Across New Worlds.* McEwan, *Gender, Geography and Empire,* 25–32, notes the role of duty in the complex mixture of motivations informing female travel in the Victorian period and the need many women felt to justify their travels.

6 PEI, *JHA* 1896, Appendix M.

7 Land Purchase Act, 1875, PEI, *Statutes of Prince Edward Island,* 1875, c. 32; Bittermann and McCallum, "Upholding the Legislation of a 'Communistic and Socialist Assembly.'"

8 Representing the Island government at most of the Land Commission hearings were Louis Davies, Samuel R. Thompson, QC, of New Brunswick, Frederick Brecken, provincial attorney general, and William Sullivan, provincial solicitor general. Edward J. Hodgson, assisted in some cases by John Longworth, represented many of the proprietors, including Charlotte Sulivan, Ponsonby Fane, and Anne Melville's son, Henry Dundas, who had inherited the estate from his father on Robert's death in 1851. A transcript of the evidence and argument was printed in MacGowan, *Report of Proceedings*; for discussion of the arguments, see McCallum, "The Sacred Rights of Property," 374–82.

9 MacGowan, *Report of Proceedings,* 99, 101, 102, 103, 113–14, 117, 122, 148–9.

10 Ibid., 78–81, 85, 92–7.

11 Ibid., 152.

12 PARO, RG 6.1, Supreme Court Records, 21/36, Estate of Charlotte Antonia Sulivan. The total award to Charlotte was $84,107, which included $2,607 in rent received prior to the transfer of title. Dividing $81,500 by the acreage for the Sulivan estate given in PEI, *JHA,* 1881, Appendix K, produces a price of $1.26 per acre rather than $1.29. The basis for the latter figure is not explained in the appendix.

13 MacGowan, *Report of Proceedings,* 256–62; PARO, RG 6.1, Supreme Court Records, 21/12, Estate of Hon. Spencer Cecil Brabazon Ponsonby Fane.

14 *Daily Examiner,* 26 Nov. 1895. Our thanks to Dr Edward MacDonald for bringing this article to our attention.

15 PEI, *JHA,* 1881, Appendix K; Robertson, "Pope, James Colledge"; Robertson, "Haviland, Thomas Heath"; Robertson, "Palmer,

Edward"; Robb, "Haviland, Thomas Heath"; Morgan, "Hodgson, Hon. Edward Jarvis."

16 MacGowan, *Report of Proceedings*, 76.

17 PEI, *JHA*, 1873, Appendix N, Copy of Correspondence Relative to the "Tenants' Compensation Act, 1872."

Bibliography

ARCHIVAL SOURCES

BRITISH LIBRARY, LONDON (BL)
Babbage Correspondence. Add. 37
Sulivan Mss. 59783

CUMBRIA ARCHIVE SERVICE (CARLISLE RECORD OFFICE)
(CAS [CRO])
Lonsdale Papers

HAMMERSMITH ARCHIVES, LONDON (HA)
Parson's Green Club Papers
Sulivan Papers

HERTFORDSHIRE ARCHIVES AND LOCAL STUDIES (HALS)
Bulwer-Lytton Papers

LIBRARY AND ARCHIVES CANADA, OTTAWA (LAC)
RG 125. Supreme Court Case Files
MG 19, E1. Selkirk Papers

LONDON METROPOLITAN ARCHIVES (LMA)
Jersey Family Papers. Acc. 1128

NATIONAL ARCHIVES, KEW (NA)
Chancery Records

CO 880. War and Colonial Department and Colonial Office: Confidential Print (North America)
CO 226. Prince Edward Island, Original Correspondence
Probate Records

NATIONAL ARCHIVES OF SCOTLAND (NAS)
Bonar, Mackenzie and Kermack Collection. GD 235
Melville Castle Muniments. GD 51
Plans for Melville Castle. RHP 6699

NATIONAL LIBRARY OF SCOTLAND (NLS)
Cochrane Papers. Mss. 2269–75
Melville Papers. Mss. 9734–5
[Miscellaneous] Ms. 9819
Scott Papers. Ms. 3884
Stuart de Rothesay Papers. Ms. 21301

NORTHAMPTONSHIRE RECORD OFFICE, NORTHAMPTON (NRO)
Westmorland (Apethorpe) Collection

NOVA SCOTIA CROWN LANDS RECORD CENTRE, HALIFAX (NSCLRC)
Grant Books

OXFORD UNIVERSITY, BODLEIAN LIBRARY (OUBL)
Letters from Laurence Sulivan, 1764–84. Mss. Eng. his.b, 190

PRINCE EDWARD ISLAND PUBLIC ARCHIVES AND RECORD OFFICE (PARO)
RG 6.1. Supreme Court Records
RG 15. Land Records
RG 16. Land Registry Records
Census of the Population and Statistical Return of Prince Edward Island, 1841 and 1861.
Crown Lands Office, Quebec, transcript. Acc. 2324
Charlottetown Camera Club Collection. Acc. 2320
Correspondence of Lady FitzRoy. Acc. 3876
Diocesan Church Society Records. Acc. 1005
H.D. Morpeth fonds. Acc. 2794

Heritage Foundation Collection. Acc. 3466
Smith, Alley Collection. Acc. 2702

PUBLIC RECORD OFFICE OF NORTHERN IRELAND, BELFAST
(PRONI)
Dufferin and Ava Papers

SOMERSET ARCHIVE AND RECORD SERVICE, TAUNTON (SARS)
Records of Bennett and Co.

YORK PROBATE REGISTRY (YPR)
Probate Records

NEWSPAPERS AND PERIODICALS

Colonial Herald (Charlottetown)
Country Life Illustrated (London)
Daily Examiner (Charlottetown)
Edinburgh Medical Commentaries
Examiner (Charlottetown)
Fulham Chronicle
Fulham Observer
Gazette (Edinburgh)
Gentleman's Magazine (London)
Herald (Charlottetown)
Islander (Charlottetown)
Monitor (Charlottetown)
Observer (Edinburgh)
Patriot (Charlottetown)
Royal Gazette (Charlottetown)
Scotsman (Edinburgh)
Summerside Journal
Times (London)
West London and Fulham Times

OTHER SOURCES

Airlie, Mabell, Countess of. *Lady Palmerston and Her Times*. Vol. 2.
London: Hodder and Stoughton, 1922

Anderson, W.E.K., ed. *The Journal of Sir Walter Scott*. London: Oxford
   University Press, 1972
Bamford, Francis, and the Duke of Wellington, eds. *The Journal of Mrs.
   Arbuthnot, 1820–1832*. 2 vols. London: Macmillan, 1950
Beck, Boyde, and Adele Townshend. "The Island's Florence Nightingale."
   Island Magazine 34 (Fall/Winter 1993): 29–36
Beck, J. Murray. "Howe, Joseph." *Dictionary of Canadian Biography*, 10:
   362–70. Toronto: University of Toronto Press, 1972
Bird, Isabella Lucy. *The Englishwoman in America*. Forward and notes by
   Andrew Hill Clark. Madison: University of Wisconsin Press, 1966
Bittermann, Rusty. *Rural Protest on Prince Edward Island: From British
   Colonization to the Escheat Movement*. Toronto: University of Toronto
   Press, 2006
– "Rural Protest on Prince Edward Island in Transatlantic Context: From
   the Aftermath of the Seven Years' War to the 1840s." In *Transatlantic
   Rebels: Agrarian Radicalism in Comparative Context*, ed. Thomas
   Summerhill and James C. Scott, 21–53. Lansing: Michigan State Uni-
   versity Press, 2004
– "Women and the Escheat Movement: The Politics of Everyday Life on
   Prince Edward Island." In *Separate Spheres: Women's Worlds in the 19th
   Century Maritimes*, ed. Suzanne Morton and Janet Guildford, 23–38.
   Fredericton: Acadiensis Press, 1994
Bittermann, Rusty, and Margaret McCallum. "The One That Got Away:
   Fishery Reserves in Prince Edward Island." *Dalhousie Law Journal* 28,
   no. 2 (Fall 2005): 385–408
– "Upholding the Land Legislation of a 'Communistic and Socialist
   Assembly': The Benefits of Confederation for Prince Edward Island."
   Canadian Historical Review 87, no. 1 (March 2006): 1–28
– "When Private Rights Become Public Wrongs: Property and the State in
   Prince Edward Island in the 1830s." In *Despotic Dominion: Property
   Rights in British Settler Societies*, ed. John McLaren, A.R. Buck, and
   Nancy E. Wright, 144–68. Vancouver: UBC Press, 2005
Blakeley, Phyllis R. "Cunard, Sir Samuel." *Dictionary of Canadian Biog-
   raphy*, 9: 172–84. Toronto: University of Toronto Press, 1976
Blessington, Countess of. *The Idler in Italy*. Paris: Baudry's European
   Library, 1839
– *The Idler in Italy: New Series*. Paris: Baudry's European Library, 1841
Bolger, Francis W.P. "Land and Politics, 1787–1824." In *Canada's Smallest
   Province: A History of Prince Edward Island*, ed. Francis W.P. Bolger, 66–94.
   Charlottetown: Prince Edward Island 1973 Centennial Committee, 1973

Borer, Mary Cathcart. *Mayfair: The Years of Grandeur.* London: W.H. Allen, 1975

Bourne, Kenneth. *Palmerston, The Early Years: 1784–1841.* London: Allen Lane, 1982

– ed. *The Letters of the Third Viscount Palmerston to Laurence and Elizabeth Sulivan, 1804–1863.* London: The Royal Historical Society, 1979.

Brighton as It Is, 1834: Exhibiting All the Latest Improvements in That Fashionable Watering Place. Wallis's Royal Edition. Brighton: The Booksellers, 1834

Buckner, Phillip. "FitzRoy, Sir Charles Augustus." *Dictionary of Canadian Biography,* 8: 295–7. Toronto: University of Toronto Press, 1985

– "Smith, Charles Douglass." *Dictionary of Canadian Biography,* 8: 823–8. Toronto: University of Toronto Press, 1985

Bumsted, J.M. "Fanning, Edmund." *Dictionary of Canadian Biography,* 5: 308–12. Toronto: University of Toronto Press, 1983

– "The Land Question on Prince Edward Island and the Quitrent Controversy of 1802–1806." *Acadiensis* 29, no. 2 (Spring 2000): 3–26

– *Land, Settlement, and Politics on Eighteenth-Century Prince Edward Island.* Montreal and Kingston: McGill-Queen's University Press, 1987

– "Stewart, Charles." *Dictionary of Canadian Biography,* 5: 775–6. Toronto: University of Toronto Press, 1983

– "Stewart, Peter." *Dictionary of Canadian Biography,* 5: 776–9. Toronto: University of Toronto Press, 1983

Burke, Bernard, and Ashworth P. Burke. *A Genealogical and Heraldic History of the Peerage and Baronetage.* 85th ed. London: Burke's Peerage Ltd, 1927

Bury, Lady Charlotte. *The Diary of a Lady-in-Waiting.* London: Jane Lane, 1908

Campbell, R.H. "The Landed Classes." In *People and Society in Scotland, 1760–1830,* ed. T.M. Devine and Rosalind Mitchison, 91–108. Edinburgh: John Donald Publishers for the Economic and Social History Society of Scotland, 1988

Canada. Registrar of the Supreme Court. *Supreme Court Reports.* Vol. 1. Ottawa: Queen's Printer, 1878

Canada. General Commission of Enquiry for Crown Lands and Emigration. *Minutes of Evidence Taken under the Direction of a General Commission of Inquiry for Crown Lands and Emigration Appointed on the 21st of June 1838 ...* Quebec: J.C. Fisher and William Kemble, 1839

Chaudhuri, Nupur, and Margaret Strobel, eds. *Western Women and Imperialism: Complicity and Resistance*. Bloomingham: Indiana University Press, 1992

Childers, Spencer. *The Life and Correspondence of the Right Hon. Hugh C.E. Childers, 1827–1896*. London: John Murray, 1901

Chilton, Lisa. "A New Class of Women for the Colonies: The *Imperial Colonist* and the Construction of Empire." *Journal of Imperial and Commonwealth History* 31, no. 2 (2003): 36–56

Clark, Andrew Hill. *Three Centuries and the Island: A Historical Geography of Settlement and Agriculture in Prince Edward Island, Canada*. Toronto: University of Toronto Press, 1959

Clive-Ponsonby-Fane, Charles. *We Started a Stately Home*. Yeovil, Somerset, 1980

Ditchfield, P.H. *London's West End*. London: Jonathan Cape, 1925

Doubleday, H.A., and Lord Howard de Weldon, eds. *The Complete Peerage*. London: St. Catherines Press, 1932

Douglass, Paul. *Lady Caroline Lamb: A Biography*. New York: Palgrave, Macmillan, 2004

Feret, Charles James. *Fulham, Old and New: Being an Exhaustive History of the Ancient Parish of Fulham*. Vol. 3. London: Leadenhall Press, 1900

Foster, Shirley. *Across New Worlds: Nineteenth Century Women Travellers and Their Writings*. New York: Harvester Wheatsheaf, 1990

Fraser, Sir William. *The Melvilles, Earls of Melville, and the Leslies, Earls of Leven*. Edinburgh, 1890

Fry, Michael. "Dundas, Robert Saunders, second Viscount Melville (1771–1851)." *Oxford Dictionary of National Biography*. Oxford: Oxford University Press, 2004

– *The Dundas Despotism*. Edinburgh: Edinburgh University Press, 1992

Goody, Jack. *The Culture of Flowers*. Cambridge: Cambridge University Press, 1993

Gordon, J.D., and D. Laird, reporters. *Abstract of the Proceedings of the Land Commissioners' Court, Held during the Summer of 1860, to Inquire into the Differences Relative to the Rights of Landowners and Tenants in Prince Edward Island*. Charlottetown: The Protestant, 1862

Grant, James. *The Great Metropolis, 2nd Series*. London, New York: Saunders and Otley, 1837

Habakkuk, John. *Marriage, Debt and the Estates System: English Landownership, 1650–1950*. Oxford: Clarendon Press, 1994

Hall, Catherine. "The Rule of Difference: Gender, Class and Empire in the Making of the 1832 Reform Act." In *Gendered Nations: Nationalisms and Gender Order in the Long Nineteenth Century*, ed. Ida Bloom, Karen Hegemann, and Catherine Hall, 107–35. Oxford and New York: Berg, 2000

Hasker, Leslie. *The Place Which Is Called Fulhanham: An Outline History of Fulham from Roman Times until the Start of the Second World War*. Fulham: Fulham and Hammersmith Historical Society, 1981

Haszard, Francis L., and A.B. Warburton. *The Prince Edward Island Reports*. Vol. 1, 1850–74; vol. 2, 1875–82. Charlottetown: J. Coombs, 1885–86

Hewitt, David. "Scott, Sir Walter (1771–1832)." *Oxford Dictionary of National Biography*. Oxford: Oxford University Press, 2004

Hibbert, Christopher. *George IV, Prince of Wales, 1762–1811*. London: Longman, 1972

Holcombe, Lee. *Wives and Property: Reform of the Married Women's Property Law in Nineteenth-Century England*. Toronto: University of Toronto Press, 1983

Holman, H.T. "Palmer, James Bardin." *Dictionary of Canadian Biography*, 6: 565–9. Toronto: University of Toronto Press, 1987

– "Townshend, William." *Dictionary of Canadian Biography*, 5: 825–6. Toronto: University of Toronto Press, 1983

Holman, H.T., and Basil Greenhill. "Lewellin, John Lewellin." *Dictionary of Canadian Biography*, 8: 505–6. Toronto: University of Toronto Press, 1985

Horstman, Allen. *Victorian Divorce*. New York: St. Martin's Press, 1985

Ilchester, Earl of, ed., *The Journal of Henry Edward Fox (afterwards Fourth and Last Lord Holland), 1818–1830*. London: T. Butterworth, 1923

Jalland, Pat. *Women, Marriage and Politics, 1860–1914*. Oxford: Oxford University Press, 1986

Johnstone, Walter. "A Series of Letters, Descriptive of Prince Edward Island, in the Gulph of St. Laurence." In *Journeys to the Island of St. John or Prince Edward Island, 1775–1832*, ed. D.C. Harvey, 87–161. Toronto: Macmillan, 1955

Kimber, Jane, and Francis Serjeant. *The Changing Face of Hammersmith and Fulham*. Derby: Breedon Books, 2002

Kurata, Marilyn J. "Wrongful Confinement: The Betrayal of Women by Men, Medicine, and Law." In *Victorian Scandals: Representations of Gender and Class*, ed. Kristine Ottesen Garrigan, 43–68. Athens: Ohio University Press, 1992

Laughton, J.K. "Saunders, Sir Charles (c. 1713–1775)." Revised by Roger Knight. *Oxford Dictionary of National Biography*. Oxford: Oxford University Press, 2004

– "Seymour, Sir George Francis (1787–1870)." Revised by Andrew Lambert. *Oxford Dictionary of National Biography.* Oxford: Oxford University Press, 2004

Lawson, John. *Letters on Prince Edward Island.* Charlottetown: G.T. Haszard, 1851

Leach, Peter. "Playfair, James (1775–1794)." *Oxford Dictionary of National Biography.* Oxford: Oxford University Press, 2004

Lewellin, J.L. *Emigration: Prince Edward Island: A Brief but Faithful Account of This Fine Colony; Showing Some of Its Advantages as a Place of Settlement; Addressed to Those British Farmers, and Others, Who Are Determined to Emigrate, and Try Their Fortune in a New Country.* Charlottetown: James D. Haszard, 1832

Lockerby, Earle. "The Deportation of the Acadians from Ile St.-Jean." *Acadiensis* 27, no. 2 (Spring 1998): 45–94

Longford, Elizabeth. *Wellington, Pillar of State.* New York: Harper and Row, 1972

MacGowan, P.S. *Report of Proceedings before the Commissioners Appointed under the Provisions of the "Land Purchase Act, 1875."* Charlottetown, 1875

Mackay, Ruddock. "Keppel, Augustus, Viscount Keppel (1725–1786)." *Oxford Dictionary of National Biography.* Oxford: Oxford University Press, 2004

Marshall, P.J. "Macleane, Lauchlin ... (1728/9–1778)." *Oxford Dictionary of National Biography.* Oxford: Oxford University Press, 2004

– "Sulivan, Laurence (c. 1713–1786)." *Oxford Dictionary of National Biography.* Oxford: Oxford University Press, 2004

McCallum, Margaret. "The Sacred Rights of Property: Title, Entitlement, and the Land Question in Nineteenth-Century Prince Edward Island." In *Essays in the History of Canadian Law: In Honour of R.C.B. Risk,* vol. 8, ed. G. Blaine Baker and Jim Phillips, 358–97. Toronto: University of Toronto Press for the Osgoode Society for Canadian Legal History, 1999

McCord, James N., Jr. "Taming the Female Politician in Early-Nineteenth-Century England: *John Bull versus Lady Jersey.*" *Journal of Women's History* 13, no. 4 (2002): 31–53

McEwan, Cheryl. *Gender, Geography and Empire: Victorian Women Travellers in West Africa.* Aldershot: Ashgate, 2000

McGilvary, George K. *Guardian of the East India Company: The Life of Laurence Sulivan.* London: Tauris Academic Studies, 2006

McNutt, W.S. "Fanning's Regime on Prince Edward Island." *Acadiensis* 1, no. 1 (Autumn 1971): 37–53

Moore, Tammy. "Common Sense and Common Practice: Custody Provisions in Deeds of Separation: England, 1705–1873." MA dissertation, University of New Brunswick, 2002

Morgan, James Henry. "Hodgson, Hon. Edward Jarvis." *Canadian Men and Women of the Time,* 470. Toronto: William Briggs, 1898

Mosley, Charles, ed. *Burke's Peerage and Baronetage.* 106th ed. Chicago: FitzRoy Dearborn, 1996–99

Musgrave, Clifford. *Life in Brighton.* Rev. ed. Rochester: Rochester Press, 1981

Nelson, Paul David. "Fraser, Simon (1729–1777)." *Oxford Dictionary of National Biography.* Oxford: Oxford University Press, 2004

Ouellet, Fernand. "Lambton, John George, 1st Earl of Durham." *Dictionary of Canadian Biography,* 8: 476–81. Toronto: University of Toronto Press, 1988

Peterson, M. Jeanne. *Family, Love, and Work in the Lives of Victorian Gentlewomen.* Bloomington and Indianapolis: Indiana University Press, 1989

Pierson, Sue. *St. Matthew's, Fulham, 1895–1995.* Elstree: The Print Room, n.d.

Pigot, F.L. "Stewart, John." *Dictionary of Canadian Biography,* 6: 735–8. Toronto: University of Toronto Press, 1987

Ponsonby, Sir John. *The Ponsonby Family.* London: Medici Society, 1929

Porter, Roy. *Mind-Forg'd Manacles: A History of Madness in England from the Restoration to the Regency.* London: Athlone Press, 1987

Prebble, John. *The King's Jaunt.* London: Fontana, 1989

Prince Edward Island. *Journals of the House of Assembly.* Charlottetown
– *Statutes of Prince Edward Island.* Annual volumes. Charlottetown

Prochaska, F.K. *Women and Philanthropy in Nineteenth-Century England.* Oxford: Oxford University Press, 1980

"Proprietor, A." *Facts versus Lord Durham.* London: Madden and Co., 1839

Rayburn, Alan. *Geographical Names of Prince Edward Island.* Ottawa: Energy, Mines and Resources Canada, 1973

Reeve, Henry, ed. *The Greville Memoirs.* London: Longman and Green, 1888

Reynolds, K.D. "Villiers, Sarah Sophia Child-, countess of Jersey (1785–1867)." *Oxford Dictionary of National Biography.* Oxford: Oxford University Press, 2004

Rigg, J.M. "Paget, Sir Arthur (1771–1840)." Revised by H.C.G. Matthew. *Oxford Dictionary of National Biography.* Oxford: Oxford University Press, 2004

Robb, Andrew. "Haviland, Thomas Heath." *Dictionary of Canadian Biography*, 12: 415–19. Toronto: University of Toronto Press, 1990

Roberts, David. "The Paterfamilias of the Victorian Governing Classes." In *The Victorian Family: Structure and Stresses*, ed. Anthony S. Wohl, 59–81. New York: St Martin's Press, 1978

Robertson, Ian Ross. "Haviland, Thomas Heath." *Dictionary of Canadian Biography*, 9: 415–19. Toronto: University of Toronto Press, 1976

– "Palmer, Edward." *Dictionary of Canadian Biography*, 9: 664–70. Toronto: University of Toronto Press, 1976.

– "Pope, James Colledge." *Dictionary of Canadian Biography*, 11: 699–705. Toronto: University of Toronto Press, 1982

– "Pope, William Henry." *Dictionary of Canadian Biography*, 10: 593–9. Toronto: University of Toronto Press, 1972

– *The Tenant League of Prince Edward Island, 1864–1867*. Toronto: University of Toronto Press, 1996

– "Whelan, Edward." *Dictionary of Canadian Biography*, 9: 825–38. Toronto: University of Toronto Press, 1976

– ed. *The Prince Edward Island Land Commission of 1860*. Fredericton: Acadiensis Press, 1988

Rogers, Irene L. *Charlottetown: The Life in Its Buildings*. Charlottetown: Prince Edward Island Museum and Heritage Foundation, 1983

Rushdie, Salman "Hobson-Jobson." In *India: True Stories*, ed. James O'Reilly and Larry Habegger, 97–8. San Francisco: Travellers' Tales, 2004

Saunders, S.A. *The Economic History of the Maritime Provinces*. Fredericton: Acadiensis Press, 1984

Schupf, H.W. "Education for the Neglected: Ragged Schools in Nineteenth-Century England." *History of Education Quarterly* 12, no. 2 (Summer 1972): 162–83

Serjeantson, Rev. R.M., and W. Ryland D. Adkins, eds. *The Victoria History of the Counties of England: Northamptonshire*. Vol. 2. London: Archibald Constable, 1906

Sheppard, F.H.W. *Survey of London*. Vol. 39, *The Grosvenor Estate in Mayfair*. London: University of London, 1977

Shteir, Ann B. "Gender and 'Modern' Botany in Victorian England." *Osiris* 12 (1997): 29–38

Simpson, A.W.B. *An Introduction to the History of the Land Law*. London: Oxford University Press, 1961

Sobey, Douglas, ed. "Prince Edward Island in 1840: The Travel Journal of Sir George Seymour." Part 1, *Island Magazine* 54 (Fall/Winter 2003): 26–33; part 2, 55 (Spring/Summer 2004): 2–7

Staves, Susan. *Married Women's Separate Property in England, 1660–1833*. Cambridge, Mass., and London: Harvard University Press, 1990

Steele, E.D. "Ireland and the Empire in the 1860s: Imperial Precedents for Gladstone's First Irish Land Act." *Historical Journal* 11, no. 1 (1968): 64–83

– *Irish Land and British Politics: Tenant-Right and Nationality, 1865–1870*. Cambridge: Cambridge University Press, 1974

Stewart, Deborah. "Robert Bruce Stewart and the Land Question." *Island Magazine* 21 (Spring/Summer 1987): 3–11

Stewart, John. *An Account of Prince Edward Island in the Gulph of St. Lawrence, North America, Containing Its Geography, a Description of Its Different Divisions, Soil, Climate, Seasons, Natural Productions, Cultivation, Discovery, Conquest, Progress and Present State of Settlement, Government, Constitution, Laws and Religion*. London: W. Winchester & Son, 1806

Stone, Lawrence. *The Family, Sex and Marriage in England, 1500–1800*. New York, Harper & Row, 1977

Stone, Lawrence, and Jeanne C. Fawther Stone. *An Open Elite: England, 1540–1880*. Oxford: Clarendon Press, 1984

Strobel, Margaret. *European Women and the Second British Empire*. Bloomingham: Indiana University Press, 1991

Stuart, D.C. "Gardens." In *A Companion to Scottish Culture*, ed. David Daiches. 146–9. New York: Holmes & Meier, 1981

Swade, Doron. "Babbage, Charles (1791–1871)." *Oxford Dictionary of National Biography*. Oxford: Oxford University Press, 2004

Taylor, M. Brook. "Johnston, William." *Dictionary of Canadian Biography*, 6: 359–61. Toronto: University of Toronto Press, 1987

– "Worrell, Charles." *Dictionary of Canadian Biography*, 8: 353–5. Toronto: University of Toronto, 1985

Thompson, F.M.L. *Hampstead: Building a Borough, 1650–1964*. London: Routledge & Kegan Paul, 1974

Thompson, Frederic F. "Cochrane, Sir Thomas John." *Dictionary of Canadian Biography*, 10: 178–80. Toronto: University of Toronto Press, 1972

– *English Landed Society in the Nineteenth Century*. London: Routledge & Kegan Paul, 1963

Thorold, Peter. *The London Rich: The Creation of a Great City, from 1666 to the Present*. London: Viking, 1999

Tipping, H. Arvay. *English Homes*. Periods I and II, *Mediaeval and Early Tudor, 1066–1558*; Period III, *Late Tudor and Early Stuart, 1558–1649*, vol. 2. London: Country Life, 1927

Trench, C.C. *The Royal Malady*. London: Longman, 1964

United Kingdom. *Acts of the Privy Council of England. Colonial Series.* Edited through the direction of the Lord President of the Council by James Munro. Vol. 5. London, 1911

Vass, Elinor. "Ready, John." *Dictionary of Canadian Biography,* 7: 740–3. Toronto: University of Toronto Press, 1988

Vicinus, Martha. *Independent Women: Work and Community for Single Women, 1850–1920.* London and Chicago: Chicago University Press, 1985

Walker, David M. *A Legal History of Scotland.* Vol. 6, *The Nineteenth Century.* Edinburgh: Butterworths LexisNexis, 2001

Webb, W.W. "Saunders, Richard Huck (1720–1785)." Revised by Jeffrey S. Reznick. *Oxford Dictionary of National Biography.* Oxford: Oxford University Press, 2004

White, Geoffrey H., and R.S. Lea. *The Complete Peerage.* London: St. Catherines Press, 1959

White, Patrick C.T., ed. *Lord Selkirk's Diary, 1803–1804: A Journal of His Travels in British North America and the Northeastern United States.* Toronto: Champlain Society, 1958

Whitting, P.D., ed. *A History of Fulham to 1965.* Fulham: Fulham Historical Society, 1970

Wilson, Philip Whitwell, ed. *The Greville Diary.* Vol. 2. London: William Heinemann, 1927

Index